NAG HAMMADI STUDIES

VOLUME XVII

NAG HAMMADI STUDIES

EDITED BY

MARTIN KRAUSE – JAMES M. ROBINSON
FREDERIK WISSE

IN CONJUNCTION WITH

ALEXANDER BÖHLIG – JEAN DORESSE – SØREN GIVERSEN
HANS JONAS – RODOLPHE KASSER – PAHOR LABIB
GEORGE W. MACRAE – JACQUES-É. MÉNARD – TORGNY SÄVE-SÖDERBERGH
R. McL. WILSON – JAN ZANDEE

XVII

VOLUME EDITOR

MARTIN KRAUSE

LEIDEN
E. J. BRILL
1981

GNOSIS AND GNOSTICISM

*Papers read at the Eighth International Conference
on Patristic Studies
(Oxford, September 3rd-8th 1979)*

EDITED BY

MARTIN KRAUSE

LEIDEN
E. J. BRILL
1981

ISBN   90 04 06399 4

CONTENTS

ABBREVIATIONS

AAG	Abhandlungen der Akademie der Wissenschaften in Göttingen
AKG	Arbeiten zur Kirchengeschichte
BA	Berliner Arbeitskreis
BG	Berolinensis gnosticus = Die gnostischen Schriften des koptischen Papyrus Berolinensis 8502 hersg., übers. u. bearb. von W. C. Till, 1955, ²1972 bearb. von H.-M. Schenke
BHTh	Beiträge zur historischen Theologie
BSAC	Bulletin de la Société d'Archéologie Copte
BZ	Biblische Zeitschrift
CBQ	The Catholic Biblical Quaterly
FKDG	Forschungen zur Kirchen- und Dogmengeschichte
GCS	Die griechischen christlichen Schriftsteller
J(b)AC	Jahrbuch für Antike und Christentum
JEH	Journal of Ecclesiastical History
JTS	The Journal of Theological Studies
MG	Migne, Patrologia, ser. graeca
ML	Migne, Patrologia, ser. latina
NHC	Codex ... der Nag Hammadi Bibliothek
NHL	Nag Hammadi Library
NHS	Nag Hammadi Studies
OLZ	Orientalistische Literaturzeitung
OrChr	Oriens christianus
REg	Revue d'Egyptologie
RechSR	Recherches de Science Religieuse
RevSR	Revue des Sciences Religieuses
RGG	Religion in Geschichte und Gegenwart
T	Torhoudt, A.
T(h)LZ	Theologische Literaturzeitung
T(h)R(u)	Theologische Revue
TU	Texte und Untersuchungen
T(h)WNT	Theologisches Wörterbuch zum Neuen Testament
V(ig)C(hr)	Vigiliae Christianae
VF	Verkündigung und Forschung
WZKM	Wiener Zeitschrift für die Kunde des Morgenlandes
ZÄS	Zeitschrift für ägyptische Sprache und Altertumskunde
ZNW	Zeitschrift für neutestamentliche Wissenschaft
ZRGG	Zeitschrift für Religions- und Geistesgeschichte

VORWORT

In diesem Band werden 8 Referate, die auf dem 8. Internationalen Patristikerkongreß in Oxford (3.-8. September 1979) gehalten wurden, publiziert, außerdem ein Referat (J. Helderman) der International Conference on Gnosticism in Yale (New Haven) vom 28.-31. März 1978.

Die Gliederung der Aufsätze entspricht den Grundsätzen, die im Vorwort der Publikation der auf dem 7. Internationalen Patristikerkongreß in Oxford gehaltenen Referate über die Gnosis genannt wurden.[1]

Mit der raschen Veröffentlichung ihrer Referate hoffen die Mitarbeiter dieses Bandes, einen Beitrag zur erfreulich lebhaften Gnosisforschung zu leisten.

MARTIN KRAUSE

---

[1] Gnosis and Gnosticism. Papers read at the Seventh International Conference on Patristic Studies (Oxford, September 8th-13th 1975) edited by M. Krause (NHS VIII), Leiden 1977, VIIf.

PART I

GNOSIS

ZUM "SIMONIANISCHEN" IN *AUTHLOG* UND *BRONTĒ*

BY

SASAGU ARAI

Im Jahre 1975 hatte ich hier in Oxford anhand meines Referates "Simonianische Gnosis und die *Exegese über die Seele*"[1] folgende These aufgestellt: Die *Exegese über die Seele* (NHC II 6) könnte in ihren Wesenszügen zumindest sachlich als simonianisch gelten, aber man darf diese nicht im historischen Sinne "vorsimonianisch" (H.-M. Schenke und K. Rudolph) bezeichnen.

Diese These hat inzwischen von Seiten Rudolphs zwar im Wesentlichen Zustimmung gefunden.[2] Rudolph kritisiert aber einige Punkte meiner Beweisführung und er hält doch an folgendem fest: "Der Stoff, den sie (sc. *ExPsych*) verarbeitet, ist unter den bisherigen gnostischen Originaltexten der einzige, der für den historischen Sinn außerhalb der häresiologischen Quellen mit gutem Gewissen für den Hintergrund seines (sc. Simons) Mythos und seiner Rekonstruktion aus der zerstörten Überlieferung herangezogen werden kann."[3]

Ich gehe hier nicht auf diese Feststellung Rudolphs ein, da ich mich schon im letzten Teil der japanischen Ausgabe meines oben genannten Aufsatzes mit Rudolph wegen dieses Problems auseinandergesetzt habe.[4] Im Folgenden möchte ich nun zur merkwürdigen Fragestellung

---

[1] Jetzt in: M. Krause (ed.), *Gnosis und Gnosticism. Papers read at the Seventh International Conference on Patristic Studies (Oxford, September 8th-13th 1975), Nag Hammadi Studies* Vol. VIII, Leiden, 1977, 185-203. Vgl. bes. 202.

[2] K. Rudolph, "Simon — Magus oder Gnosticus? Zum Stand der Debatte", *ThR* 42 (1977) 354ff., bes. 358.

[3] Rudolph, *ThR* 42, 359.

[4] Jetzt in: *Mediterraneum* (Annual Report of the Collegium Mediterranistarum) Vol. II, Tokyo 1979, 3-25, bes. 15ff (mit deutscher Zusammenfassung: 24f.). Hier werden meine Gegenargumente gegenüber Rudolph nur zusammenfassend dargestellt:

1. Gegen meine Auffassung, daß Simonianer "Simon einerseits mit Christus und Ennoia andererseits mit Helena in Verbindung gebracht, und somit Simon und Helena als irdisches Paar historisiert haben" (*NHS* VIII, 193f.), behauptet Rudolph folgendes: "Eine derartige 'Historisierung' auf seiten der Simonianer halte ich allerdings für nicht erweisbar und sehe dahinter eher eine häresiologische Persiflage" (*ThR* 42, 356). Man könnte zwar hinter Schilderung des Just., apol. I, 26, 3 und des Iren. adv. haer. I, 23, 2 eher eine "häresiologische Persiflage" als eine simonianische "Historisierung" des Simon/Ennoiamythos sehen. Aber wäre ersteres beweisbarer als letzteres? Rudolph müßte

Schenkes, die auch Rudolph im Zusammenhang unseres Problems unterztützt,[5] ob nicht neben *ExPsych* auch *Brontē* (NHC VI 2) und

---

dazu für seine Behauptung Belege anführen. Andererseits nimmt Schenke, "Die Relevanz der Kirchenväter für die Erschließung der Nag Hammadi-Texte", in: J. Irmscher, K. Treu (ed.), *Das Korpus der Griechischen Christlichen Schriftsteller, Historie, Gegenwart, Zukunft*, (*TU*, Bd. 120), Berlin 1977, 218, Simon und seine Gefährtin Helena wie Rudolph als "polemische Umstellung und Persiflage" von seiten der Haeresiologen an, die allerdings nach Schenke "auch die entsprechenden Züge des Selbstverständnisses Simons mitbetroffen haben müßte."

In diesem Zusammenhang verweist Schenke, "Bemerkungen zur Apokalypse des Petrus", in: M. Krause (ed.), *Essays on the Nag Hammadi Texts, In Honour of Pahor Labib, NHS* Vol. VI, Leiden 1975, 282f. mit Recht darauf, daß Simon sich auch nicht als Bräutigam verstanden hätte, wenn es keine Braut gegeben hätte. Allerdings darf man meiner Meinung nach hier nicht vom historischen Simon, sondern lediglich von Simon im Sinne der Simonianer (s.u.) sprechen. Dann dürften wir hinter der "häresiologischen Persiflage" doch wenigstens sachlich Ansätze der "Historisierung" von seiten der Simonianer annehmen.

2. Im Unterschied zu meiner früheren Meinung verzichte ich in meinem Aufsatz (in: *NHS* VIII, 196, Anm. 53) auf die Annahme einer "Grundschrift" der *ExPsych*, da ich mit M. Krause inzwischen überzeugt bin, daß es sich um einen bereits christlich-gnostisch konzipierten Traktat handelt. Nach Rudolph bleibt ihm "unverständlich", warum ich dann trotzdem die exegetischen Partien der *ExPsych* als "zweitrangig" betrachte (*ThR* 42, 356). Zwar habe ich nirgendwo in meinem Aufsatz das Wort "zweitrangig" gebraucht. Wenn ich mir aber erlaube, es hier aufzunehmen, betrachte ich die exegetischen und ermahnenden Partien gegenüber den Wesenszügen des Seelenmythos der *ExPsych* als "zweitrangig", gebrauche dies Wort also nicht im Sinne der Quellenscheidung. Der Verfasser der *ExPsych* hat seinen gnostischen Seelenmythos konzipiert, indem er Zitate aus der Bibel und der Odyssea in den exegetischen und ermahnenden Partien als Stoffe gebraucht hat. In diesem Sinne bin ich mit Krause u.a. heute noch überzeugt, daß es sich um einen bereits christlich-gnostisch konzipierten Traktat handelt. Die exegetischen und ermahnenden Partien, die ausgesprochen christlich sind, sind also insofern "zweitrangig", als diese dem Verfasser nur als Material dienen, mit dem er seine gnostische "Daseinshaltung" objektiviert und somit sein "Sein" mythologisch macht.

3. Nach Rudolph bin ich "nicht folgerichtig", da ich einerseits von einer "gnostisch-platonischen Seelenfallgeschichte" spreche, die "als Vorlage" für *ExPsych* in Frage komme, andererseits "(gleichzeitig (202!)" dazu geneigt bin, den Seelenmythos der *ExPsych* gerade ihrer einfachen und klaren Gestalt als Folge einer Anpassung auch an die platonische Seelengeschichte zu betrachten (*ThR* 42, 357). Ich habe aber nirgendwo in meinem Aufsatz eine "gnostisch-platonische Seelengeschichte, die als Vorlage für *ExPsych* in Frage kommt", angenommen!

4. Rudolph ermahnt mich folgendermaßen: "Eine Erlösungsgestalt fehlt im Platonismus, und auch der Seelenbegriff ist eng mit der Idee von der Weltseele verbunden, so daß eine direkte gegenseitige Abhängigkeit nur über gewisse Zwischenglieder gegeben ist". (*ThR* 42, 357f.). Das weiß ich auch! Aber könnten wir nicht tatsächlich den Seelenmythos, der dem der *ExPsych* insofern ähnelt, als es sich um den Abfall der Seele handelt, im orphisch-pythagoräisch geprägten Mittel-, bzw. Neuplatonismus ausfindig machen? In diesem Milieu wird sogar auch Helena als Inkarnation des Schicksals der Seele interpretiert. Die "Erlösungsgestalt", die in der Form des "Bräutigams" zur Rettung der Seele abgesandt wird, gilt natürlich als Postulat von seiten des Gnostizismus der *ExPsych*.

5. Rudolph kritisiert meine Auffassung, indem er "wesentliche Unterschiede", die ich zwischen *ExPsych* und dem Simonianismus ausfindig gemacht habe, zu einer Synopse zu-

AuthLog (NHC VI 3) "viel simonianischer sind als der Simonianismus der Kirchenväter",[6] Stellung nehmen.

1

Bevor ich mich in diesem Zusammenhang mit Schenke (und Rudolph) konfrontiere, müßten wir uns zu allererst darüber im Klaren sein, was eigentlich Charakteristica des Simonianismus sind. Und es wäre doch m.E. methodologisch vernünftig, mittels des Simonianismus der

---

sammensetzt (357). Aber diese Synopse selbst ist z. Teil auf dem Mißverständnis meiner Darstellung aufgebaut. Vor allem ist im 3. Unterschied meine Meinung über Helena in 136, 35 der *ExPsych* von Rudolph nicht exakt wiedergegeben, "Helena in 136, 35 nicht sicher emendierbar; wenn, dann nicht zum ältesten Teil gehörig (200)" (357). Ich habe zwar geschrieben, daß ich selbst die Lesung [Hele]nē an der Facsimilie-Ausgabe des Original-Textes nicht klar verifizieren konnte. Ich habe aber letzten Endes diese Lesung anerkannt: "Aber sowohl die Länge als auch der Kontext der zerstörten Zeile machen — so scheint mir — die Lesung "Helenē" wahrscheinlicher" (S. 210). Deswegen trifft die Kritik Rudolphs, die auf Grund dieses Mißverständnisses geübt wird (358), überhaupt nicht zu. — Jedenfalls kann ich nicht verstehen, warum Rudolph die Auffassung des Berliner Arbeitskreises für koptisch-gnostische Schriften (BA), nach der die paränetische Partie 135, 4-137, 26 — "Helenē" kommt doch 136, 35 vor! — von der "Grundschrift" her gesehen, der 4. und zwar letzten "Stufe" der *ExPsych* zugehört, nicht kritisiert, wenn er Helena als das dem Psychēmythos der *ExPsych* unentbehrliche Element ansieht. Meine Meinung, daß die Helenagestalt im Simon-Ennoia/Helenamythos des Iren. sekundär sei, der jetzt auch Rudolph mit seinem eigenen Grund zustimmt (*ThR* 42, 309), entspricht genau der sekundären Stellung der Helena, die sie innerhalb der Paränese der *ExPsych* einnimmt.

6. "Simon und Ennoia sind" nach Rudolph "nicht", wie ich meine, "als Syzygos aufzufassen, sondern eher, wie in der *ExPsych* als 'Bräutigam' (Erlöser) und 'Seele' (Ennoia), da die Vergottung Simons zum 'Urvater' (in seiner Gemeinde und sicher bei den Häresiologen) keine älteste simon. Lehre gewesen ist. Man muß damit rechnen, daß Simon als Inkarnation der 'großen Kraft', als Bote eines höheren Wesens auftrat, mit dem er im Laufe der Divinisierung verschmolz" (*ThR* 42, 358). Dieser Ansicht Rudolphs kann ich mich überhaupt nicht anschließen, da sie der Entwicklungslinie der simonianischen Lehre von Simon als Gottheit zum Boten Gottes zuwiderläuft, was ich unten erörtern werde.

Schließlich behauptet Rudolph, daß auch ein Zusammenhang von "überkosmischer" und "kosmischer" Seele im Simonianismus greifbar ist, und zwar in der "Metempsychose" der Ennoia (*ThR* 42, 358). Ich bin gerne bereit, dieser Behauptung Rudolphs zuzustimmen, zumal ich in meinem Aufsatz (200) nicht einen "Zusammenhang", sondern eine einzigartige Einheitlichkeit von überkosmischer und kosmischer Seele, zwar in der *Ex-Psych*, aber nicht im Simonianismus für aufweisbar gehalten habe. Im Simonianismus bleibt Ennoia duchgehend als überkosmische Seele und steht nur prototypisch für das menschliche Selbst, so daß er menschliche "Leiber", und zwar letzten Endes den Leib der Helena postuliert, die er zur "Metempsychose" der Ennoia nötig hat, während das menschliche Selbst in *ExPsych* nicht nur in der oberen, sondern auch in der unteren Welt von Anfang an bis zum Ende "Seele" genannt wird und diese mit Helena nicht wie im Simonianismus durch "Metempsychose", sondern einfach gleichgesetzt wird.

[5] *ThR* 42, 359, Anm. 37.
[6] in Irmscher, Treu (ed.), a.a.O., 218.

Kirchenväter dessen Charakterzüge zu klären, zumal es beim heutigen
Stand der Forschung, wie ich es nachher zeigen werde, noch in der Luft
hängt, ob sowohl *Brontē* als auch *AuthLog* in den Simonianismus einge-
ordnet werden können.

Wenn wir den "Simonianismus" nennen, müssen wir in diesem
wenigstens drei Phasen unterscheiden, ganz abgesehen vom
"historischen" Simon.[7] Simonianer haben also ihre Simonverehrung,
die der Apg 8,10f zugrundeliegt, mittels des Sophia/Ennoiamythos, den
wir z.B. aus den ältesten Schichten des *ApcJoh* ausfindig gemacht
haben,[8] gnostisiert, indem sie zuerst den "Vater" mit Simon, und dann
diesen einerseits mit "Christus", andererseits "Sophia/Ennoia" mit
Helena in Verbindung gebracht haben. In dieser ersten und zweiten
Phase (Just., apol. I, 26, 2f; Iren., adv. haer. I 23, 1-3) steht Gott Simon
als Erlöser im Vordergrund. Die Simonianer haben also die Funktion
des Erlösers, die in den ältesten Schichten des *ApcJoh* nicht nur
"Vater" und "Sohn" der "Sophia" gegenüber innegehabt haben, sondern auch diese den Menschen gegenüber innegehabt hat, auf Simon
allein konzentriert, so daß Ennoia, bzw. Helena hier in diesen Phasen
als salvanda, also noch nicht als "Salvator", bleibt. Erst in der dritten
Phase des Simonianismus, dem wir in Hipp.ref. begegnen, ist diese
"schwache" Helena als "mächtig" in den Vordergrund gerückt worden, die allerdings schon in der zweiten Phase des Simonianismus, z.B.
in der Stesichoros-Legende immanent vorhanden war. Und Simon gilt
hier in der dritten Phase nicht mehr als Gott selbst, sondern als der von
Gott ausgesandte Offenbarer oder Erlöser.

Wenn die Sache sich so verhält, dann müßten wir als das Primäre der
simonianischen Charakteristica die merkwürdige Gestalt Simons nennen, der als Gottheit die Rolle des Erlösers spielt. Simon als den von
Gott Ausgesandten können wir zwar in der späteren, oder sogar der spä-
testen Phase des Simonianismus ausfindig machen, aber eine derartige
Erlösergestalt dürfen wir nicht mehr ausschließlich als "simonianisch"

---

[7] Ob Simon Magus oder Gnosticus war, lasse ich hier offen. Allerdings halte ich noch
mit R. Bergmeier, K. Beyschlag und G. Lüdemann daran fest, daß bei Simon selbst keine
gnostischen Charakterzüge beweisbar sind. Vgl. Arai, in: Krause (ed.), a.a.O., 189. So
auch jetzt B. Aland, "Gnosis und Philosophie" in: G. Widengren (ed.), *Proceedings of
the International Colloquium on Gnosticism, Stockholm August 20-25 1973*, Stockholm,
1977, 59ff., bes. 62.

[8] H.-M. Schenke, "Nag Hammadi-Studien III: Die Spitze des dem Apokryphon Johannis und Sophia Jesu Christi zugrundeliegenden Systems", *ZRGG* XIV (1962), 352-361,
bes. 356; S. Arai, "Zur Christologie des Apokryphons des Johannes", *NTS* 15 (1969),
302-318.

bezeichnen, da diese vielmehr allgemein im Gnostizismus, vor allem —
verbunden mit Christus — im christlichen Gnostizismus ihren Platz
hat.[9]

Der zweite der simonianischen Wesenszüge ist ohne Zweifel die En-
noiagestalt, da der Simonianismus erst dann zur "simonianischen Gnosis" wird, wenn er die Gestalt der Ennoia als *prima salvanda* der Menschen in sich aufnimmt. Man darf aber dabei folgendes nicht vergessen:
Wie Simon in der ersten Phase mit dem höchsten Gott des gnostischen
Sophia/Ennoiamythos in Verbindung gebracht wurde, so wurde Helena
mit seiner "ersten Ennoia" erst in der zweiten Phase des Simonianismus
identifiziert. Mit Aland zu sagen: "Sachlich hat der gnostische Mythos
mit der Helenageschichte nichts zu tun, sondern beides ist sekundär verbunden worden. Dazu mag beigetragen haben, daß sich das Bild der
Dirne, die in einem Bordell letzte Zuflucht findet, besonders gut dazu
eignete, die äußerste Schmach und Verlassenheit zu demonstrieren, der
das Göttliche in dieser Welt, die es nicht kennt, ausgesetzt ist".[10] Jedenfalls gilt "das Bild der Dirne", die im Bordell steht, nicht primär als
simonianisch, da es nicht nur im simonianischen, sondern auch in
anderen gnostischen Mythos, ja darüberhinaus weit in altorientalischen
wie hellenistischen Legenden verbreitet war.[11]

2

Vom oben ausgeführten Standpunkt her gesehen, zögere ich,
zunächst *AuthLog* mit Schenke (und Rudolph) als "simonianisch"

---

[9] Diese "Entwicklung" der simonianischen Gnosis hat Aland (in: Widengren ed., ibid.)
unabhängig von mir mit Recht hervorgehoben. Allerdings halten Rudolph einerseits (*ThR*
42, 309f) und J. Frickel andererseits (*ThLZ* 102, 1978, 733ff) heute noch daran fest, daß
die simonianische *Apophasis Megalē* (*AM*) des Hipp. doch Recht hat, das Primäre des Simonianismus zu vertreten. Aber dürfen wir der Chronologie des Lukas (Ende des 1. Jhr.),
des Just. (Mitte des 2. Jhr.), des Iren. (2. Hälfte des 2. Jhr.) und des Hipp. (Anfang des 3.
Jhr.) ohne genügende Beweismaterialien zuwider laufen? Z.B. ist erst der "Nachfolger Simons" Menander nicht mehr die "erste Kraft, die allen unbekannt ist", d.h. Gott selbst,
sondern nur noch ein von ihm ausgesandter Erlöser der Menschen (Iren. adv. haer. I 23,
5). "Aus diesem einen Punkt zeigt sich aber, daß offenbar spätestens zu Irenäus' bzw.
Justins Zeit wahrscheinlich noch früher die Identifikation der höchsten, unendlichen
göttlichen Kraft mit dem als Mensch erschienenen Simon als Sakrileg empfunden und
aufgegeben wurde. Der Apophasisbericht steht, wie nicht anders zu erwarten, ganz in dieser Linie" (Aland, in: Widengren ed. a.a.O., 62).
[10] In: Widengren (ed.), a.a.O., 60. Vgl. auch 65.
[11] Vgl. G. Quispel, Jewish Gnosis and Mandaean Gnosticism, in: J.-É. Ménard (ed.),
Les Texts de Nag Hammadi, Colloque du Centre d'Historie des Religions (*Strasbourg,
23-25 octobre 1974*), *NHS* VII, Leiden 1975, 82-122, bes. 89-103.

oder sogar "simonianischer als der Simonianismus der Kirchenväter" zu bezeichnen.

Es ist zwar richtig zu sehen, daß auch in *AuthLog* wie in *ExPsych* eine Geschichte der in diese Welt, bzw. in die Hylē gefallenen und zu erlösenden Seele andeutungsweise vorausgesetzt wird.[12] Aber diese Seelengeschichte an sich ist nicht speziell simonianisch, sondern vielmehr ein in der hellenistischen, bzw. mittelplatonischen Religions- und Geistesgeschichte weit belegbarer Topos, der z.B. in *Hermetica* wiederkehrt.[13]

Andererseits dürfte das leitende Bildmotiv für die Erlösungsmöglichkeit der Seele, wie der BA mit Recht aufweist, "das des Logos sein, der ihr, wie ein Heilmittel, — sei es 'auf die Augen' (p. 22, 27; 27, 31; 28, 12), sei es 'auf den Mund' (p. 22, 24; vgl. p. 31, 3f) — von ihrem 'Bräutigam' (p. 22, 23) verabreicht wird. (der 'Logos' nimmt also hier gleichsam die Stelle von Gnosis oder Pistis ein, während der Erlöser der Bräutigam der Seele bzw. der zu ihr gehörige Nūs ist. vgl. 28, 25)."[14] Die Vorstellung des "Bräutigams" als Erlösers der "Braut" Seele könnten wir wiederum als Gemeinsames mit dem gnostischen Seelenmythos der *ExPsych* hervorheben. Aber der der Seele zugehörige "Nūs", den man mit BA funktionell mit ihrem Bräutigam gleichsetzen kann, fehlt in *ExPsych* völlig. Außerdem wird in *AuthLog* dieser Nūs andererseits als eine im Menschen immanente, höhere Substanz vorgestellt (22, 28ff; vor allem 24, 26.29).

Das Motiv des "Logos" scheint uns in diesem Zusammenhang noch wichtiger zu sein, zumal dieses das leitende Bildmotiv für die Erlösungsmöglichkeit der Seele sein dürfte. Dieser "Logos" wird hier in *AuthLog* vom "Bräutigam", also vom Erlöser der Seele separat vorgestellt. Er gilt nämlich als das vom "Bräutigam" der Seele dargebotene Erkenntnismittel oder sogar als Erkenntnismöglichkeit. Von diesem "Logos"

---

[12] So BA, "Authentisches Logos". Die dritte Schrift aus Nag Hammadi-Codex VI, *ThLZ* 98 (1973), 251; Schenke, in: Irmscher, Treu (ed.), a.a.O., 216; G. W. MacRae, A Nag Hammadi Tractate on the Soul, in: *Ex orbe religionum, Studia G. Widengren oblata I*, Leiden, 1972, 478; J. É. Ménard, L'authentikos Logos, Texte établi et présenté, Québec, 1977, 4; K. Koschorke, " 'Suchen und Finden' in der Auseinandersetzung zwischen gnostischem und kirchlichem Christentum", in: *Wort und Dienst, Jahrbuch der Kirchlichen Hochschule Bethel*, Neue Folge 14 (1977), 51f.

[13] So MacRae, ibid. Zur hellenistischen Seelenlehre, die in *Hermetica* vorausgesetzt wird, vgl. A.-J. Festugière, *La révélation d'Hermès Trismégiste III: Les doctrines de l'âme*, Paris, 1953. Zu platonischen, bzw. mittelplatonischen Elementen in *AuthLog* vgl. R. van den Broek, The Authentikos Logos: A New Document of Christian Platonism, *VigChr* 33 (1979), 260ff.

[14] In: *ThLZ* 98, 251f.

ist weder in *ExPsych* noch im Simonianismus der Kirchenväter die Rede.

Allerdings kommt der "Logos" in der *AM* des Hipp. oftmals zur Sprache. In unserem Zusammenhang fällt vor allem die Vorstellung auf, daß der Mensch zum "Baum des Lebens" gelangen kann, wenn ihn das ihm "zukommende Wort" (λόγου τοῦ προσήκοντος VI 16, 5; 17, 7) trifft. Ohne dieses Wort ist der Graben zwischen ihm und Gott unüberspringbar.[15] Aber dieses "Wort" in der *AM*, das dem Menschen über sein Wesen aufklärt, würde höchstwahrscheinlich mit Simon als Offenbarer und Erlöser identifiziert vorgestellt sein.[16] Dieses ist also nicht, wie in *AuthLog*, die Erkenntnismöglichkeit, die in der *AM* eher eine im Menschen als "Möglichkeit" (δυνάμει) innewohnende göttliche "Kraft" sein könnte.

Die Termini "Logos" und "Nūs" könnten m.E. an sich der mittelplatonisch, bzw. stoischen Anthropologie entstammen, die z.B. auch im 4. christlichen Traktat aus NHC VII, nämlich *Silv* wiederkehrt (85, 25f; 92, 25-27; 102, 13-16; vor allem 86, 24-27).[17] Allerdings steht es von diesen "Lehren des Silvanus" fest, daß sie nicht gnostisch sind, zumal die Schöpfung hier in *Silv* nicht einem niedrigen Gott, sondern dem Vater selber zugeschrieben wird, wobei Christus in biblischem Sinne als Schöpfungsmittler auftritt (115, 3-6; 116, 7-9).[18] Unser *AuthLog* ist zwar nicht wie *Silv* ausgesprochen christlich, aber es scheint auch in ihm vorausgesetzt zu sein, daß der himmlische Vater mit dem Schöpfergott identisch ist, wenn wir die Aussage in 26,6f, "nichts ist ohne seinen (des Vaters) Willen entstanden" im Licht von 26,10ff, "er setzte diesen großen Kampf in der Welt ein" lesen. Ich weiß, daß dies eine durchaus auch innergnostisch annehmbare Möglichkeit ist.[19] Aber die Einheitlichkeit des himmlischen Vaters mit dem Schöpfergott verträgt gerade der Simonianismus nicht, den wir oben in seiner ersten und zweiten Phase

---

[15] Vgl. Aland, in: Widengren (ed.), a.a.O., 57.

[16] Vgl. E. Haenchen, Gab es eine vorchristliche Gnosis?, in: *Gott und Mensch, Gesammelte Aufsätze*, Tübingen 1965, 270.

[17] Vgl. J. Zandee, " 'Die Lehren des Silvanus' als Teil der Schriften von Nag Hammadi und der Gnostizismus", in: *NHS* VI, 239-252, bes. 242ff., 249ff.; Ders., "*The Teaching of Silvanus*" and *Clement of Alexandria, A New Document of Alexandrian Theology*, Leiden, 1977, bes. 134ff.

[18] Vgl. Zandee, in: *NHS* VI, 239.

[19] So BA, in: *ThLZ* 98, 254. Broek, *VigChr* 33, 260ff., hält *AuthLog* für "a new document of christian Platonism", indem er unserer Schrift gnostische Züge von vorneherein abspricht. Wie kann man aber vor allem es als nicht gnostisch, sondern platonisch bezeichnen, dem "Entstandenen" abzusagen (26, 14ff.)? Nach *AuthLog* ist also zwar nichts ohne den Willen des Urvaters entstanden, aber man muß die "Entstandenenen", bzw. die-

ausfindig gemacht haben. Dem simonianischen Mythos in diesen Phasen liegt doch genau umgekehrt ein "Bruch in der Gottheit" zugrunde und der göttliche Simon selbst steigt zu Ennoia ab, die aus ihm "hervorsprang" und von den Schöpfermächten in die menschen Körper, bzw. in Helena eingefesselt wurde, damit er sie von den Fesseln befreie und somit den Menschen Rettung gewähre (Iren. adv. haer. I 23, 3). Diesem typisch simonianisch-gnostischen Erlösungsmythos steht der Gedanke des Schöpfergott des *AuthLog* zuwider, da dieser hier mit dem himmlischen Vater identisch sein kann und die Funktion eines Erlösers hier nicht wie im Simonianismus der Gottheit selbst (Simon), sondern dem "Bräutigam" zugeschrieben worden ist, der wie in *ExPsych* als der von der Gottheit Ausgesandte vorgestellt zu sein scheint.

Wenn die Sache sich so verhält, dann ist es kein Zufall, daß Schenke als Argumente für die simonianischen Charakterzüge des *AuthLog* nur eine einzige Stelle nennt, das heißt 24, 5-10: "[Wenn nun] eine (Seele), d[ie unverständig ist], sich einen tr[enn]enden [Geist erwä]hlt, so schließt er [sie] aus [und w]irft sie ins *Hurenhaus*. Denn [er brach]te ihr die Last[erhaftig]keit, [weil sie] die Sittsamkeit ab[legte]."[20]

Aber "Hurenhaus" (πορνεῖον) als Metapher für die untere Welt hat, wie wir oben in Bezug auf "Dirne" (πορνεία) festgestellt haben, ursprünglich mit dem Simonianismus nichts zu tun.

3

Zum Schluß bringe ich die Sprache auf die Schrift *Brontē*. Es ist auch schwer, diese Schrift wie *AuthLog* einer ganz bestimmten Schulrichtung zuzuweisen, zumal sie ein einziger Monolog eines mannweiblichen Wesens ist, das sogar als Allgöttin alle Gegensätze zu umfassen scheint: "Ich bin die Weisheit der Griechen und die Erkenntnis der Barbaren" (16, 3ff); "Ich bin .... die Dirne und die Ehrbare" (13, 18) usw. Eben deswegen weichen die Meinungen über die religionsgeschichtliche Einordnung dieser Schrift weit voneinander ab. Einmal wird behauptet, daß unsere Schrift nicht gnostisch oder sogar vorgnostisch und im 1. Jahrhundert vor Chr. in jüdischen Kreisen Alexandriens unter Einfluß

---

jenigen, die aus den Schöpfern der Leiblichkeit entstammen (32, 16ff.), hinter sich lassen und sie verachten "in einem erhabenen Wissen und ... hineineilen zu dem, der existiert" (26, 14-20). In diesem Sinne nenne ich *AuthLog* — mit Zögern — gnostisch. Vgl. dazu Koschorke, *Wort und Dienst* 14, 51f, bes. Anm. 3, der allerdings vom "Willen" des Urvaters schweigt.

[20] Nach Übersetzung Schenkes, in: Irmscher, Treu (ed.), a.a.O., 217.

vom Isisaretalogien entstanden sei.[21] Dem wird entgegengestellt, daß *Brontē* ein "philosophisches" Spätprodukt, das den gnostischen Mythos vom Fall und der Errettung der Seele voraussetzt, ist.[22]

Auch in unserer Schrift wird der Fall der Brontē zwar nicht explizit erwähnt. Deswegen wird so weit gegangen zu behaupten, daß hier überhaupt kein "Bruch in der Gottheit" vorhanden sei.[23] Und doch, genau gesehen, werden Ichaussagen unserer Schrift von den soteriologischen Aussagen eingerahmt: Herabgesandtwerden (13, 2ff), Niedergeworfensein auf die Erde (15, 2ff) und Aufsteigen des "Ich", bzw. der von diesem befreiten Seelen zu ihrem Ruheplatz, wo man keinen Tod mehr kennt (21, 26-32).[24] Vom Blickpunkt dieser Rahmenhandlung her gesehen, werden in den Ichaussagen ambivalente Charakterzüge eines weiblichen, bzw. mannweiblichen Prinzips im gnostischen Sophiamythos zum Ausdruck gebracht.

Nun ordnet Schenke *Brontē* in den Simonianismus ein, indem er uns die Frage stellt, ob nicht diese Schrift neben *ExPsych* und *AuthLog* viel simonianischer als der Simonianismus sein könnte.

Als Indizien für seine These führt er zunächst 13, 15-18 an:

> "Ich bin die Erste
> und die Letzte.
> Ich bin die Geehrte
> und die Verachtete.
> Ich bin *die Dirne*
> und die Ehrbare."[25]

Wie ich wiederholt festgestellt habe, macht Helena als Dirne noch keinen Simonianismus aus. Das weiß freilich auch Schenke. Deswegen untermauert er dann seine These mit einer anderen Stelle, die mit seiner Ergänzung lautet:

---

[21] So Quispel, in: *NHS* VII, 82-122, bes. 86; Ders., "Origen and the Valentinian Gnosis", *VigChr* 28 (1974), 29-42, bes. 31.

[22] So BA, in: K.-W. Tröger (ed.), *Gnosis und Neues Testament, Studien aus Religionswissenschaft und Theologie*, Berlin 1973, 48; G. W. MacRae, "Discourses of the Gnostic Revealer", in: Widengren (ed.), a.a.O., 110-112, bes. 121.

[23] So Quispel, in: *NHS* VII, 101.

[24] Vgl. R. Unger, "Zur sprachlichen und formalen Struktur des gnostischen Textes »Der Donner: der vollkommene Nous«, *OrChr* 59 (1975), 82.

[25] Nach Übersetzung Schenkes, in: Irmscher, Treu (ed.), a.a.O., 216.

"Bei [dem Namen] der *großen Kraft*
und (bei) dem, dessen [Ergreifung] den Namen nicht erschüttern
   wird:
[*Der Ste*]*hende* ist es, der mich geschaffen hat." (21, 7-10).[26]

Die "große Kraft" ist, wie bekannt, das Epitheton Simons, das der
Apg 8, 10 entstammt und in der 1. und 2. Phase des Simonianismus mu-
tatis mutandis den höchsten Gott bedeutet. Andererseits bezeichnet die
"große Kraft" in der 3. Phase des Simonianismus, also in der *AM*, eine
im Menschen als "Möglichkeit" (δυνάμει) innewohnende, göttliche
Potenzialität, die höchstwahrscheinlich mit der von ihr ausgegangenen
"Kraft", also mit Simon, nicht identisch ist.[27] Wir kennen dagegen den
Titel eines "Stehenden" (ἑστώς) sowohl für den höchsten Gott als auch
für den vergöttlichten Simon aus der *AM*, aber auch aus nicht gnostischen Quellen. Es ist allerdings gerade wegen des häufigen Vorkommens
des Begriffs nicht möglich, von der Bezeichnung ἑστώς her auf die
Herkunft der simonianischen Gnosis zu schließen, wie immer wieder
versucht worden ist.[28]
   Jedenfalls hat Schenke insofern Recht, als er die "große Kraft" in der
ersten Zeile und den "Stehenden" in der letzten Zeile des oben ange-
führten Passus für den höchsten Gott hält, da sie beide tatsächlich im
Simonianismus als Gottesbezeichnung gelten. Es scheint mir aber sehr
problematisch, wenn Schenke in die mittlere Zeile mit einer gewaltigen
Ergänzung den vom höchsten Gott unterschiedenen Erlöser hineinzu-
lesen und diesen "in doketistischer Weise" zu verstehen sucht, indem er
als Para 'ele dazu eine verchristlichte Form des Gedankens des Irenäus,
adv. haei. I 23, 3 anführt: et passus autem in Judaea putatum, cum non
esset passus.[29] Meiner Meinung nach verträgt diesen doketistischen
Simon weder der Simonianismus der ersten Phase noch der der dritten,
da im ersteren Simon mit Christus nichts zu tun hat und der letztere sehr
monistischen Charakter in sich trägt. Dann könnte dieser Simon dem
Simonianismus der 2. Phase entsprechen, den ich aber für die Folge
einer Anpassung an das Christentum, also nicht primär für simonianisch halte.
   Bis jetzt habe ich versucht die Meinung Schenkes über den Passus 21,
7-10 nachzuprüfen, und zwar vorausgesetzt, daß seine Ergänzung in die

---

[26] Nach Übersetzung Schenkes, ibid.
[27] So Aland, in: Widengren (ed.), a.a.O., 66.
[28] So Aland, in: Widengren (ed.), a.a.O., 53. mit Anm. 72.
[29] in: Irmscher, Treu (ed.), a.a.O., 216.

lacunae richtig sei. In der Tat haben weder die Ergänzung noch die Rekonstruktion des Textes noch die dementsprechende Interpretation Schenkes bis heute bei irgendjemandem (außer bei Rudolph)[30] Unterstützung gefunden. Auch ich selbst konnte die von Schenke ergänzten Lesungen wie "Bei [dem Namen]", "und (bei) dem, dessen [Ergreifung]" und "[Der Ste]hende" an der Fascimilie-Ausgabe des koptischen Originaltextes[31] überhaupt nicht verifizieren.[32] Wenn der Text selbst sich so verhält, hängt die These Schenkes, die er auf Grund des von ihm ergänzten Textes aufstellt, ganz in der Luft. Allerdings bleibt das Wort der "großen Kraft" als einziger Anhaltspunkt für den Simonianismus. Aber die "große Kraft" ihrerseits ist als Bezeichnung des göttlichen Wesens in der hellenistischen Religionsgeschichte sehr weit verbreitet.[33] Nur zwei Termini "Dirne" und "große Kraft" allein scheinen mir als Belege für den Simonianismus allzu schwach zu sein.

Eben deswegen beruft sich Schenke schließlich auf die "Gesamteinschätzung" von *Brontē*, um somit seine These "entscheidend" zu bekräftigen: "Wenn man sich nämlich fragt, in den Mund welcher der bekannten gnostischen Sophia-Gestalten diese dialektische Offenbarungsrede am ehesten paßt, dann muß man eben die simonianische Ennoia, deren Geschick die größte Spannweite hat, nennen."[34]

Wie wir gesehen haben, hatte die "Ennoia" in der 1. Phase des Simonianismus noch keinen "dialektischen" Charakter, da sie dort nur als *prima salvanda* der menschlichen Seelen angesehen wurde. Diese "schwache" Ennoia, verbunden mit Helena, wurde in der 2. bzw. 3. Phase des Simonianismus des Hipp. "mächtig". Die "Gesamteinschätzung" Schenkes über *Brontē* ist also insofern richtig, als in der späteren Phase des Simonianismus Ennoia/Helena beinahe als "Salvator salvan-

---

[30] Rudolph schweigt dazu!

[31] *The Facsimile Edition of Nag Hammadi Codicis*, Codex VI, published under the Auspices of the Department of Antiquities of the Arab Republic of Egypt in Conjunction with the United Nations Educational, Scientific and Cultural Organization, Leiden, 1972, 25 (VI, [21]).

[32] Nicht nur die editio princeps von M. Krause, P. Labib (ed.), *Gnostische und hermetische Schriften aus Coder II und Codex VI*, Glückstadt, 1971, 132, sondern auch die neue deutsche Edition und Übersetzung von R. Unger, *OrChr* 59, 104 und die neueste englische Edition und Übersetzung von G. W. MacRae, The Thunder: Perfect Mind, VI, 2: 13, 1-21, 32, in: D. M. Parrott (ed.), *Nag Hammadi Codices V 2-5 and VI with Papyrus Berolinensis 8502, 1 and 4*, *NHS XI*, Leiden, 1979, 252 lassen die Ergänzung der lacunae unseres Passus offen. Nach Unger, *OrChr* 59, 104, Anm. 336 und 337 "kann die Lücke nicht ergänzt werden", oder "Ergänzung nicht möglich". Mir scheint, daß es sich hier bei unserem Passus um eine Spekulation über den Namen der "großen Kraft" (?) handelt.

[33] Vgl. Beyschlag, a.a.O., 106ff.

[34] In: Irmscher, Treu (ed.), a.a.O., 216.

da" bezeichnet werden könnte, was ich allerdings nicht für primär simonianisch halte.[35]

Immerhin müßten wir uns hier die Frage stellen, warum man als Spre-
cher der dialektischen Offenbarungsrede in *Brontē* ausschließlich "die
simonianische Ennoia" nennen muß. Gilt das nicht auch von der So-
phiagestalt, die dem barbelo-gnostischen Mythos des *ApcJoh* zugrundeliegt, da sie hier ausgerechnet die Rolle des zu erlösenden Erlösers spielt,
oder auch von Sophia-Achamot im Valentinianismus, die sowohl als
mater als auch als *prunicus* bezeichnet wird? Ich möchte hier vor allem
die 5. titellose Schrift aus NHC II (sog. *UW*) nennen, zumal in dieser
Schrift die dialektische Ichaussage der Sophia-Eva eben zu der der
Brontē eine treffende Parallele darstellt:[36]

UW 114, 4-15	*Brontē* 13, 2-14
Eva nun ist die erste Jungfrau (παρθένος). Wenn diese ohne Mann gebiert, ist sie es, die sich selber geheilt hat. Deswegen sagt man von ihr, daß sie gesagt hat: "Ich bin der Teil (μέρος) meiner Mutter und ich bin die Mutter, ich bin das Weib, ich bin die Jungfrau (παρθένος), ich bin die Trösterin der Wehen; mein Gatte hat mich erzeugt und ich bin seine Mutter und er ist mein Vater und mein Herr; er ist meine Kraft; was er will, sagt er. Vernünftig werde ich. Aber ich habe einen Herrenmenschen er-zeugt.[37]	Ich bin die Frau und Jungfrau (παρθένος). Ich bin die Mutter und die Tochter. Ich bin die Glieder (μέλος) meiner Mutter. Ich bin die, deren Hochzeiten (γάμος) zahlreich sind, und ich habe nicht geheiratet. Ich bin die Hebamme und die, die nicht gebiert. Ich bin der Trost meiner Geburtsschmer-zen. Ich bin die Braut und der Bräutigam. Und mein Mann ist es, der mich gezeugt hat. Ich bin die Mutter meines Vaters und die Schwester meines Mannes, und er ist mein Abkömmling ...[38]

---

[35] Neuerdings versucht Schenke, "Die Tendenz der Weisheit zur Gnosis", in: B. Aland
(ed.), *Gnosis, Festschrift für Jonas*, Göttingen, 1978, 353 ein anderes Indiz für das "Simonianische" unserer Schrift gerade in deren Titel "βροντή" ("Donner") ausfindig zu machen: Der Donner wäre ursprünglich im Name der Athena, die ihr als Tochter des Zeus,
des Donnerers, von dem der Donner eben ausgeht, sinnvoll zukommt. In diesem Licht be-
käme auch die Notiz des Iren. adv. haer. I, 23, 4, nach der die Simonianer Simon und Helena in den Bildern des Zeus und der Athena verehrt hätten, eine neue Perspektive. —
Athena (Minerva) ist tatsächlich in der griechischen Mythologie Tochter des Zeus, und
zwar des Juppiter tonans. Ist es aber folgerichtig, daß hier Schenke Zeus/Athena in diesem Sinne mit dem Zeus/Athenakult der Simonianer in Verbindung bringt und somit den
simonianischen Charakter unserer Schrift zu bekräftigen versucht, während er einmal die
Gestalt Helena als Partnerin Simons für nicht simonianisch, sondern für die Folge einer
"Persiflage" der Häresiologen gehalten hat? (So auch Rudolph, Literatur s. oben S. 3,
Anm. 4). Außerdem war möglicherweise der Titel "Brontē" ursprünglich in unserer
Schrift nicht vorhanden, zumal dieser außer im Titel nirgendwo erwähnt worden ist.
Jedenfalls ist der Simon (Zeus)/Helena (Athena)-Kult m.E. im Simonianismus
sekundär. Vgl. Arai, in: *NHS* VIII, 189f.

[36] Vgl. vor allem MacRae, in: Widengren (ed.), a.a.O., 119f.

[37] Nach der Übersetzung Böhligs, in: A. Böhlig, P. Labib (ed.), *Die koptisch-gnostische
Schrift ohne Titel aus Codex II von Nag Hammadi im Koptischen Museum zu Alt-Kairo*,
Berlin, 1962, 75.

[38] Nach der Übersetzung Krauses, in: Krause, Labib (ed.), a.a.O., 122f.

Die Schrift *UW* hat ihrerseits nicht nur valentianische, sondern auch sethianische und sogar mandäische Züge, aber fast keinen Zug des Simonianismus.[39]

Die Spannweite des dialektischen Monologs der *Bronte* ist also allzu breit, als daß man diese Schrift einer ganz bestimmten Schulrichtung zuweisen könnte, geschweige denn dem Simonianismus. Deswegen scheint mir die Meinung des BA um Schenke viel sachgemäßer als Schenkes selbst zu sein: "Die Schrift ist eine 'philosophische' Abstruktion, die erst auf Grund der Entwicklung des gnostischen Sophia-Mythos und anderer Mythen möglich wurde, die die verschiedensten Elemente in sich vereinigt."[40]

Zusammenfassend läßt sich Folgendes sagen: Schenke hat insofern Recht, als er in den drei Schriften, nämlich *Bronte*, *AuthLog* und *ExPsych*, beinahe "einen und denselben Seelenmythos" ausfindig gemacht hat und in jeder Schrift einigermaßen simonianische Motive hervorgehoben hat.[41] Ich bin aber nicht im Stande, methodologisch und sachlich mit Schenke (und Rudolph) so weit zu gehen und mich zu fragen, ob nicht neben *ExPsych* auch *Bronte* und *AuthLog* "am Ende vielleicht viel simonianischer sind als der Simonianismus der Kirchenväter."

---

[39] Vgl. H.-G. Bethge, in: J. M. Robinson (ed.), *The Nag Hammadi Library in English*, New York, Hagerstown, San Francisco, London, 1977, 161.

[40] In: Tröger (ed.), a.a.O., 49.

[41] In: Irmscher, Treu (ed.), a.a.O., 216ff.

AUTOGENES AND ADAMAS

The Mythological Structure of the Apocryphon of John

BY

R. VAN DEN BROEK

The development of the Pleroma as described in the *Apocryphon of John* (AJ) is the result of the mergence of quite different traditions into a complicated, incoherent and contradictory system. Our sources reflect different stages of this merging process. These sources are two recensions of AJ, preserved in four Coptic versions,[1] Irenaeus' report on the Barbelo Gnostics in his *Adversus Haereses*, I, 29, certainly based upon a recension which considerably differed from those we know,[2] and related myths in other gnostic texts, in particular the *Gospel of the Egyptians*.[3] In this paper I want to argue that the embarrassing structure of the first, metaphysical part of AJ is mainly due to a fusion of two originally separate and independent conceptions of God. In order to show this we have to clarify the original position of the lower aeons Autogenes and Adamas.

According to all witnesses, the apex of the spiritual world is formed by a Trinity consisting of the Unknowable Father or the Invisible Spirit, the Mother (Ennoia or Barbelo), and the Son (the Light or Christ). To

---

[1] W. C. Till, *Die gnostischen Schriften des koptischen Papyrus Berolinensis 8502*, 2nd rev. ed. by H.-M. Schenke (TU 60²), Berlin, 1972; M. Krause and P. Labib, *Die drei Versionen des Apokryphon des Johannes im Koptischen Museum zu Alt-Kairo* (Abhandlungen des Deutschen Archäologischen Instituts Kairo, Koptische Reihe, I), Wiesbaden, 1962. The three versions from Nag Hammadi are contained in Codices II, III, and IV; the long version is found in Cod. II and IV, the short one in Cod. III and in the Berlin text (abbreviated: BG).

[2] For a discussion of the differences between Irenaeus and the extant versions of AJ, see C. Schmidt, "Irenäus und seine Quelle in adv. haer. I, 29", in *Philotesia, Paul Kleinert zum 70. Geburtstag dargebracht*, Berlin, 1907, 315-336; H.-M. Schenke, "Nag Hammadi Studien I: Das literarische Problem des Apokryphon Johannis", *Zeitschrift für Religions- und Geistesgeschichte* 14 (1962) 57-63; M. Krause, "The Relation of the Apocryphon of John to the Account of Irenaeus", in W. Foerster, *Gnosis. A Selection of Gnostic Texts*, English Translation edited by R. McL. Wilson, I, Oxford, 1972, 100-103.

[3] A. Böhlig and F. Wisse, *Nag Hammadi Codices III, 2 and IV, 2: The Gospel of the Egyptians (The Holy Book of the Great Invisible Spirit)* (Nag Hammadi Studies, IV), Leiden, 1975.

both the Mother and the Son, the Father grants three other hypostases. The result is that there are two tetrads which subsequently are combined into an ogdoad of four pairs. The further development of the Pleroma proceeds through the generation of new aeons by these pairs. The original scheme can be still more clearly seen in Irenaeus than in the extant versions of AJ, as appears from the following juxtaposition.

Irenaeus	AJ
In the Virginal Spirit the Father manifests himself to Barbelo as Ennoia, to whom are added:	The Invisible Spirit (= the Father) manifeste himself as Ennoia (= Barbelo), to whom are added:
Prognosis	Prognosis
Aphtharsia	Aphtharsia
Aeonia Zoe	Eternal Life
The Father and Barbelo generate the Light, who is	The Father and Barbelo generate the Light, the divine Autogenes, who is
Christ, to whom are added:	Christ, to whom are added:
Nous	Nous
—— (see below sub c.)	Thelema
Logos	Logos
The two tetrads are combined into an ogdoad of four pairs:	———
	———
a. Ennoia and Logos	a. ———
b. Aphtharsia and Christ	b. ——— (see below sub bb.)
c. Aeonia Zoe and Thelema	c. Eternal Life and Thelema
d. Nous and Prognosis[4]	d. Nous and Prognosis
These pairs glorify the great Light (= the Father) and Barbelo.	These pairs glorify the Invisible Spirit and Barbelo.
aa. Ennoia and Logos produce	aa. ———
Autogenes "ad repraesentationem magni luminis";	The Autogenes, Christ, was perfected "eouparastasis of the great Invisible Spirit" (III, 11, 5); the Inv. Spir.
he was greatly honoured and all things were subjected to him. Together with Autogenes Aletheia was emitted and both formed a new pair.	honoured him with great honour, set him over everything and gave him all power, and subjected to him the Truth which is in him.
bb. Aphtharsia and Christ produce the four great Lights[5]	bb. From Christ and Aphtharsia, throught the Invisible Spirit and through Autogenes, the four great

---

[4] In the *Gospel of the Egyptians* this ogdoad is described as the Ogdoad of the Father; the Mother and the Son each having an ogdoad of their own. In the Ogdoad of the Father the sequence of the aeons is identical with that of Irenaeus and AJ, the only differences being the omission of Christ and the addition, at the end, of the androgynous Father (III, 42, 5-11; IV, 51, 22-52, 2 Böhlig-Wisse 58-59). Just as in Irenaeus and AJ, only in the fourth pair, Nous and Prognosis, the male aeon is mentioned first, whereas in the other cases the female aeon precedes the male one. This points to a fixed, literary tradition.

[5] The *Gospel of the Egyptians* does not mention the generation of aeons from the four pairs but only speaks of the appearances, one after another, of the divine hypostases,

"ad circumstantiam Autogeni"

cc. Aeonia Zoe and Thelema produce four emanations *"ad subministrationem quatuor luminaribus"*.

Each Light receives one aeon.
dd. All aeons having thus been established, Autogenes emits the perfect and true Man,

who is called Adamas.[7]

Together with him Perfect Knowledge is emitted, by which Adamas also knows him who is above all things. He was given an invincible power by the Virginal Spirit. All things rejoiced over him and praised the great Aeon. In this way was manifested the Mother, the Father, and the Son.[8]

Lights came forth *"euparastasis* for him" (III, 11, 19).
cc. — — (Thelema, Ennoia and Life are mentioned, with the names of the four ministers, but the text is apparently in disorder)[6]
Each Light receives three aeons.
dd. All things became established. From Prognosis and perfect Nous the perfect, true Man came forth, through the good pleasure of the Invisible Spirit and of Autogenes, and was called Adam.

The Invisible Spirit gave him an invincible, intellectual power.
Adamas glorified the Invisible Spirit, and Autogenes, and the aeons, the three: the Father, the Mother, the Son.

mostly brought forth by a special power. After Autogenes Logos there appears a living power, "the mother of the incorruptible ones", who gives birth to Adamas. Autogenes and Adamas give praise to the Father and then ask for a power and strength for Autogenes and a son for Adamas. A power comes forth and begets the four Lights and Seth (III, 49-51, 22; IV, 60, 30-63, 17 Böhlig-Wisse 90-101). Thus Adamas comes into being before the servants of Autogenes, and Seth together with these servants. The figure of the heavenly Seth plays an important role in the *Gospel of the Egyptians*; in AJ's myth of the Pleroma his birth is not mentioned but he still holds the position in the second Light which tradition assigned to him (comp. BG 35, 20-36, 2 and GEgypt III, 65, 16; IV, 77, 12-13 Böhlig-Wisse 152-153).

[6] Cod. II, 8, 1-2 and BG 33, 4-5 mention "the Will, the Ennoia, and the Life"; Cod. IV, 12, 6 omits the whole passage and Cod. III, 11, 20-21 reads: "The Thelema, the Eternal Life and the Ennoia". I would suggest that in this passage Ennoia is not original but intruded into the textual tradition through an early Greek scribe's error: θέλημα καὶ αἰώνια ζωή probably was erroneously read as θέλημα καὶ ἔννοια καὶ ζωή. This would explain why in BG and Cod. II the word Life lacks its usual qualification "Eternal"; the text of Cod. III looks like a partial return to the original. In the *Gospel of the Egyptians*, the four servants of the four Lights are said to be their consorts; together they form "the first ogdoad of the divine Autogenes" (III, 52, 3-16; IV, 63, 24-64, 10 Böhlig-Wisse 102-103). A second ogdoad of Autogenes is formed by four Ministers of the great Lights and the consorts of these Ministers (III, 52, 16-53, 12; IV, 64, 10-65, 5 Böhlig-Wisse 104-105). The second ogdoad is not mentioned in Irenaeus or AJ but the names of three consorts of the Ministers appear among the 12 aeons assigned to the four Lights in AJ. These traditions deserve a special investigation which I intend to present in the near future.

[7] Irenaeus' source contained a pun on the name Adamas, which was brought in connexion with the word ἀδάμας, "unconquerable" (more usual ἀδάμαστος, "unsubdued", "untamed"): *"quem et Adamantem vocant, quoniam neque ipse domatus est, neque ii ex quibus erat."*

[8] In addition to this Irenaeus says that from the Anthropos (= Adamas) and Gnosis a Tree is born which is called Gnosis too, whereas AJ, presupposing the heavenly Seth to be

In AJ the birth of Autogenes from Ennoia and Logos has been suppressed because Autogenes is identified with the third person of the
Trinity, Christ, the son of the Father and Barbelo. This procedure
eliminated the difficulty, still conspicuously present in Irenaeus, that the
dignity, honour and sovereignty attributed to Autogenes are quite
unusual for an aeon which came into being after the completion of the
first stage of the divine world, but wholly characteristic of a first
hypostasis after the Unknowable Father. However, comparison with the
parallel passage in Irenaeus shows that AJ is secondary here. The high
position of Autogenes suggests that this figure derives from quite
another context and that he was only secondarily allotted an inferior
p'ace in the trinitarian system of AJ.

Another important difference between Irenaeus and AJ is that the
former says that Adamas is the son of Autogenes, while the latter states
that he was born from the fourth aeonic pair, Prognosis and Nous. The
view in AJ is more consistent with the myth of the four pairs than that in
Irenaeus. If Autogenes comes forth from such a pair it may be expected
that also Adamas, who apparently is of lower rank, is born in a similar
way. It seems possible, however, that at this point the source of Irenaeus
had retained a more primitive and original element of the myth of
Autogenes. Comparison with other texts shows that Autogenes is the
heavenly Anthropos, Man, and Adamas the Son of Man.

In *Eugnostos the Blessed*, the all-embracing, unknowable God is called *Agennetos* (III, 72, 22) and *Propatôr* (74, 22). His first manifestation
is called *Autopatôr* and *Autogenetôr* (75, 6-7) and also *Immortal Man*
(76, 23-24) and *Autopatôr-Man* (77, 14-15). Immortal Man produces
with his consort the Son of Man, called *Progenetôr-Father* and *Adam of
the Light*. This Adam and his consort emit the *Son of the Son of Man*,
called the *Saviour*, the *Begetter of All Things* (= *Pangenetôr*) (81,
22-83, 3).[9] The Autogenes and Adamas of AJ correspond to the Immor-

---

the son of Adamas, speaks about the positions assigned to Adamas, Seth, the Sons of Seth
and other souls within the Pleroma. The basic myth presented above apparently could be
developed in quite different directions. The Tree of Knowledge played an important part
in Ophite speculations, while Seth was the central figure in Sethian Gnosticism.

[9] The Saviour in his turn reveals six androgynous spiritual beings "whose type is that of
those who preceded them." Their male names are: *Agennetos*, *Autogennetos*, *Genetôr*,
Protogenetôr, *Pangenetôr*, and *Archigenetôr* (82, 7-18). Of these beings *Agennetos* and
Autogennetos correspond to the Unknown Father and Immortal Man; the third and the
fourth names seem to refer to the Son of Man or Adam, and the fifth and the sixth names
to the Saviour. But their female names do not correspond in the same way to the female
aspects of the four highest beings.

tal Man or Autogenetôr and the Son of Man or Adam of Eugnostus. In AJ's short recension the name Autogenetôr is even repeatedly used instead of the usual Autogenes (BG 34, 8; 34, 11 = III, 12, 20; 35, 8).

Though there are other texts which declare the second divine hypostasis to be Autogenes, it is obvious that this name was only secondarily attached to the heavenly Man. The term αὐτογενής could also be used to indicate the supreme God, which made it virtually identical with ἀγένητος or ἀγενής.[10]

In the Hermetic writing *On the Ogdoad and the Ennead*, NH Cod. VI, 6, the highest God, the *Agennetos*, is distinguished from the *Autogennetos* and the *Genneton* (57, 13-18; 63, 21-23).[11] What is meant by these terms can be deduced from the doctrine of the gnostic Peratae, described in Hippolytus, *Ref.*, V, 12, 1ff. The universe is a triad of which the first 'part' is unoriginate (ἀγέννητον) and perfectly good; the second is self-originate (αὐτογενές), containing an infinite number of self-originate powers, and the third is the particular and originate (γεννητόν; *Ref.*, V, 12, 1-3). This triad can also be described as the Father, the Son, and Matter (V, 17, 1). The Peratae identified the Self-originate Son with Christ, the Saviour (V, 17, 8), just as in AJ Autogenes is considered identical with Christ, the Son.

These ideas were explicitly applied to the myth of the Anthropos by the Naassenes. According to Hippolytus, they revered beyond all others Man and the Son of Man (V, 6, 4). Man is said to be androgynous and called Adamas (V, 6, 5; 7, 2.14); the Son of Man is identified with Christ, the Saviour, and is in fact the earthly manifestation of Man, Adamas (V, 7, 33). The Naassenes adhered to the same doctrine of the tripartite universe as was taught by the Peratae. They were uncertain whether the soul comes from the Pre-existent (ἐκ τοῦ προόντος) or from the Self-originate (ἐκ τοῦ αὐτογενοῦς) or from outpoured Chaos (ἐκ τοῦ ἐκκεχυμένου χάους), i.e. formless matter (V, 7, 9). The Father of the universe, the Pre-existent One, has begotten "that invisible,

---

[10] Αὐτογενής as a predicate of the supreme God in *Orphic fragm.* 245, 8 (Kern 257); in *Orac. Sibyll.*, fragm. 1, 17 (Geffcken 228) he is called αὐτογενής, ἀγένητος, and in *Hermetic fragm.* 23, 58 (Nock-Festugière IV, 19) αὐτόγονος or (var. lect.) αὐτογενής. In Synesius, *Hymni* I, 146-148 (Terzaghi 11) God is addressed as αὐτοπάτωρ, προπάτωρ, ἀπάτωρ, υἱὲ σεαυτοῦ. In *Zostrianus*, a gnostic writing which shows a close relationship with Eugnostus and AJ, the pre-existent, Unknown Father, his Son, and Geradamas, the Perfect Man, are all called Autogenes (NH Cod. VIII, 6, 21; 20, 5ff; 30, 6; 127, 15ff).

[11] See J.-P. Mahé, *Hermès en Haute-Égypte. Les textes hermétiques de Nag Hammadi et leur parallèles grecs et latins*, I (Bibliothèque Copte de Nag Hammadi, Section: "Textes", 3), Quebec, 1978, 48-52, 110.

unnameable, and unutterable Son of his'', viz. Adamas (V, 9, 1). From these texts we may infer that the heavenly Anthropos was called Autogenes by the Naassenes too.

That the Autogenes and Adamas of AJ originally were the highest divine beings after the Unknowable Father, Man and the Son of Man, explains also Autogenes' high position, of which three aspects are mentioned by both Irenaeus and AJ.

The first aspect is that Autogenes is allowed to stand near the Great Light (Irenaeus) or the great Invisible Spirit (AJ). The word used for this in the original Greek text of AJ is preserved in III, 11, 5: Autogenes was perfected *eouparastasis* of the great Invisible Spirit. The same word is used in III, 11, 19 to describe the position of the four great Lights: they appeared *euparastasis* of Autogenes. If derived from παρίσταμαι the word παράστασις can mean the act of standing near a king, "a position or post near a king".[12] In this sense the word was translated in the other Coptic versions of AJ, and also the Latin translator of Irenaeus interpreted in this way the word παράστασις (or: περίστασις?) which he found used with respect to the four Lights in the Greek original: they were emitted *"ad circumstantiam Autogeni"*. But the word παράστασις can also be taken as a substantive derived from παρίστημι, meaning *int. al.* "manifestation", "representation".[13] Irenaeus' Latin translator took it in this sense when he found it used with respect to Autogenes: he was emitted *"ad repraesentationem Magni Luminis"*. But it seems more plausible that the word παράστασις, used twice in the same construction, in III, 11, 5 and 19, should be interpreted in the same way, as was done by the Coptic translators. The heavenly world is visualized as a royal court: God is the king and Autogenes his first servant, holding the highest rank with the right to stand beside the throne, the four great Lights being his ministers.

According to Irenaeus, the second and third aspects of Autogenes' dignity are that he was greatly honoured and that all things were subjected to him: *"et valde honorificatum dicunt, et omnia huic subiecta."* The same is said in the short version of AJ: "It is the divine Autogenes, Christ, whom he has honoured with a great honour because he had come forth from his first Ennoia, (Autogenes) whom the Invisible Spirit has set as God over everything. The true God gave him all power

---

[12] H. G. Liddell and R. Scott, *A Greek-English Lexicon*, New Edition by H. St. Jones and R. McKenzie, Oxford, 1940, 1325a.

[13] Liddell and Scott, *o.c.*, 1325a, and G. W. H. Lampe, *A Patristic Greek Lexicon*, Oxford, 4th impr. 1976, 1025.

(ἐξουσία) and subjected to him the Truth which is in him in order that he
should know everything, he whose name will be said to those who are
worthy" (III, 11, 6-14). The sudden introduction of Truth in this
context is explained by Irenaeus, who after the words *"omnia huic
subiecta"* continues with the birth of Autogenes' consort: *"Coemissam
autem ei Alethiam et esse coniugationem Autogenis et Alethiae."* Having already suppressed the birth of Autogenes from Ennoia and Logos,
AJ accordingly had also to leave out that of his consort, but seems to
have retained Aletheia by making her subject to Autogenes.

These three aspects of Autogenes' dignity, his position near to God,
his being honoured by God and the subjection of all things to him, have
their ultimate source in that Psalm of David on the dignity of man,
Psalm 8:

> What is man that thou art mindful of him,
> and the son of man that thou dost care for him?
> Yet thou hast made him *little less than God* (1),
> and dost crown him with *glory and honour* (2),
> Thou hast given him *dominion over the works of thy hands*;
> thou hast *put all things under his feet* (3).
>
> (vss. 4-6, RSV)

That this Psalm played a part in the speculations on the Son of Man
appears from Daniel 7, 14 which speaks of the honouring of the Son of
Man by the Ancient of Days: "Sovereignty and glory and kingly power
were given to him so that all people and nations of every language
should serve him." Saint Paul, who does not mention the title of Son of
Man, nevertheless was familiar with the conception as is shown by his
quotations of Ps. 8, 6 in 1 Cor. 15, 27 and Eph. 1, 22: "He (God) has
put all things in subjection under his (Christ's) feet."[14] The glory of the
Anthropos as described in Ps. 8, 5-6 seems to have found a succinct and
fixed expression in the notion that he has been given all power (πᾶσαν
εξουσίαν). This formula is found in AJ (see above) and is also repeatedly
used with respect to the Anthropos in the Poimandres;[15] but it was also
applied to Christ as the Son of Man (Matth. 28, 18; 11, 27; John 3, 35;

---

[14] See C. H. Dodd, *According to the Scriptures*, London, 1952, 19-20, 32-34, who also
adduces other scriptural passages in which Ps. 8, 4ff. is used, and B. Lindars, *New Testament Apologetic*, London, 1961, 50, 168.

[15] *Poimandres*, 12, 14, 15, 32 (Nock-Festugière, I, 10, 11, 19); cf. H. Windisch,
"Urchristentum und Hermesmystik", *Theologisch Tijdschrift* 52 (1918) 213.

13, 3; 17, 2). That Ps. 8,4-6 as a whole was applied to the Anthropos can also be seen from Hebrews 2,6ff., where these verses are cited in the version of the Septuagint. The Seventy had interpreted the word *elohim* in vs. 5 as "angels".[16] The author of the Epistle to the Hebrews says that now we do not yet see all things subjected to Man, but we see Jesus who for a short while was made lower than the angels but through the suffering of death was crowned with glory and honour. This interpretation of Ps. 8,4ff. obviously represents a Christian adaptation of the Myth of the heavenly Anthropos, provoked by the reading "angels" and made acceptable by taking the words βραχύ τι ("a little") in a temporal sense ("for a short while"). But the view that Ps. 8, 4ff. refer to the Anthropos must have been developed from the reading *elohim*, "God". For those who read in the Psalm that man was made little less than the angels there was no reason to interpret this man as Man, the first manifestation of God's glory.[17] This idea must have originated in a Jewish, Hebrew-speaking milieu. We have already seen that also in Dan. 7, 14 the glory and the all-dominating power, which in Ps. 8, 5-6 are attributed to man, are given to the Son of Man.

All these considerations lead to the conclusion that the whole passage on Autogenes and Adamas in AJ was not conceived by the composer of the original Apocryphon but that this writer made use of an originally independent Jewish myth of the heavenly Anthropos. This myth already distinguished between Man and the Son of Man, who was called Adamas and apparently held to be the prototype of earthly man, "the perfect and true man".

That the tradition concerning Autogenes and Adamas originally only knew of the Unknowable Father above them and in AJ was only secondarily combined with the conception of a Trinity of Father, Mother, and Son can still clearly be seen in the praise of Adamas after his creation. He first glorifies the Invisible Spirit, Autogenes, and the aeons (probably the four Great Lights and their servants), and then, without any transition or explanation, adds the Father, the Mother and the Son: "And he spoke, glorified and praised the Invisible Spirit, saying: 'Because of you everything has come into being and everything will

---

[16] The same in the Targum (*mal'akajja'*); but the Rabbis took the word *elohim* in the sense of God; cf. P. Billerbeck, *Kommentar zum Neuen Testament aus Talmud und Midrasch*, III, Munich, 1926, 681-682.

[17] For the origin of the doctrine of the Anthropos, see G. Quispel, "Ezekiel 1, 26 in Jewish Mysticism and Gnosis", *Vigiliae Christianae* 34 (1980) 1-13.

return to you. I, then, I shall[18] praise and glorify you and Autogenes
and the aeons; the three: the Father, the Mother, and the Son, the
perfect power' " (II, 9, 5-11).

The disclosure of the original mythological background of Autogenes
and Adamas sheds some new light on the problem of the relationship
between the two parts of AJ, which correspond to Irenaeus, *Adv.
Haer.*, I, 29 and I, 30, respectively.[19] An important difference between
the two parts is that the first part and Irenaeus, I, 29 teach a Trinity of
Father, Mother and Son, and that the second part, beginning at BG 44,
19 parr., clearly presupposes a myth of the Anthropos, which indeed is
found in Irenaeus, I, 30.

In I, 30, 1, Irenaeus relates the following doctrine of the Ophites: In
the power of the Deep (Bythos) there is a first light, the Father of All,
called the First Man. His Ennoia which proceeds from him is his Son,
called the Son of Man or the Second Man. Below these there is the Holy
Spirit, called the First Woman. From her the First and the Second Man
beget an incorruptible light, the Third Male, called Christ.

This myth is pressuposed in the second Part of AJ. The Demiurge and
his Archons conceive the idea to create man when they hear a voice from
heaven, saying: "Man exists, and the Son of Man". The short version
of AJ, BG 42, 20-43, 4, adds that through this voice "the holy, perfect
Father, the *First Man* taught this in the form of a man, the Blessed One
revealed to them his shape." The long version, IV, 14, 18-24, reads:
"And the holy Mother-Father taught them, and the complete
foreknowledge, the image of the Invisible One, who is the *Father of the
All* through whom everything came into being, the *First Man*, for he
revealed his appearance in a human form."[20] It is clear that we meet
here the *Pater omnium* or *Primus Homo* and the *Filius Hominis* of
Irenaeus I, 30, 1. There must have been a time when the second part of
AJ was preceded by a myth of the Anthropos which at least was closely
related to that of Irenaeus I, 30.

We have seen that the original myth of Autogenes and Adamas
indeed was such an Anthropos myth. But in contrast to that of Irenaeus

---

[18] The other versions (IV, 14 hiat) have the present tense, which seems to be the better
reading.

[19] The studies mentioned in note 2 primarily deal with the differences between AJ and
Irenaeus, whereas few attention has been paid to those between the two parts of AJ itself.

[20] Of these explanations there is no trace in Irenaeus, I, 30, 6. There it is the Mother
who calls out against the Demiurge: "Do not lie, Ialdabaoth, for there is above you the
Father of all, the First Man, and the Man, the Son of Man."

I, 30, 1, this myth had been developed into a system of tetrads forming ogdoads. A discussion of the original meaning of these tetrads will be given elsewhere. Here, I only suggest that the starting point for this development lay in the figure of Ennoia, who originally was conceived of as the consort of the Father, the female aspect of the androgynous God.[21] By making her an independent hypostasis she could easily be interpreted as the Spouse of God and the Mother of the Son. This is what happened in AJ and Irenaeus I, 29, though not in exactly the same way. How easily this could be done appears from Irenaeus I, 30, 1 itself.

According to Irenaeus, the *Primum Lumen* and *Pater omnium* (said to be the *Primus Homo*) and his Ennoia (called the *Secundus Homo*)beget a *Lumen Incorruptibile*, Christ, from the Holy Spirit. One has only to leave out the Holy Spirit or to identify her with Ennoia in order to arrive at the trinitarian myth of the first part of AJ: The Father, who is all Light (BG 25, 9-15; 26, 15-21; Irenaeus: *"magnum Lumen"*) and his Ennoia (= Barbelo) produce the Light, Christ. The myth of the Pleroma in the *Apocryphon of John* can be characterized as an elaborate myth of the heavenly Anthropos pressed into a trinitarian scheme.

---

[21] The Anthropos myth in Irenaeus, I, 30, 1 cannot represent the original version: the *Pater omnium*, who is described as the supreme God (*"primum lumen in virtute Bythi, beatum et incorruptibile et interminatum"*), is said to be the *Primus Homo*, and his Ennoia the *Filius Hominis* or *Secundus Homo*. The identification of the supreme God and the Anthropos (the first type of the Anthropos doctrine distinguished by H.-M. Schenke, *Der Gott "Mensch" in der Gnosis*, Göttingen, 1962, 64-68) seems to be a secondary development. That God's Ennoia is interpreted as the Son of Man, and also that the First and the Second Anthropos together generate the *Tertium Masculum*, Christ, from the Holy Spirit are quite singular views. Most probably, this myth originally taught four androgynous highest beings, just as is done in *Eugnostus*: the Unknowable Father, Man, the Son of Man, and the Saviour (Christ).

ISIS AS PLANE IN THE GOSPEL OF TRUTH?*

BY

JAN HELDERMAN

The aim of this article is to try to trace the mythographic figure behind the *Plane*, Error, in the Gospel of Truth. Whereas R. Haardt[1] spoke of the *disiecta membra* of a myth regarding the Plane-figure, we will try—following the pattern of the Osiris/Isis/Horus-myth—to connect if possible, these loose parts of a myth to the presupposed myth again. We believe we have found this myth in Plutarch's *De Iside et Osiride*, following some leads as given by some scholars in the past.

As to the Plane and her activities in the *Gos. Truth* the following points could be summarized.

On p. 17 of the MS we meet the Plane in the center of a larger part of cosmogonic character. First of all, we can state that she is Ignorance personified, nearly made an ὑπόστασις.[2] *Ignorance* with her consequences *Fear* (ⲚⲞⲨϢⲠ) and *Fright* (ϨⲢⲦⲉ) causes the appearance of *Plane*, p. 17: 14. We are informed that she, becoming strong, fashioned her matter (ὕλη) in emptiness, without knowing the Truth. This emptiness[3]—compare p. 26:26 Error is empty—is as such the antithesis to the Pleroma and in the Pythagorean tradition connected with the Dyas, the number 2, an important quality of Plutarch's Isis, as we shall see. Essential in our search for the mythological figure upon which Plane

---

* Extended version of a paper read at the International Conference on Gnosticism at Yale University (USA), 28-31 March 1978. Abbreviations following JBL 95 (1976) p. 335-346.

[1] R. Haardt, "Zur Struktur des Plane-Mythos im Evangelium Veritatis des Codex Jung", *WZKM* 58 (1962) 25.

[2] See n. 74 below.

[3] As to the Valentinian emptiness see, apart from the commentary re p. 17:16 in the *editio princeps* of the *Gos. Truth* (M. Malinine a.o., *Evangelium Veritatis*, Zürich: Rascher, 1956; Supplement 1961—the edition used here), R. Kasser a.o., *Tractatus Tripartitus* pars I *De Supernis* (Bern: Francke, 1973) 351 and H. Jonas, *Gnosis und spätantiker Geist*. I, Die mythologische Gnosis (Göttingen: Vandenhoeck & Ruprecht, 1964³) 366. As to the Pythagorean tradition see W. Möller, *Geschichte der Kosmologie in der griechischen Kirche bis auf Origenes* (Halle: Minerva, 1860; reprinted, Frankfurt/Main 1967) 43. S. Arai, *Die Christologie des Evangelium Veritatis. Eine religionsgeschichtliche Untersuchung* (Leiden: Brill, 1964) 55, translates adverbial: *vergebens*.

was modelled is the interpretation of p. 17:15 she (Plane) worked at her matter and fashioned it. We think it is stated clearly here that Plane created matter while simultaneously working on it and fashioning it. Further on we learn that Plane applied herself to the modeling of a creature (πλάσμα) in order to achieve an *Ersatz*[4] of Truth. Though this work (πλάσμα) of Falsehood did not mean anything to the Father, Plane is nevertheless engaged in modeling her work (ἔργον) p. 17:15. 18-20. 24. 32. An important parallel to Plane's matter (ὕλη) is found in Fragment 23 of Heracleon on John 4:23 where it is said that men, relative to God, are lost in the *depth of the matter* (ὕλη) *of the Plane.*[5] Now the Aeons themselves are exposed to Ignorance. They search the Father in vain (p. 17:5-10; 18:8-12; 24:16-18), though they are in him: "this was a great marvel that they were in the Father without knowing him" (p. 22:27-30).[6] Peculiar to the *Gos. Truth* is the fact that the Aeons and Pneumatics are interchangeable. After Plane's appearance, Oblivion (ⲃ ⲱ ⲉ) results as one of her consequences (p. 17: 24; 21:36). Another aspect of the same situation of forlornness is described by Deficiency (ⲱⲧⲁ) (p. 24:21-26). In the world two classes of people exist (metaphorically defined as "jars"): filled ones: the Pneumatics; empty ones: the Hylics (p. 25 & 26 passim).

As a matter of fact the empty jars belong to the empty Plane (p. 26:18-19). Finally Plane and her consorts (the Hylics) will be destroyed (p. 21:36-37). Still one point has to be dealt with in this connection: the Pneumatics are not only exposed to the activities of Plane; they even received Plane/Error (p. 22:24) and committed sins in *their* Plane/Error (p. 32:37). Now one could say that in these places it is made clear that so to say the state of consciousness of the Aeons/Pneumatics is substantialized into Plane as such.[7] This is however only partly true because on the other hand the Aeons/Pneumatics are called upon exactly to engulf (to eat) matter (ὕλη) in themselves as by a flame

---

[4] Cf. Arai, *Christologie* p. 56 concerning ⲭⲃ̄ⲃ ⲓ ⲱ (*Ersatz*). N. B. Plane created matter and in some way formed it afterwards. Cf. Isis in *De Iside*; see below.

[5] Cf. as to this fragment: W. Völker, *Quellen zur Geschichte der christlichen Gnosis* (Tübingen: Mohr, 1932) 75 (text); W. Foerster, *Von Valentin zu Herakleon.* Untersuchungen über die Quellen und die Entwicklung der valentinianischen Gnosis (Giessen: Töpelmann, 1928) 22; F. M. M. Sagnard, *La Gnose Valentinienne et le témoignage de Saint Irénée* (Paris: Vrin, 1947) 495 and Y. Janssens, "Héracléon. Commentaire sur l'Evangile selon Saint Jean", *Le Muséon* 72 (1959) 137.

[6] Concerning the *liberum arbitrium* of the aeons cf. R. Kasser, *Tract. Trip.* I, 334; 340.

[7] Haardt, Plane-Mythos, p. 38: (Plane as:) *die Hypostase des Zustandes der Selbstentfremdung* (Hypostasified selfastrangement).

(p. 25:15-17). They so destroy Plane's creation by purifying themselves of her: a known Valentinian concept: the consumption of the material element as by fire.[8]

As to Plane however one should emphasize her hypostatic character, her activities as a person. Not only from the point of view of her creational work, her personality is stressed too in the way of contrast to the figure of the Logos/Sōter. So on p. 35:18-20 it is said †ⲠⲖⲀⲚⲎ ⲞⲨϨⲰϥ ⲚⲤϨⲘ ⲠⲈ ⲞⲨϨⲰϥ ⲈϥⲘⲀⲦⲚ ⲚⲤⲈϨⲰϥ ⲀⲢⲈⲦϤ ⲠⲈ: "Plane, something that has fallen it is, something, that easily draws itself up", when encountering him (i.e. the Redeemer) who came to him whom he wants to bring back. This difficult phrase would in all probability mean that Plane, when encountering the Redeemer, stands up and asserts herself in a rebellious way, see p. 18: 22 too.[9] Another example in the same sphere however is p. 26:16-26: when the Redeemer appears, the Plane is greatly disturbed; and when the Gnosis approaches her, the Plane becomes empty. Here Plane cannot bear the confrontation with the Logos, the context stressing the mighty revelation of the Logos.[10] It is obvious that Plane in the *Gos. Truth* is the embodiment of evil and mischief.

Interestingly the well-known parable of the "lost sheep" is found in *Gos. Truth* p. 31:35-32:15.[11] Now this parable was a favorite one in gnostic circles, especially with the Valentinian *Marcosians*. Irenaeus deals on several occasions with *Achamoth* as the *erring sheep* (*Adv. haer.* I, 8, 4; 16, 1-2; 23, 2 and II, 5, 2) or *Sophia errans* (ibid. II, 10, 2;

---

[8] See commentary in *editio princeps*. As to Irenaeus, *Adv. haer.* I, 3, 5: Sagnard, *La Gnose* 154 and 250-252.

[9] For the expression ⲤⲞⲞϨⲈ ⲈⲢⲀⲦ⸗ see Crum, *Coptic Dictionary*, 380b-381a cf. 537b.

[10] Cf. the great disturbance among the Archonts when Ennoia passes by in *Trim. Prot.* 43:14.16 and 44:9. See J. Helderman, "In Ihren Zelten... Bemerkungen zu Codex XIII Nag Hammadi p. 47:14-18 im Hinblick auf Joh. 1: 14'', *Miscellanea Neotestamentica* Studia ad Novum Testamentum praesertim pertinantia a sociis sodalicii Batavi c.n. Studiorum Novi Testamenti Conventus anno MCMLXXVI quintum lustrum feliciter complentis suscepta (ed. T. Baarda a.o. Leiden: Brill 1978), vol. I, 193.

[11] The verb ⲤⲰⲠⲘ is used here. The sah. and boh. text of Matt 18: 12ff. have ⲤⲰⲠⲘ too. The same verb occurs in Luke 15:4ff sah., whereas boh. has ⲦⲀⲔⲞ. Cf. as to *Gos. Truth* p. 31 W. C. van Unnik, "Het kortgeleden ontdekte 'Evangelie der Waarheid' en het Nieuwe Testament", *Mededelingen Koninklijke Nederlandse Akademie van Wetenschappen, afd. Letterkunde*, N. R. Deel 17 nr. 3, p. 21 and in relation to *Gos. Thom* log. 107, W. Schrage, *Das Verhältnis des Thomas-Evangeliums zur synoptischen Tradition und zu den koptischen Evangelienübersetzungen* (Berlin: Töpelmann, 1964) 193-196. The verb ⲤⲰⲠⲘ is applied for rendering of πλανᾶν, ἀπόλλυεσθαι; ⲦⲀⲔⲞ for ἀπολλύναι, διαφθείρειν.

12, 1; 17, 8 and 24, 6).[12] In I, 16, 1 we meet the significant combination of erring and audacity regarding the lost sheep (τό πρόβατον ἀποσκιρτῆσαν πεπλανῆσθαι), audacity also being of great moment in connection with the Isis-figure of *De Iside*, as we shall see.

Meanwhile we should not overlook the different scopus of the NT-parable and of the Plane in the *Gos. Truth*; on the one hand, the idea of guilt, inherent in the figure of the lost sheep but absent in the Plane; and on the other hand, Plane as essence of evil as she appears in the *Gos. Truth* but not occurring in this sense in the NT. Though the idea of erring and deceit more or less frequently does appear in gnostic writings,[13]

---

[12] As is known H.-M. Schenke criticised in his *Die Herkunft des sogenannten Evangelium Veritatis* (Berlin: Evangelischer Verlag, 1958) 21-22 the labelling of the *Gos. Truth* as Valentinian especially in view of several pecularities in e.g. Irenaeus, *Adv. haer.*, I, 16, 1, where the Marcosians used 11 instead of 99 lost sheep. Or I, 8, 4 where the fallen Sophia is meant, while in the *Gos. Truth* unredeemed Pneumatics are focussed. Now one should not forget that Sophia-though not figuring as such in the Gos. Truth-at last always represents the *salvandi* in an inclusive way. Further on Schenke is stressing the point that the Marcosians proclaimed one should fly over to the Father (the number 1) on the right hand (place of completion), whereas with the Valentinians the right side meant the psychic abode. Moreover the 99 lost sheep (in Schenke's view the still in the higher world existing Aeons) have to await the deliverance of the missing 1 sheep (in his view the most deeply fallen Aeons in the world of man). After the redemption however *all* Aeons will return to the Father (symbolized by the number 100, the right hand). This is the heart of the matter with the Marcosians too: passing over to the number 1, respectively 100, the Father, the right hand. And at last as to *Adv. haer.* I, 16, 2 Schenke concludes that Irenaeus would have combined the number-speculation there with the Marcosian interpretation of the parable mentioned in *Adv. haer.* I, 16, 1. This is not right because I, 16, 1 (end) has to be translated in this manner: (the Marcosians)" say in a prophetic way that so the remaining numbers-with the drachme the 9, with the sheep the 11-when connected-produce the number 99, because 9 times 11 is 99". Therefore the combination originated rather with the Marcosians themselves.

[13] Concerning the idea of the lost and erring sheep as a favorite one with the Gnostics, cf. Sagnard, *La Gnose* 197, 276 (erroneously *Adv. haer.* II, 10, 3-4 in stead of II, 10, 2) and 393; Haardt, Plane-Mythos 36 n. 39. See further, *Adv. haer.* II, 24, 6 and I, 23, 2 (on this place Jonas, *Gnosis* I, 355). As to the plane-motif in other gnostic writings we list the following examples. In *Tri. Trac.* p. 122: 4: "the path unto error" (concerning the Hylics); in *Ap. John* (BG 8502, 2 on p. 67:18 cf. parallels): the soul, seduced by the Antimimon Pneuma, "will err"; in *Gos. Phil.* p. 66:20ff (log. 63): "many people are erring on the Way" (cf. the so called *Psalm of the Naassenes* (Hippolytus, *Ref.* V, 10, 2): the unfortunate soul was erring into a labyrinth full of misery, See Jonas, *Gnosis* 99 & 103) in *Exeg. Soul* p. 135:10 and p. 136:15.27: concerning men as deceived by worldliness (which therefore causes to err). Very interestingly Homer's *Odyssey* is quoted here (regarding which see F. Wisse in *NHS* VII, p. 77-78 and M. Scopello in *NHS* VIII, p. 5-10). In *Gos. Eg.* p. 61:22 (Codex III), respectively p. 73:6 (Codex IV) error is related to the Diabolos. In the *Auth. Teach.* p. 34:28 it is talked about the "demon of error". In the same sense in the *Paraph. Shem* p. 27:20 it is said the demon is "a deceiver" (πλανός). In the *Apoc. Pet.* p. 77:24f the "messengers of error" are attacking truth. Nowhere however is a demonic person as Plane met with as is the case in the *Gos. Truth*.

the figure of a personlike, a mythological *nomen agentis*, as Plane is, does not occur, as far as we know. Moreover one should note that in the *Gos. Truth* the verb cⲱpⲙ̄ is used for the erring of Aeons/men (p. 31:23.29; 32:1.3), their seeking for truth being frustrated by ignorance as caused by Plane, who acts as "misleader" (see below re *Umdeutung* of Plutarch's Isis). For an adequate evaluation of Plane, a useful startingpoint is the way in which the topic of erring (πλανᾶσθαι) appears in contemporary literature and philosophical tradition.

The characteristic of πλάνη/πλανᾶσθαι in philosophical tradition is that of tragedy, mostly without any reference to human responsibility or guilt. So in classical tragedies, one could mention the role of Io (Aeschylus, *Prometheus Vinctus* or of Oedipus (Sophocles, *Oedipus Coloneus*). In philosophy one could mention Plato: the erring of the soul caused by corporal bonds (*Phaedo* 79C) or erring as basis for any evil (*Republ.* IV, 444B).[14]

The Hermetic literature is very interesting. The feature of tragedy is clearly stressed here. So the tragedic corporal bonds in the sphere of death are emphasized too. (C.H. I, 19) or the astrological bonds that cause human erring (C.H. XIII, 11).[15] It is no surprise that πλάνη/πλανᾶσθαι have many synonyms, especially ignorance, ἄγνοια. In the *Hermetica* we find notions as Knowledge, Life, Light etc. not so much as divine powers but more as moral virtues, whereby we note that Truth e.g. has as her antithesis notions as Deceit (ἀπάτη) and Envy (φθόνος).[16] Remarkably we learn that finally Error and her associates will be destroyed by the Demiurge (*Asclepius*, 26). In de *Odes of Salomon* we meet personifications of Error and Truth e.g. in Ode 38:4.7-15 so that one has observed: "by a sudden personification, Truth and Error acquire human forms and we have before us what looks like a pair of heretical teachers".[17] In this connection we notice that in the Odes we do not find however the idea of Error as Demiurge or the notion of

---

[14] See especially I. von Loewenclau, "Die Wortgruppe πλάνη in den Platonischen Schriften", *Synousia*. Festgabe W. Schadewaldt (ed. H. Flashar and K. Gaiser; Pfullingen: Neske, 1965) 111-123; likewise *TWNT* VI, 241.

[15] As for the astrological bonds cf. A. J. Festugière, *La Révélation d'Hermès Trismégiste*, I (Paris: Gabalda, 1950) 87-88; III (Paris: Gabalda, 1953) 154. Ignorance is not a question of human guilt but of tragedy, cf. Festugière, III, 104; compare C. H. XVI, 11.

[16] As to notions opposed to truth, cf. Festugière, III, 155.

[17] R. Harris & A. Mingana, *The Odes and Psalms of Solomon* II (Manchester: University Press, 1920) 394. Cf. for the same dualism of opposite forces Error and Truth *Gos. Phil.* p. 84:3-7 (log. 123).

Aeons as *salvandi*, the object of redemption rather being the imprisoned soul.[18] Plane and Truth as personifications are found in the *Testaments of the XII Patriarchs* too, e.g. in *T. Benj.* 6:1, where Beliar appears as πνεῦμα πλάνης. This is however in the context of the Dualism of the two Spirits, as known from the writings of Qumran. At this point we should remember that in the *Gos. Truth* we do not find Plane and Truth as opposite powers: rather Truth is there an emanational quality of the Father and specified either as *way* (to knowledge) p. 18:20 or as the *mouth of the Father* p. 26:34.

Neither should one overlook the fact that p. 17:20 Plane creates an *Ersatz* for Truth (ⲭ̄Ⲃ̄ⲃⲓⲱ)[19] the latter being subordinated in a sense to Plane as it is in reality to the Father.

Now the aspect of tragedy is not absent in the *Gos. Truth*. We need only mention the famous passage on p. 22:27-28 (the great marvel of the aeons being *in* the Father without knowing him) and the bonds of Plane with which she keeps the Aeons/men in ignorance and doom (p. 17:35; 31:24-25). One should however in our opinion clearly distinguish this background of tragedy concerning the gnostic view of the crucial problem of how the good God could possibly be related to the origin of cosmic tragedy *from* the figure of Plane as a *nomen agentis* of evil, a personal "Anti-creator" so to say.

Here we should consider first the frequent opinion that Plane should display the qualities of the Valentinian Demiurge.[20] It is evident however that the Demiurge is far too positive as compared with Plane, who is thoroughly negative, demonic in a way. Moreover one should notice the essential connection between Plane and ὕλη in the *Gos. Truth*, a fundamental observation in our opinion. Plane has a real hylic aspect in the *Gos. Truth*. It is not surprising that Haardt in his study made the following remark: "dass die Plane-Erzählung im EV.—phänomenologisch betrachtet—die Stelle eines gnostischen Weltschöpfermythos einnimmt".[21]

---

[18] Cf. Arai, *Christologie*, 54 (versus Schenke). Moreover one should not forget that in *Gos. Truth* no essential dualism occurs, Plane being finally destroyed, p. 26:25.

[19] Cf. Crum, *Coptic Dictionary*, 552[b] and Arai, *Christologie*, 56.

[20] Cf. Haardt, Plane-Mythos 38; J. E. Ménard, L'Evangile de Vérité, *NHS* II p. 36; R. Kasser, *Tract. Trip.* I, 377 and Jonas, *The Gnostic Religion* (Boston: Beacon, 1958) 316 n. 48; compare his *Gnosis* I, 412. The Demiurge belongs in a way to Sophia, who as Aeon— though the last one—emanated from the Father. Plane on the contrary far more clearly resembles the Valentinian Kosmokrator or Diabolos cf. Ménard, *L'Evangile de Vérité* 157; R. Kasser, *Tract. Trip.* II, 204 and Jonas, *Gnosis* I, 372. See n. 13 above on Gos. Eg.

[21] Haardt, Plane-Mythos 38.

And as already said, he speaks about the *disiecta membra* of a myth, in which the Plane-idea is playing a central part, although he expresses as his opinion that it is impossible to say anything specific about origin and function in Gnosticism of this myth.

In our opinion however one should look in the direction once pointed out by Albert Torhoudt in his study: *Een onbekend gnostisch systeem in Plutarchus' De Iside et Osiride.*[22] As we will see Torhoudt asserts in his study that Plutarch's Isis-interpretation is not only remarkable but also contains gnosticizing elements; especially in ch. 54. It is this idea in Torhoudt's work—not his connection of the Valentinian Sophia with Isis—which makes his work really a pioneering one. It is a pity that Torhoudt's work is mostly overlooked and unknown, perhaps on account of his difficult German flavoured Flemish language. Apart from some scattered references as noted above, it is only in John Gwyn Griffiths' book Plutarch's *De Iside et Osiride* that Torhoudt receives deserved attention and recognition.[23]

Before taking a closer look at T.'s interpretation of *De Iside*, we should observe that a possible relation between the Plane-figure and the Isis of *De Iside* is not that strange or farfetched, when one considers some general perceptions as to second century spiritual and philosophical trends. First, this period has been given the justified qualification of being *isiaque par excellence.*[24] To the Greeks of the Hellenistic era Isis is identified with most of the forces of nature and equated at the same time as the *Myriad-named* with a large number of other deities (as for Greek goddesses with e.g. Demeter, Artemis, Selene; as for Egyptian goddesses with Bubastis, Hathor, Maat a.o.).[25]

---

[22] A. Torhoudt, *Een onbekend gnostisch systeem in Plutarchus' De Iside et Osiride* (Gembloers: Duculot, 1942; vol. 1 of *Studia Hellenistica*, Leuven, 1942). Torhoudt's work is shortly mentioned only by Y. Janssens, Héracléon 295; W. Theiler, *Forschungen zum Neuplatonismus* (Berlin: de Gruyter, 1966) 110 n. 12 (compare the latters recension of Torhoudt in *Erasmus*. Speculum Scientiarum 2 (1948-1949) Sp. 396-399) and U. Wilckens, *Weisheit und Torheit* (Tübingen: Mohr, 1959) 156-157 (compare his article in *TWNT* VII, 501 n. 233. Torhoudt hereafter: T.

[23] J. Gwyn Griffiths, *Plutarch's De Iside et Osiride* (Cambridge: University of Wales Press, 1970). The known classicist/egyptologist Griffiths mentions Torhoudt's work on pp. 13, 49, 354, 504-505 and 535. We use his edition of De Iside.

[24] Leclant in *Bull. Fac. Lett. Strasbourg*, March 1959, 306. See R. E. Witt, "The importance of Isis for the Fathers", *Studia Patristica* VIII (Berlin, 1966 ed. by F. L. Cross) part VI, 135.

[25] For the Greek goddesses see e.g. Witt, 140; Griffiths, 43, 51, 57, 309, 390 446 and 502-503 and H. Conzelmann, "Die Mutter der Weisheit", in: *Zeit und Geschichte* (Festschrift R. Bultmann ed. E. Dinkler; Tübingen: Mohr 1964) 227. As to the egyptian goddesses see e.g. Witt, 141; Griffiths, 264-265.

In the Roman era this identification persisted. One may conclude however that the Greek element in all this was overwhelmingly preponderant. Furthermore, during the Ptolemaic era mysteries were attached to the cult of Isis and Osiris in the full sense of the Greek term.[26] Secondly we should notice the peculiar topics and special characteristics of Plutarch's *De Iside*, that make this work a tractate *sui generis*. Though *De Iside* cannot be treated as a coherent and logically built up treatise in our sense of the word, it can—as Griffiths rightly concluded—"scarcely be denied that the core of the work consists of an interpretation of the Osiris-myth in which a dualistic emphasis accompanies an elaborate daemonology"; a dualism that one should not soft-pedal, especially regarding chaps. 45-49. Plutarch's philosophical interpretations of the known myth are Greek indeed and derive principally from two traditions: the Neoplatonic and the Stoic; the former expressly applied to the myth in chaps. 53-54, where "a creation-system is elaborated in which Osiris is the pure creative Logos, Isis the material and receptive element and Horus, their offspring, is the world".[27] It is on these chapters that our study is mainly focussed.

Whereas H. D. Betz in an article written in 1972 stated he had discovered a *seltsames mysterientheologisches System* in ch. 2, an observation in reality made already 25 years earlier,[28] it was Albert Torhoudt who dealt with an unknown gnostic system discovered by him especially in ch. 54, in the allegory of the so called Elder Horus. For apart from the relationship *Isis-Hyle* in *De Iside*—a question to be discussed hereafter—it is in this chapter that we meet the nucleus of T.'s Unknown Gnostic System. T. states that only here and in Valentinian gnosticism primitive matter is *not* pre-existent (a current idea in philosophical tradition of that time)[29] but brought forth by *Hyle*, as her

---

[26] Griffiths, 24 cf. as for Plutarch's dualistic flavored thinking 20, 28 and 48. H. D. Betz rightly remarks that Plutarch especially in his dialog *"De E apud Delphos"* is showing a certain affinity with gnostic (dualistic) thinking: "He is certainly ready for it, because he basically agrees with the gnostic 'Daseinshaltung'....and yet...he has not crossed the Rubicon. He still holds on to one of the central concepts of the religion of the Greeks, the presence of the deity in the cosmos", H. D. Betz, "Observations on Some Gnosticizing Passages in Plutarch", *Proceedings of the International Colloquium on Gnosticism* (Stockholm 1973) (Stockholm: Almqvist/Leiden: Brill, 1977) 177-178. Betz is not dealing with *De Iside* in this article. See n. 78 below.

[27] Griffiths, 48 (compare 60).

[28] H. D. Betz, "Ein seltsames Mysterientheologisches System bei Plutarch", *Ex Orbe Religionum*, Festschrift G. Widengren (Leiden: Brill, 1972) I, 347-354. See on *De Iside* chap. 2 already Sagnard. *La Gnose*, 587.

[29] See T. 104. On the pre-existence of matter in later Platonism cf. S. R. C. Lilla, *Clement of Alexandria. A Study in Christian Platonism and Gnosticism* (Oxford: Univ.

first creation being εἴδωλον and φάντασμα, the Elder Horus. The allegory on the Elder Horus was influenced, T. states, by an Alexandrian doctrine concerning the problem of the *unde malum*, where *matter* would have been evil as such.[30] The passage in ch. 54 reads as following:

"ἡ μὲν γὰρ ἔτι τῶν θεῶν ἐν γαστρὶ τῆς 'Ρέας ὄντων ἐξ "Ισιδος καὶ 'Οσίριδος γενομένη γένεσις 'Απόλλωνος αἰνίττεται τὸ πρὶν ἐκφανῆ γενέσθαι τόνδε τὸν κόσμον καὶ συντελεσθῆναι [ὑπὸ] τοῦ λόγου τὴν ὕλην φύσει ἐλεγχομένην ἐπ' αὐτὴν ἀτελῆ τὴν πρώτην γένεσιν ἐξενεγκεῖν· διὸ καί φασι τὸν θεὸν ἐκεῖνον ἀνάπηρον ὑπὸ σκότῳ γενέσθαι καὶ πρεσβύτερον ὧρον καλοῦσιν· οὐ ὑὰρ ἦν κόσμος, ἀλλ' εἴδωλόν τι καὶ κόσμου φάντασμα μέλλοντος·"

"For the procreation of Apollo by Isis and Osiris, which occurred when the gods were still in the womb of Rhea, intimates that before this world became manifest and was completed by Reason (Logos), *matter*, being shown by its nature to be incapable of itself, *brought forth the first creation*. For this reason they declare that god to have been born maimed in the darkness and they call him the Elder Horus; for he was *not the world, but only a picture and a vision of the world to come*".[31]

This εἴδωλον and φάντασμα, picture and vision, of the world to come, means that the Elder Horus is *imperfect cosmos, a failure*.

Here we have to deal with the crucial point of the two Horuses: *Horus the Young* (Child), *Har-pi-chrod*: *Harpocrates* and the *Elder Horus, Ḥr Wr: Haroëris*. The latter is in ch. 54 equated with Apollo. So in ch. 12 Apollo/Haroëris is described as originated from Rhea, born in darkness from Osiris and Isis, who were united in Rhea's womb. In any case Haroëris is maimed (ἀνάπηρος). It is indeed very puzzling, that, in contrast with this negative Apollo-image, in chaps. 10 and 75 Apollo is depicted in a very positive way as a symbol for unity, the *Monad*! Here we are confronted with discrepancies in *De Iside*, due to compilations

Press, 1971) 193-194; J. Zandee, Les "Enseignements de Silvain" et le Platonisme, *NHS* VII, 165 and H.-F. Weiss, *Untersuchungen zur Kosmologie des hellenistischen und palästinischen Judentums* (Berlin: Akademie, 1966) 168. Note that in *Tri. Trac.* p. 53:31 the idea of pre-existent matter is *denied* (cf. R. Kasser, *Tract. Trip.* I, 315 and 338). See n. 51 below.

[30] On the Alexandrian theory of matter being evil, cf. T. 23, 36, 62-63 and 99.

[31] Cf. as to this translation Möller, *Kosmologie*, 46 n. 2; same translation gives J. Pascher, Η ΒΑΣΙΛΙΚΗ ΟΔΟΣ. *Der Königsweg. Zu Wiedergeburt und Vergottung bei Philon von Alexandreia* (Paderborn: Schöningh, 1931) 73 and J. Dillon, *The Middle Platonists. A Study of Platonism 80 B.C. to A.D. 220* (London: Duckworth, 1977) 204 (compare pp. 373 & 385-386).

and sources used by Plutarch.[32] The former, Horus the Child, was born, as the famous Egyptian myth has it, from Isis and Osiris posthumously, his member being revivified by her.[33] In chaps. 19 and 65 Harpocrates/Horus the Child *therefore* receives negative qualifications such as ἀτελής, imperfect and prematurely born (ch. 65) and weak in his lower limbs (ch. 19). However one should notice that befóre the above quoted passage in ch. 54 Horus (the Child) is pictured as the good perceptible world—the κόσμος νοητός; especially ch. 56: Horus perfected achievement and directly áfter it, at the beginning of ch. 55, the resemblance of Horus the Child, weak in his lower limbs etc. ánd Haroëris, the Elder Horus maimed as he is, is unmistakable! It stands to reason therefore that T. stressed these resemblances and, on account of the imperfectness common to *both*, explained the pejorative interpretation of the birth of both Horuses (against the original meaning of the myth) as due to that gnosticising theory of evil that influenced the philosophical interpretation of the Osiris-Isis-Horus-myth.[34] We meet, in the opinion of T., this gnosticising theory in the allegory on the Elder Horus in ch. 54. Many inadequacies still remain, e.g. the three different Logoi in *De Iside*. Two of them we meet in ch. 54 Logos as Osiris, symbol of eternal good and Logos as Hermes/Thoth who defends Horus against the charge of illegitimacy by Typhon, symbol of evil.[35] On the other hand however we meet Harpocrates/Horus the Child as Logos himself in a sense, a very positive and perfect Harpocrates-figure. T. makes a very important point here in our opinion. For in ch. 68 we learn that Harpocrates should *not* be regarded simply as an imperfect and weak god...but as the patron and teacher of the doctrine (Logos) among men concerning the gods: a doctrine, which is still young (νεαρός), imperfect (ἀτελής) and in-

---

[32] As to the compilations cf. Griffiths, 99-100 (compare pp. 84 & 88). Concerning both Horuses cf. Griffiths, 59-60 and 337-338; regarding Haroëris, Griffiths, 300 n. 5 and 561; regarding Harpocrates, T. 37 n. 3. The genealogy of Harpocrates and especially of Haroëris is very conflicting indeed, see Th. Hopfner, *Plutarch über Isis und Osiris*, vol. I: Die Sage (Prag: Orientalistisches Institut, 1940); vol. II Die Deutung der Sage (Prag: Orientalistisches Institut, 1941). On this point I, 87 and II, 229.

[33] As to Osiris revivified by Isis see Hopfner I, 82-85; Griffiths, 284 (N.B. "In a Late-Egyptian text to which Spiegelberg called attention, Isis claims to have given birth to a son without male cooperation") and 353 and 464.

[34] As to the pejorative interpretation, see T. 30, 39 and 41-43; the original meaning of the myth, see T. 39 and 44 (re Horus' tenderness (positive!) and his birth-though abnormal-not illegitimate); as the theory of evil is concerned see ibid. 36, 39, 43 (N.B.: Harpocrates' birth (in a pejorative sense now) being related to Haroëris in the so called allegory, see ibid. 27 and 32, where it is rightly pointed out that the γάρ has an explaining, combining function).

[35] Cf. Griffiths, 505.

articulate. One is struck by the fact that in the description of human knowledge concerning the gods the *same* traits occur as was the case with the imperfect, untimely born Horus, weak in his lower limbs, inarticulate in fact. There is on the basis of the macro-microcosmos-idea correspondence between the *imperfect cosmos* (the maimed, imperfect Horus combined with Haroëris as we saw) ánd *imperfect man* with respect to his insight. This means: as the highest god (Osiris) produces from nature (Isis) the perfect completed world (Horus, ch. 56), we see here that this formation, articulation of nature as receptive element is done by the Logos of the highest god. That the Logos as form-principle is bearing the *name* Harpocrates is thoroughly reasonable, because Horus/Harpocrates as perfect achievement, cosmos, is the *result* of the activity of the Logos as the Demiurge in the Philonian sense.[36] When thus the formal element of the Logos is lacking, the result is an imperfect, maimed world. No wonder T. confirmed and illustrated his statement by referring to the Valentinian Sophia who on account of her recklessness (τόλμα) created *alone* but thérefore created a miscarriage (ἔκτρωμα).[37] It is true that recklessness, τόλμα is not expressly mentioned in ch. 54, but the creation of Haroëris as εἴδωλον, φάντασμα by Hyle (Isis) alone, together with the use of the verb ἐλέγχειν in the sense of refuting proof sufficiently demonstrates that the idea as such is present here. In this regard it is necessary to deal briefly with the statement Hyle, Matter, created Haroëris/Elder Horus *alone*, whereas in ch. 54 yet it is clearly professed that Haroëris originated from the union of Isis *and Osiris* in Rhea's womb. Though it is clear that in the myth as such Osiris and Isis figured both together,[38] in the "Horus-allegory", however, Isis as Hyle acts alone in accordance with a theory of evil, matter being evil. This is also evident from the following facts. First of all, it is on a first look somewhat strange that Rhea bearing Osiris and Isis is mentioned alone too without the name of her male partner. It is not that strange, that he is not mentioned, because Rhea's consort Cronus is god of primitive matter too (he being equated with water, sea) and considering

---

[36] See T. 83, 87 and 92; Griffiths, 535 as to the relationship Harpocrates-Logos.

[37] As to the Valentinian ἔκτρωμα idea, cf. T. 85 (compare 45-46 & 101 and Griffiths, 354 summarizing T.'s thoughts in a pointed way). Concerning the recklessness of the Valentinian Sophia, see Irenaeus, *Adv. haer.* I, 2, 2—to that point Sagnard, *La Gnose*, 33 and Kasser. *Tract. Trip.* I, 343. The Marcosians typified Sophia even as: ἡ μεγαλότολμος ἐκέινη, *Adv. haer.* I, 13, 6; cf. T. 51-52. It is clear that the Valentinian Sophia-concept is much more pessimistic than Isis-Hyle is in *De Iside* here. T. rightly concludes one meets a transitional phase in *De Iside* as to this point (pp. 32, 57, 63-64, 92 and 105. See n. 20 above.

[38] So T. 35, 41 and 44 too.

the fact, that he is sometimes characterised as hermaphrodite (ἀρσενόθηλυς).[39] Then the darkness of the womb reminds one of primaeval darkness (cf. Egyptian *Kuk, Keku*) and other data as connected with matter (evil) too.[40] Osiris and Isis being in Rhea's womb further has a predestinational connotation, leading to their essential *unity* as gods of matter and nature.[41]

For it is important to notice, in the fourth place, that Osiris can stand for primaeval water too, as Isis for primaeval earth arising from the water.[42] Thereby it is of great moment that Isis, equated with Selene and so related to (primaeval) water too, is hermaphrodite because of Selene's bisexuality.[43] One cannot help thinking that in the light of the foregoing, since Isis, Osiris, Rhea resp. Cronus are strongly related, almost identified in many currents of tradition (Gnostic ones too), *Hyle* acting in the allegory of ch. 54 is not so abnormal. This is all the more evident, when one observes the identification of Isis with Rhea resp. nature in the context of the Neopythagorean *Dyas* as symbol for matter and recklessness (τόλμα).[44] On the other hand, however, there is a possibility too to elucidate Osiris' and Isis' procreation of Haroëris, by

---

[39] The gnostic sect of the Perates considered Cronus as hermaphrodite equated with the sea, primitive element (see Hippolyt *Ref.* V, 14). Rhea too can be characterized as a goddess of earth (cf. Grimal, *Dictionaire de Mythologie grecque et romaine*, 408).

[40] Cf. the syzygy of *Kuk* & *Kauke* belonging to the old Egyptian divine ogdoad in the doctrine on creation of Hermopolis, meaning primaeval darkness in which primitive matter also is potentially present (cf. coptic ΚΑΚΕ), see J. Zandee, Das Schöpferwort im alten Ägypten, *Verbum*. Festschrift H. W. Obbink (Utrecht: Kemink, 1964) 34; V. von Strauss und Torney, *Die altägyptische Götter und Göttersagen* (Heidelberg: Winter, 1889) I, 422-423 (who interestingly relates these gods to Valentinian *Bythos* and *Sige*). As to the connection of primaeval darkness and water cf. Berosus, *Historiae quae supersunt* (ed. Richter) 49-50; moreover—concerning the relation darkness and matter (Hyle)—Alexander of Lycopolis (anti-manichaean author, 4th century), reporting Manichaeans would combine darkness and matter (see Jonas, *Gnosis* I, 291 n. 3).

[41] See Griffiths, 307 and 57 (Osiris and Isis as earth-gods).

[42] As for the equation of Osiris and (Nile) water, see Griffiths, 304; 421. According to Hippolyt the gnostic sect of the Naassenes made the same equation (*Ref.* V, 7). Isis meaning primitive earth rising from the water, see Griffiths, 421 and 445-446; J. Bergman, *Ich bin Isis*. Studien zum memphitischen Hintergrund der griechischen Isisaretologien (Uppsala: Berlingska, 1968) 282.

[43] The equation Isis-Selene (bisexual moongoddess) cf. Griffiths, 465, 500-501 and G. Vandebeek, *De interpretatio graeca van de Isisfiguur* (Gembloux: Duculot, 1946; *Studia Hellenistica*, 4 Leuven) 128. This equation elucidates again Isis' role in her acting over Osiris, see n. 32 above. Isis as moisture, cf. Griffiths, 304 n. 4 and 444 (by means of the star Sothis/Sirius). Isis meaning primitive water and earth, Bergman, *Ich bin Isis*, 282.

[44] See for Nicomachus, the second century Pythagorean, equating Dyas-Isis-Nature-Rhea. T. 103 and G. C. Stead, "The Valentinian Myth of Sophia", *JTS* 20 (1969) 100 n. 1 & 2.

subsuming Osiris *in* Isis as Hyle, though in this subsumption *Osiris could represent the worldsoul acting with Hyle*, Matter.[45] For, as we shall demonstrate, in *De Iside* Isis stands too for the good worldsoul *united with* Isis as (Platonic) matter. Their being mentioned apart in ch. 54 could therefore have meant to clarify the aspect of Isis as *worldsoul* ánd Isis as *Hyle*.

With regard to the pecularities of the Isis-interpretation in *De Iside*, it is interesting to note how some observations made already to that point by T., were confirmed from another point of view by H. J. Krämer in his 1967 published work on the history of Platonism, *Ursprung der Geistmetaphysik*, unaware of T.'s study. Krämer proved that Plutarch was thoroughly influenced in his Platonic interpretation of Isis by Xenocratic traditions, Xenocrates being Plato's nephew and successor. Now it was exactly Xenocrates, who introduced the *Dyas* as *positive* worldsoul, who worked between the highest God (here Osiris) and the force radically opposed to him (here Typhon), the unlimited Dyas (ἀόριστος δυὰς). In *De Iside* the worldsoul had to form, correct and arrange that Unlimited Dyas, the evil demon, Matter, principle of disorderliness and pathetic a-logical forces. Longing for the highest god, the *Monad*, she was in her work threatened too by Typhon.[46] The unique characteristic of *De Iside* however is that *with this good worldsoul another entity is combined*: namely *Hyle*, Matter, *an idea totally strange and uncommon to Xenocrates*.[47] Isis therefore is here the Platonic ὑποδοχή, χώρα, ὕλη, δεκτικόν etc.[48] Whereas Plutarch in his óther works recognizes only *one* soul connected with matter, here in *De Iside*, a good *and* a bad soul (Typhon) are functioning. This, therefore, is a peculiar trait of *De Iside*.[49] Naturally one has asked whether this combination was made by Plutarch himself or whether it was already found by him in his *Vorlage*.

It is likely indeed, that Plutarch did find this peculiar Isis in sources used by him, as Krämer, Torhoudt and Quispel pointed out, an Alexandrinian milieu lying behind this gnosticising source.[50]

---

[45] So Möller, *Kosmologie*, 46; a very ingenious observation.

[46] H. J. Krämer, *Der Ursprung der Geistmetaphysik*. Untersuchungen zur Geschichte des Platonismus zwischen Platon und Plotin (Amsterdam: Grüner, 1967), see pp. 92-101, especially 94 (on Typhon) and 39, 82 (on the worldsoul functioning between the highest god en the *un*-limited, bad force below); cf. *De Iside* ch. 48 as to Isis, a: φύσις μεταξύ.

[47] Cf. Krämer, 97. Already T. made this observation (pp. 20, 28 and 69).

[48] See De Iside ch. 53, 57, 59 and 77 (on this topic: Griffiths, 58, 502, 511-512, 562; Krämer, 96-97).

[49] Cf. Krämer, 97 and T. 14, 17-19.

[50] As to the *Vorlage*: Krämer, 97 and G. Quispel, "Jewish Gnosis and Mandaean Gnosticism. Some reflections on the Writing Brontè", *NHS* VII 88 n. 7. On gnosticising

It is essential now to realize what were the implications of this combined Isis-figure in *De Iside* with regard to gnostic writers who may have
read this treatise of Plutarch. Now first we should remember that matter
acquired connotations of evil, a rather negative evaluation in the period
concerned.[51] Further on one should be conscious about the fact that the
idea of the Dyas as such was exposed to negative appraisals, the Dyas
being opposed to the Monad. Especially in Neopythagorean tradition
the Dyas was identified with ἔρις and still more τόλμα, quarrel and
recklessness, as is also seen in *De Iside* ch. 10: Dyas-Artemis-Isis.[52]

For the Neopythagoreans the Dyas was considered as Unlimitednes
(ἀπειρία), movement, principle of separation and τόλμα.[53] And so the
good and positive worldsoul was just by her being Dyas, exposed to
degradation, τόλμα being inherent in the Dyas as such.[54] Together with
the Hyle-character of Isis, it is thoroughly understandable that *this* Isis-
figure could easily be "gnostified" so to say. By her hylic identity she
became entangled against her will in the Typhonic sphere of ignorance,
ἄγνοια.[55] Once subjected to such a process of degradation, one can easily
ascertain the difference with the positive Demiurge of Valentinianism.

In our opinion there is a relationship between the mitigated gnostic
character of Isis in *De Iside* ch. 54 especially and the clearcut negative
character of the Plane in the *Gos. Truth*, both earmarked by the reckless
will to create alone, without a partner.

It is in this connection we have to deal now with the phenomenon of
gnostic *Protestexegese*.[56] As is known this type of exegesis or allegorizing is marked on the one hand by valuation in strictly positive sense of
original negative phenomena (such as the Serpent in Paradise, Sodom

---

elements in *De Iside*, see Griffiths, 49, 51 60 and 99. On the "theory of evil" in *De Iside*
ch. 54, T. 23, 84-85 and 95.

[51] Cf. Sagnard, *La Gnose*, 296 n. 7; W. Theiler, *Forschungen zum Neuplatonismus*.
(Berlin: de Gruyter, 1966), 106, 108 and J. Zandee (n. 29 above).

[52] See T. 59 and as to Neopythagorean thinking ibid. 99-103.

[53] With regard to the Pythagorean Dyas, cf. Krämer, 49-50, 93, 95, 98, 320-322 and
329; Griffiths, 484 and Sagnard, *La Gnose*, 260, 342 and 348. As to the recklessness of the
Valentinian Sophia n. 36 above. The idea of τόλμα in contemporary philosophical and
gnostic traditions, cf. Jonas' comment in *Le Origini dello Gnosticismo* (Leiden: Brill,
1967) 213-214.

[54] Cf. Krämer, 50, 321-322.

[55] It has to be noticed that in *De Iside* even the cosmos (Horus) is in his lower parts
mixed with κακία; the highest god only gets the better of Typhon (see Krämer, 94, 98 and
Griffiths, 486).

[56] This terminology was coined by K. Rudolph, "Randerscheinungen des Judentums",
Kairos 9 (1967), 117. As to the element of rebellion and protest in gnosticism, see Jonas,
Le Origini, 102 and 105.

and Gomorrah) and on the other hand by devaluation, degradation of original positive phenomena (such as God in the OT). A meaningful example would be the case of the radically degraded *Zeus*, identified with *Heimarmene* in a notice of the Alchemist Zosimus.[57] This rebellious allegorizing, in the literature mostly called *Umdeutung*, created in our opinion the demonic, evil Plane in the *Gos. Truth* too. One could understand that the author of the *Gos. Truth* experienced the famous goddess Isis, celebrated and worshipped in her mysteries in Alexandria in súch a way, that he as a christian Gnostic would have degraded her from the positive goddess of wisdom to the extremely negative Plane...

Therefore, it is no wonder that in *Gos. Truth* p. 17:28 we hear the summons to despise (καταφρονεῖν) Error because she is very dangerous for the Aeons/men, exposed to ignorance regarding the Father, tragic victims of a tragic seeking for God, gripped by her (cf. *Gos. Truth* p. 31:21-22, punishments and tortures being inflicted upon them by Plane). The tragedy of the Aeons/men is clearly marked in p. 31:22-23: "for they really wandered far from His Face".[58]

Plane is the evil demon, who keeps the Aeons/men in the bonds of ignorance. Not shé is tragic, but théy are tragic figures. This is obvious because Plane is not (as Sophia) an erring Aeon, always still being in- and returning to the Father. She is outside God, opposed to Him, an agent of evil.

Here we reach the key-problem: *why* was it then that this evil character was described and indicated especially as *Plane*? The more so where we learned that the verb πλανᾶσθαι did have in the philosophical tradition the clear connotation of tragedy (see above). Why was it then that the Isis as we met her in *De Iside*, especially in ch. 54, was degraded, *umgedeutet* exactly to *Plane*?

In our opinion this was done by the author of the *Gos. Truth* on the basis of the wanderings (πλάναι) Isis had to make in her seeking for Osiris. First of all we would like to emphasize that one should therefore

---

[57] See Jonas, *Gnosis*, I, 217-233. Concerning the third century Alchemist Zosimus, cf. A. J. Festugière, *Hermétisme et Mystique Païenne* (Paris: Aubier-Montaigne, 1967) 209-210. As to the relation Alchemy-Valentinian Gnosticism, cf. Sagnard, *La Gnose*, 120 and 243-44. Examples of gnostic *Protestexegesis* in general: A. Böhlig, "Hintergründe in gnostischen Texten von Nag Hammadi", *Le Origini*, 113 and E. H. Pagels, *The Johannine Gospel in Gnostic Exegesis* (Nashville: Abingdon, 1973) 68.

[58] The German and English translation in the *editio princeps* implicate that punishments and tortures caused the wandering, but this is not meant by the Coptic ΝΕΥϹⲀⲢⲘ p. 31:23.

not relate the Valentinian Sophia (not figuring at all in the *Gos. Truth*) to the Ἶσις πλανωμένη (as is sometimes suggested, incidentally),[59] but rather the Plane.

Now the *"wandering"-theme* regarding Isis—we should stress this observation—does *not* convey moral error on her side in *De Iside*.

Her painful, hard seeking for Osiris and therefore her wanderings, πλάναι, are not negatively characterized in Plutarch's treatise.[60] Meanwhile the *plane-or wandering-motif* was very popular and extensively used in Antiquity. We learned already the tragic aspect. Further on it occurred not only as a permanent topic in the romance-literature of Antiquity, but also it was positively valued as an indispensable element in the searching after the truth as done in philosophy.[61] Now as for Isis the wandering-motif is really playing a central part. This is all the more remarkable where πλάνη as such, apart from Demeter's search for Persephone, was denied to other gods.[62] In *De Iside* however we find the idea of wandering expressed in chaps. 14, 25 (Demeter), 27 and ch. 54: the Ἶσις πλανωμένη. Isis' wandering is focussed on the seeking and finding of the badly mutilated Osiris on the banks of the river Nile, according to the famous myth. In the second instance the ζήτησις καὶ εὕρησις Ὀσίριδος, seeking and finding of Osiris, meant the disappearance and reappearance of Osiris in the sense of the Nile-water (ch. 39 and 52).[63] Plutarch himself adds a cosmic interpretation when stating in ch. 54 that the reassemblance of the lacerated Osiris meant establishing the cosmos as such. In this connection we should be aware of the fact that one could assert Plutarch would rationalize the traditional myths in a way of *Entmythologisierung* (see chaps. 11, 20 and 58), especially where the ἀληθής

---

[59] Cf. L. Schottroff, *Der Glaubende und die feindliche Welt*. Beobachtungen zum gnostischen Dualismus und seiner Bedeutung für Paulus und das Johannesevangelium (Neukirchen-Vluyn, Neukirchener Verlag, 1970) 54; B. L. Mack, *Logos und Sophia*. Untersuchungen zur Weisheitstheologie im hellenistischen Judentum (Göttingen: Vandenhoeck, 1973) 70 and Griffiths, 504.

[60] Griffiths made a mistake when stating in his work on p. 504: "A fundamental idea in Plutarch's account is that matter (ὕλη) is the result of error (πλάνη)". Most likely G. made this erroneous observation under influence of the Valentinian Sophia-topic and did read this concept in *into De Iside*. In reality however Isis herself is the Hyle and the imperfect hylic product (Haroëris as phantasm of the world to come) results from her *recklessness*.

[61] With regard to the wandering-motif in the romance-literature, see H. Braun s.v. πλανάω *TWNT* VI, 234 (end) and Mack, *Logos und Sophia*, 135 n. 12 and 153 n. 135. As to the topic in contemporary philosophy Braun ibid.

[62] Braun ibid. and Griffiths, 386.

[63] Cf. Hopfner, *Plutarch über Isis und Osiris*, 22, 31, 180-182 and 225; Griffiths, 63-65, 315, 405 and 450-452.

δόξα περὶ θεῶν, the true belief about gods, is concerned (ch. 11).[64] Now Isis' laborsome wanderings, while searching for Osiris, signify in the Isis-mysteries the road of salvation, leading to the τόποι καθαροί, the places of purity, as ultimate goals. This way of painful wandering and searching had to be imitated in the cult by the initiates.[65]

The language of the mysteries in turn acted upon philosophical ideas as not in the least in the case of Plato, who especially took the complex topic of wandering and finding from there.[66]

Here we should be aware too of the fact that a clear dividingline between Gnosticism and mysteries cannot be easily drawn because—apart from important differences—both religious phenomena had much in common (the *Zeitgeist*, a peculiar *Weltgefühl*) and moreover the widespread mysteries will have affected as a matter of course gnostic circles too.[67] Finally we recall against the background outlined above, the famous and beautiful first three chapters of *De Iside*, especially ch. 2. It is there that Plutarch gives a special philosophical explanation of Isis' wandering and searching: it properly meant the search for liberating truth. On account of this aspect it is no wonder that the Isis-mysteries, "Isis-movement", attracted in that age of deep spiritual uncertainty especially people searching for the essential knowledge concerning God, Truth, the *studium veri*, etc. The θειότητος ὄρεξις, longing for the divine world (De Iside ch. 2), certainly appealed to large groups of people.[68]

---

[64] Cf. Griffiths, 513-514.

[65] See on the painful wanderings, πλάναι...περιδρομαὶ κοπώδεις, A. Dieterich, *Eine Mithrasliturgie* (Leipzig: Teubner, 1910) 164 and Braun ibid. As to the imitation by the initiates, cf. H. D. Betz, "Ein seltsames... System", 350 and the articles s.v. γεννάω in *TWNT* I, 668 and s.v. μεταμορφόω in *TWNT* IV, 764.

[66] See von Loewenclau, *Die Wortgruppe πλάνη*, 118-119 and E. v. Ivánka, "Religion, Philosophie und Gnosis: Grenzfälle und Pseudomorphosen in der Spätantike", *Le Origni*, 321. Interestingly J. E. Ménard in his otherwise with our opinion differing article "La πλάνη dans l'Evangile de Vérité", *Studia Montis Regii* (Montréal) 7 (1964) p. 4-5, however stresses this background for the *Gos. Truth* too.

[67] See H. G. Gaffron, *Studien zum koptischen Philippusevangelium unter besonderer Berücksichtigung der Sakramente* (Bonn: Universität Bonn, 1969) 87 as to the resemblance of gnosticism and the mysteries; with regard to the differences, things are complicated. Usually both movements are distinguished by observing that, whereas in the mysteries the prospect of *deification* is the main motive, the essential *Anliegen* in gnosticism could be indicated as the conviction *to become God again*. See e.g. for the discussion Gaffron, 98, 284 and 287-288.

[68] The general outlook of ch. 1-3 of *De Iside* is marked in a pithy way by Griffiths, 70: "To Plutarch the Osirian mysteries are a means of achieving philosophical truth, and Isis is the repository of wisdom which makes this possible....Isis leads the initiate to *gnôsis* of the supreme being.." See as to the *studium veri* ibid. 256 and further 258 and 390 with

Taking all these factors into account, we think that the author of the *Gos. Truth* could readily have been tempted to reverse Isis' honorable but laborious wandering and searching into a radically negative circumstance: imitating *her* would never grant wisdom and insight. On the contrary, men would in this way for ever be kept in the bonds of meaningless wandering; searching in vain.

An *Umdeutung* of Ἶσις πλανωμένη therefore. An example of *Protestexegese* that has however more far reaching implications. In speaking about deep spiritual uncertainty as affecting people of the first centuries within the borders of the immense *Imperium Romanum*, we have to keep in mind a remarkable distrust in the liberating and salutary possibilities of philosophy with her many ramifications. It is therefore too that an author as the one of the *Gos. Truth* judged the promising words regarding the search for truth and wisdom in *De Iside* ch. 2, as purely negative. Philosophical tradition did not give any real deliverance from the pessimistic *Weltgefühl*. Confidence in philosophy collapsed within the gnostic movement, along with a plain aversion of corporal existence as human condition.[69] As to the *debacle of philosophy* one can refer to many *loci probantes* such as *Gos. Truth* p. 19:20 (regarding the teachers in the temple, full of self-conceit); *Treat. Res.* p. 43-44:3 especially, disavowing Greek philosophical thinking with deep animosity and *Tri. Trac.* II, p. 108: 36-109:24 and 110:11-18.[70] One wonders what were the impulses that caused this negative judgment. Though the Gnostics as a matter of fact *did* use philosophical terminology,[71] their contempt of philosophy as a way out

---

regard to Ἶσις σόφη. Considering the attraction of an Isis thus qualified for people so deeply moved about the basic questions of life in the context of religion, one will not be astonished to learn that for a man as Valentine the basic problem concerned the *unde deus* (Tertullian, *De praescr. haer.* VII) cf. Sagnard, *La Gnose*, 588.

[69] A fine example as to the spiritual climate is *Corpus Hermeticum* I, 19: ὁ δὲ ἀγαπήσας ἐκ πλάνης ἔρωτος τὸ σῶμα, οὗτος μένει ἐν τῷ σκότει πλανώμενος, αἰσθητῶς πάσχων τὰ τοῦ θανάτου, he who has loved his body, that originated from the error of love, remains in the darkness, erring, suffering in his senses the things of death.

[70] See e.g. the *editio princeps* of the *Treat. Res.* (M. Malinine a.o., *De Resurrectione* (Stuttgart: Rascher, 1963) XXVI; L. H. Martin, "The anti-philosophical polemic and gnostic soteriology in 'The Treatise on the Resurrection", *Numen* 20 (1973) 20-37; J. Zandee, "Gnostic ideas on the fall and salvation", *Numen* 11 (1964) 23-24 and J. Zandee", L'Exemplarisme du monde transcendant par rapport au monde visible dans le Tractatus Tripartitus du Codex Jung", *REg* 24 (1972) 225-226.

[71] Cf. A. Böhlig, "Die griechische Schule und die Bibliothek von Nag Hammadi", *Göttinger Orientforschungen* VI (Hellenistica), 2, pp. 9-53; cf. his article in *NHS* VII, 41-44. See especially H. Jonas, *Gnosis* I, 6, 45-48, 56, 144-146, 168, 245-247 and his "Delimitation of the Gnostic Phenomenon", *Le Origini*, 101.

was occasioned by political, sociological and economical circumstances in the states of Alexander's *Diadochi*, where paternal traditions, manners and customs were swept away by the waves of unification, reducing people to colourless big masses. One was tired of philosophical quibbling. One had no longer confidence in the idea that the νοῦς was the ordering principle of the world; on the contrary, the world, gripped and forlorn as it was, was made and controlled by a deplorable or even evil Demiurge.[72]

Conclusion

In view of the observations made above, I therefore think it thoroughly feasible that the author of the *Gos. Truth devaluated Isis*, goddess of wisdom, harmony and tenacious seeking for truth (the highest god) *towards the opposite: Error embodied.* The Gnostic, disappointed in philosophy, mysteries etc. as a means to reach ultimate certainty concerning the questions of life, sought in *another* direction. Isis underwent an unlimited *Metamorphose*[73] and became an evil demon, personification of restlessness and instability, whereas the revealed truth

---

[72] A special *agendum* in the field of gnostic studies still remains making an inventory and evaluation of the sociological aspects of Gnosticism cf. e.g. P. Pokorný, "Der soziale Hintergrund der Gnosis", *Gnosis und Neues Testament* (ed. K.-W. Tröger; Berlin: Evangelische Verlagsanstalt, 1973) 77-87. Further K. Rudolph, "Gnosis und Gnostizismus, ein Forschungsbericht" *TRu* 38 (1973) 17 reviewing H. G. Kippenberg's article "Versuch einer soziologischen Verortung des antiken Gnostizismus" *Numen* 17 (1970) 22ɔ 229. An important aspect too is the political one, see e.g. Jonas, *Gnosis*, I, 254-255 (the *Griechenhass* in the eastern part of the Mediterranean basin). A. J. Festugière strikingly characterised the debacle of contemporary philosophy: "Bref, il s'agit de notre bonheur, de notre tout. Voilà ce que l'élite demande aux philosophes. Des négations, des doutes, des sourires, un cliquetis de mots, ne suffisent point. On veut une certitude" (*L'Ideal religieux des Grecs et l'Evangile* (Paris: Gabalda, 1932) 99). A special problem is the disillusion concerning wisdom in the Jewish communities. One has eventually spoken about gnosticism as being an inner Jewish revolt, cf. the Quispel-Jonas debate (see for a summary K. Rudolph, Gnosis.. *TRu* 36 1971) 114-115.

[73] Many words are used interchangeably to depict this gnostic phenomenon as "transmutation of ideas", "convergence" (McL. Wilson in *Kairos* 13 (1971) 284-285) and often "Pseudomorphose" (as coined by O. Spengler and taken over by Jonas, see his *Gnosis* I, 74, 88 and 255) I would rather prefer the use of this particular word for the *general* characteristic gnostic usage of existing notions and conceptions, giving those however a new meaning. "Metamorphose" could better be used to indicate gnostic transformations of a *special* idea; the more so, when we become conscious again of the meaning of the greek preposition μετά in the sense of *Umdeutung* (cf. Jonas, *Gnosis* I, 205 n. 1) remembering too Irenaeus' remark Valentine adapted, μεθαρμόσας, general (gnostic) principles for his doctrine, *Adv. haer.* I, 11, 1 (cf. Sagnard, *La Gnose*, 446 n. 1 and 590).

is unshakable, leading to the ultimate goal of gnostic salvation: *Rest*.[74]
So Isis became Plane. Not her quality as Hyle—how very essential that
really was (ch. 54: leading to miscarriage)—but *her wandering was*
stressed and *selected, because that would not lead to the truth in gnostic
opinion*. The so devaluated Isis could therefore best be denoted by
Plane: an interesting example of gnostic *Protestexegese*, striking the
goddess exactly thére, where her encouraging pains to reach truth and
harmony in the most positive way were originally indicated. She was
transformed into a negative hypostasis.[75]

F. M. M. Sagnard made in his known work on Valentinian
gnosticism, the suggestive remark that the hymn to knowledge in chaps.
1-2 of *De Iside* could readily serve as a preface to an esoteric treatise of
Valentinian gnosticism.[76] I believe one can go further. The author of the
Gos. Truth should very well have experienced the influence of *De Iside*
as such, so suitable for his purpose as Isis-Hyle-Plane was concerned. It
is not our aim to discuss literary dependences or traditio-historical con-
nections in the *Gos. Truth* here. *De Iside* could however very feasibly
have served as an essential, though not the only, source of the *Gos.
Truth*, looking upon the fact in which way and how frequently Gnostics
did use highlights of classical literature, ranging from comedies to
philosophical treatises as e.g. witnessed by Irenaeus (*Adv. haer.* II, 14,
1-2).[77] This counts even more when we refer to the syncretistic atmosphere of Alexandria—so stimulating for gnostic authors.[78] Espec-

---

[74] In the *Gos. Truth* p. 17:26; 26:16-19; 29:2-3 error is typified by restlessness,
ϢΤΑΡΤⲢ̄. As to ἀνάπαυσις / Μ̄ΤΟΝ, rest, see my study on this topic.

[75] The word hypostasis is commonly used for qualities of the high God (cf. e.g. A. J.
Festugière, *Révélation* III, 153-174; *RGG* III, 505-506) especially for God's Wisdom,
Chokma. When *metamorphosed* however, positive hypostases became naturally negative
ones.

[76] So Sagnard, *La Gnose*, 588. L. Cerfaux, "La Gnose, essai théologique manqué",
Irénikon 17 (1940) 5-6 evidently thought in the same direction, though with even more cer-
tainty (cf. also Cerfaux' "Un thème de mythologie gnostique dans le De Iside et Osiride de
Plutarque", *Chronique d'Egypte* 11 (1936) 42-43.

[77] Cf. e.g. Sagnard, *La Gnose*, 117; R. Crahay, "Une mythopée gnostique dans la
Grèce classique", *Le Origini*, 336 and B. Aland, "Gnosis und Philosophie", *Proceedings
of the International Colloquium on Gnosticism* (Stockholm), 39 n. 21.

[78] The peculiar, syncretistic atmosphere of second century Alexandria is e.g. in a most
significant way demonstrated by the so called letter of the Emperor Hadrian, where it is
reported one could not possibly find there a single christian or a bishop not affected by
several cults or quackery or even not devoted to the cult of Serapis (Fl. Vopiscus, *Vita Fir-
mi...* 8; see H. Leisegang, *Die Gnosis* (Stuttgart: Kröner, 1955) 281 and W. C. van Unnik
a.o., *Evangelien aus dem Nilsand* (Frankfurt/Main: Scheffler, 1960) 43); cf. Stead, "The
Valentinian Myth", 92. As to Plutarch, he wrote *De Iside* ± 118 in Delphi after however

ially however when we would assume *Valentine* being the author of the *Gos. Truth*. Not discussing that point here, one can very well defend such an assumption in the light of several indications as to his life and thoughts. According to Tertullian in *Adv. Valent.* 4: Valentine would have found the "seed of an older doctrine". Many had affirmed that this "older doctrine" was the Apocryphon of John. Be that as it may, though we cannot possibly be sure which one was source of the "older doctrine", the fact remains, that Valentine lived in Alexandria, where he very well could have read *De Iside*.[79] Thereby one has to be aware too about the circumstance, that he as a Christian almost likely was acquainted with the figure of the Jewish Chokma, who has so many traits in common with Isis, if not finally derived from the latter...

In any case the Plane-figure has not contributed in the last place to the unique and appealing character of the *Gos. Truth*.

---

having visited Alexandria in the years before (see Griffiths, 17 n. 3, 94, 98, 101 n. 2 and 540); he passed through a development towards a certain mysticism (cf. Griffiths, 25; n. 26 above).

[79] With regard to the relationship of Valentine and Alexandrian culture, cf. G. Quispel, *Gnosis als Weltreligion* (Zürich: Origo, 1972) 111; Sagnard, *La Gnose*, 610-612 and Krämer, *Ursprung*, 251. Especially a combination with the famous place Irenaeus, *Adv. haer.* I, 21, 4 would make his authorship of the *Gos. Truth* very probable (see re I, 21, 4: Jonas, *Gnosis*, I, 206, 375, 411; II, 162; his *Gnostic Religion*, 176 and 312 and Krämer, *Ursprung*, 259). One could refer to the Fragments 7 and 8 (Völker, *Quellen*, 59) of Valentine too, in connection with Harpocrates/Karpocrates as Torhoudt, 93 in a very inventive way did. An idea corroborated by the combination of the two fragments by R. M. Grant, "Notes on Gnosis", *VC* 11 (1957) 151.

CHRISTLICH-GNOSTISCHE TEXTE ALS QUELLEN FÜR DIE AUSEINANDERSETZUNG VON GNOSIS UND CHRISTENTUM*

VON

MARTIN KRAUSE

Seit dem Erscheinen des letzten Facsimilebandes 1977[1] ist die gesamte Nag Hammadi Bibliothek[2] allen Wissenschaftlern, die über Koptisch-kenntnisse verfügen, zugänglich. Seit Ende 1977 gibt es auch die erste englische Übersetzung des Gesamtfundes.[3] Leider bietet diese Überset-zung — wohl aus Platzgründen — auch an Stellen, die verschieden über-setzt werden können, nur *eine* Übersetzungsmöglichkeit im Gegensatz zu den Übersetzungen der Coptic Gnostic Library in den Nag Hammadi Studies, wo mehrere Übersetzungsmöglichkeiten[4] im Apparat erörtert werden. Die Coptic Gnostic Library hat auch die älteren Codices, die Codices Brucianus[5] und Askewianus[6], sowie den Berliner gnostischen Codex[7] aufgenommen, um deutlich zu machen, daß auch diese schon länger bekannten aber jüngeren Schriften Teile der christlich-gnostischen Texte sind und bei der Erforschung dieser Textgruppe mit berücksichtigt werden müssen.

Mein heutiges Anliegen ist es, Ihnen zu zeigen, daß in den christlich-gnostischen Texten die Auseinandersetzung zwischen Gnosis und Chri-

---

* Dieses Referat habe ich vor dem 8. Internationalen Patristikerkongreß bereits auf der Exegetentagung "Gnosis. Geschichte und Texte in frühchristlicher Zeit" in Einsiedeln am 26.9.1978 gehalten.

[1] The Facsimile Edition of the Nag Hammadi Codices, Codex I, Leiden, 1977.

[2] Die Facsimile Bände der übrigen Codices II-XIII sind bekanntlich seit 1972 erschie-nen.

[3] The Nag Hammadi Library in English translated by Members of the Coptic Gnostic Library Project of the Institute for Antiquity and Christianity James M. Robinson, Direc-tor, Leiden, 1977.

[4] Vgl. z. B. D. M. Parrott (Vol. Ed.), Nag Hammadi Codices V, 2-5 and VI with Papy-rus Berolinensis 8502, 1 and 4 (NHS XI), Leiden, 1979, 51ff.

[5] The Books of Jeu and the Untitled Text in the Bruce Codex. Text edited by C. Schmidt. Translation and Notes by V. MacDermot (NHS XIII), Leiden, 1978.

[6] Pistis Sophia. Text edited by C. Schmidt. Translation and Notes by V. MacDermot (NHS IX), Leiden, 1978.

[7] Vgl. A. 4.

stentum überwiegend *nicht polemisch*[8] geführt wurde. Der Grund hier-
für ist m. E. das synkretistische Denken der Gnostiker, ein Erbe der
pharaonischen Ägypter. Die Gnostiker versuchten, durch Anpassung,
durch die gnostische Allegorese von Bibeltexten, in denen sie ihre Lehren wiederfanden, durch die Anfertigung christlich-gnostischer Schriften, die sie auf Christus selbst zurückführten, und durch die Übernahme, Umdeutung und Erweiterung christlicher Sakramente die Christen
für eine christlich gefärbte Gnosis zu gewinnen.

1. Als Grund für das weitgehende Fehlen von Polemik in den
christlich-gnostischen Texten sehe ich das *synkretistische* Denken an,
das sich fundamental von dem jüdischen monotheistischen Denken unterscheidet. Dieses synkretistische Denken hat seine Heimat in Ägypten
und ist fest in der ägyptischen Geschichte und Religion verankert: Ägypten ist bekanntlich aus einer Vielzahl von Gauen mit je einem Gaugott
zu einem Einheitsstaat vereinigt worden. Die Gaugötter mußten in ein
Verhältnis zueinander gebracht werden. Es wurden einerseits *Götterfa-
milien* gebildet (einzelne Götter wurden Söhne, Töchter, Väter oder
Mütter anderer Götter), andererseits übernahmen Götter ein bestimmtes Gebiet, Resort (so wurde z. B. Thot Gott der Weisheit), und
schließlich — was uns interessiert — gingen Götter ineinander auf, es
entstanden die sogenannten Bindestrich-Götter: z. B. Ammon-Re oder
Sobek-Re. Bei dieser Gleichsetzung des Krokodilgottes Sobek mit dem
Sonnengott Re als neuen Gott Sobek-Re wurden einerseits beide Götter
miteinander vereint (der größere Gott Re läßt bei seiner Einwohnung in
Sobek diesem seine größere Kraft einfließen) und andererseits existieren
sie auch getrennt weiter, verlieren nicht ihre personale Existenz. Dieses
Phänomen ist seit dem bahnbrechenden Aufsatz von Hans Bonnet[9] in
alle Monographien über die ägyptische Religion aufgenommen
worden.[10]

Diese genannten Beispiele, die leicht vermehrt[11] werden könnten, sollen zeigen, daß der Ägypter von Haus aus kein Vertreter des Monotheis-

---

[8] Zur Polemik der Gnostiker vgl. K. Koschorke, Die Polemik der Gnostiker gegen das
kirchliche Christentum unter besonderer Berücksichtigung der Nag-Hammadi-Traktate
"Apokalypse des Petrus" (NHC VII, 3) und "Testimonium Veritatis" (NHC IX, 3) (NHS
XII), Leiden, 1978.

[9] H. Bonnet, "Zum Verständnis des Synkretismus", ZÄS 75 (1935), 40-52; ders., Real-
lexikon der ägyptischen Religionsgeschichte, Berlin, ²1971, 237ff.

[10] S. Morenz, Ägyptische Religion (Die Religionen der Menschheit 8), Stuttgart, 1960,
147ff.; E. Hornung, Der Eine und die Vielen. Ägyptische Gottesvorstellungen, Darmstadt, 1971, 82ff., vgl. auch A. 11.

[11] Weitere Beispiele werden in den A. 10 zitierten Arbeiten genannt, vgl. jetzt auch E.
Hornung, Monotheismus im pharaonischen Ägypten in: O. Keel (Hrsg.), Monotheismus
im Alten Israel und seiner Umwelt (Biblische Beiträge 14), Fribourg, 1980, 83-97.

mus, sondern des Synkretismus war und daß er gleichsam erst zum Monotheismus[12] erzogen werden mußte. Von daher verstehe ich auch die Kritik, die in den gnostischen Texten am Gott des Alten Testamentes geübt wird. Er kennt nicht den höchsten Gott und hält sich — weil er Engel schafft — für den alleinigen Gott. In der "Hypostase der Archonten"[13] wird er wie eine Fehlgeburt beschrieben, als selbstgefälliges Tier in Löwengestalt, das spricht: "Ich bin Gott, und außer mir gibt es keinen anderen" (Jes. 45, 5; 46, 9b). Er wird von einer Himmelsstimme belehrt und als blinder Gott bezeichnet. Auch im "Apokryphon des Johannes" sagt er zu den Engeln: "Ich bin ein eifersüchtiger Gott (2. Mose 20, 5), außer mir gibt es keinen" (Jes. 45, 5; 46, 9 b),[14] und der Verfasser bemerkt dazu: "womit er schon den Engeln, die bei ihm sind, anzeigte, daß es einen anderen Gott gibt; denn, wenn es keinen (anderen) gäbe, auf wen sollte er eifersüchtig sein?"[15]

Selbst in Ägypten ansässige Juden dachten synkretistisch, nicht monotheistisch und sind offenbar von diesem ägyptischen Denken beeinflußt worden. Ich verweise auf die Juden in Elephantine, die ihren Gott Jahwe mit anderen Göttern gleichsetzten.[16] Im Hellenismus wirkt diese Gabe Ägyptens weiter: andere Gottheiten werden nicht bekämpft, sondern miteinander gleichgesetzt.[17] So läßt man sich z. B. in verschiedene Mysterienkulte[18] einweihen.

In den gnostischen Texten finden wir, vor allem in den kosmogonischen Texten, immer wieder Gleichsetzungen von Äonen, ausgedrückt durch 'das ist' ετε παϊ πε bzw. ετε ταϊ τε oder ετε ναϊ νε. Ich will aus dem "Apokryphon des Johannes" nur ein Beispiel nennen: als Gott sein eigenes Abbild in reinem Lichtwasser erkannte, trat seine Ennoia in Erscheinung, die anderen Äonen gleichgesetzt wird: "Und seine *Ennoia* wurde wirksam. Sie trat in Erscheinung. Sie trat vor ihn

---

[12] Der Versuch Echnatons, den Monotheismus in Ägypten einzuführen, scheiterte, vgl. den Exkurs "Der Ansatz Echnatons", Hornung, Der Eine und die Vielen, 240-246.

[13] II, 4: 94, 14ff.

[14] BG 44, 14f. u. Par.

[15] BG 44, 15ff. u. Par.; zum "Zweiten Logos des großen Seth" vgl. M. Krause, "Aussagen über das Alte Testament in z.T. bisher unveröffentlichten gnostischen Texten aus Nag Hammadi", Ex orbe religionum. Studia Geo Widengren, Leiden 1972, 449-456, 450f.

[16] Z.B. Anath mit Jahwe, vgl. zuletzt F. Stolz, Monotheismus in Israel in: O. Keel (Hrsg.), Monotheismus im Alten Israel und seiner Umwelt (Biblische Beiträge 14), Fribourg, 1980, 143-189, 166 u. A. 66 (mit der älteren Lit.).

[17] Vgl. M. P. Nilsson, Geschichte der griechischen Religion, Bd. 2, Die hellenistische und römische Zeit, München, ²1961, 573ff.

[18] J. Leipoldt, Von den Mysterien zur Kirche. Gesammelte Aufsätze, Leipzig, 1961, 47f. (mit Belegen).

hin in seinen Lichtglanz — sie ist die Kraft, die vor allen Dingen ist, die *Pronoia des Alls*, die erstrahlt in dem Lichte des Abbildes des Unsichtbaren, die *vollkommene Kraft, die Barbelo*, der vollkommene Äon der Herrlichkeit'' usw.[19]

In der ''Titellosen Schrift von Codex II'' wird eine Gleichsetzung Christi mit den gnostischen Soter vorgenommen: ιнс πεχс εϥτнтωn επсωтнр ''Jesus Christus, der dem Soter gleicht''.[20]

Dieses synkretistische Denken spiegelt sich auch in der Zusammensetzung der Bibliothek von Nag Hammadi wider, wo m. E. vier Hauptgruppen[21] unterschieden werden können: neben nichtchristlichgnostischen Schriften christlich-gnostische Abhandlungen, hermetische Traktate und philosophische Schriften und Weisheitslehren. Wenn auch das Zustandekommen und der Besitzer der Bibliothek noch kontrovers[22] diskutiert werden, ist Codex VI das beste Beispiel für dieses Denken, denn die 8 in ihm niedergeschriebenen Werke lassen sich auf alle vier Gruppen[23] verteilen: zu den nichtchristlich-gnostischen Texten gehört die 2. Schrift, die ''Bronte'' betitelt ist, zu den christlich-gnostischen Abhandlungen die ''Akten des Petrus und der 12 Apostel'', der ''Authentikos Logos'' und ''der Gedanke unserer großen Kraft'', zu den hermetischen Texten gehören die 6.-8. Schrift und zu den philosophischen Werken die 5. Schrift, ein Auszug aus Platons Staat. M. E. kann nur ein synkretistisch denkender Mensch den Auftrag zum Abschreiben dieser verschiedenen in Codex VI vereinigten Schriften erteilt haben.

Diesen ''praktizierten'' Synkretismus spiegeln auch mehrere Berichte aus Ägypten wider, von denen einige Beispiele genannt werden sollen. Aus dem Anfang des 2. Jh.s ist uns ein Brief des Kaisers Hadrian an den Konsul Servian[24] erhalten, in dem es u. a. heißt: ''Hier (nämlich in

---

[19] III, 1: 7, 12-20 u. Par.

[20] II, 5: 105, 26.

[21] M. Krause, ''Die Texte von Nag Hammadi'', Gnosis. Festschrift für Hans Jonas, Göttingen, 1978, 216-243, 238ff.; vgl. auch G. Kretzschmar, Gnosis III, RGG II, ³1958, 1660: ''Ein gutes Beispiel für den hier im 3./4. Jh. verbreiteten hemmungslosen Synkretismus zwischen christlicher, nichtchristlicher und philosophischer Gnosis gibt die um 1946 bei Nag Hammadi aufgedeckte koptisch-gnostische Bibliothek.''

[22] Krause, aO. 241ff.

[23] Vgl. Krause, aO. 242.

[24] Er ist erhalten bei Flavius Vopiscus, Vita Saturnini 8 in: Scriptores historiae Augustae ed. E. Hohl, 1927. Zum Brief vgl. W. Weber, Untersuchungen zur Geschichte des Kaisers Hadrianus, 1907, 97ff.; W. Bauer, Rechtgläubigkeit und Ketzerei im ältesten Christentum, Göttingen, ²1964, 51 hält ihn für ganz unsicher. A. v. Harnack. Die Mission und Ausbreitung des Christentums in den ersten drei Jahrhunderten II, Leipzig, ⁴1924, 703 A. 3 nennt ihn ''umstritten'' und läßt ihn als Quelle für das 3. Jh. gelten. Dagegen ha-

Alexandrien) sind die Serapisverehrer [gleichzeitig] Christen und, die sich Christi Bischöfe nennen, verehren auch den Serapis. Hier gibt es keinen jüdischen Synagogenvorsteher, keinen Samariter, keinen christlichen Priester, der nicht Astrolog, Opferdeuter und Salber wäre''. Vom 1. Viertel des 2. Jh.s an haben in Alexandrien bedeutende Denker versucht, Christentum und Gnosis miteinander zu verbinden. Ich erinnere an Basilides[25], der von 120-145 in Alexandrien lehrte, ebenso an seinen Schüler Isidor.[26] Ebenfalls in Ägypten geboren und in Alexandrien erzogen ist Valentin,[27] der von 135-160 seine christlich-gnostischen Lehren in Rom vertrat und eine Schule gründete, die sich in eine westliche und eine östliche teilte.[28] Zeitgenosse Valentins in Ägypten war Karpokrates, der ebenso wie sein Sohn Epiphanes[29] in Alexandrien lehrte. Der junge Origines[30] wuchs nach dem Märtyrertod seines Vaters im Hause einer reichen Dame in Alexandrien *zusammen mit einem Gnostiker* auf,[31] ohne daß daran Anstoß genommen wurde.

Ein weiteres Jahrhundert später, zwischen 330 und 340, trifft der in Judäa geborene junge Epiphanius,[32] später Bischof von Salamis, in Ägypten Christen an, die gleichzeitig aktive Mitglieder einer gnostischen Sekte sind. Da ihr Treiben dem Epiphanius wenig christlich erscheint, erstattet er dem Bischof Bericht, 80 Anhänger dieser Sekte werden unter den Gemeindechristen ermittelt und aus der Kirche ausgeschlossen.[33] Dieser Bericht zeigt m. E., daß die Gnostiker an den Gottesdiensten der Großkirche teilnahmen und versuchten, Christen — wie im Falle des Epiphanius — für ihre in Konventikeln praktizierten Lehren zu gewinnen.

2. Als Folge dieser synkretistischen Denkweise übernahmen die Gnostiker die heiligen Schriften der Christen, die sie gnostisch allegorisch

---

ben H. Gelzer (S. Julius Africanus I, 1880, 16) und J. Leipoldt ("Zur Ideologie der frühen koptischen Kirche", BSAC 17 (1964), 102) ihn für echt gehalten.

[25] Zu Basilides vgl. B. Altaner — A. Stuiber, Patrologie, Freiburg, ⁸1978, loo u. 563 und K. Rudolph, Die Gnosis. Wesen und Geschichte einer spätantiken Religion, Leipzig, 1977, 330-334.

[26] Zu Isidor vgl. Altaner-Stuiber, aO. loo f. und Rudolph, aO. 334.

[27] Zu Valentin vgl. Altaner-Stuiber, aO. lol u. 563 und Rudolph, aO. 339-342.

[28] Altaner-Stuiber, aO. lol u. 563.

[29] Zu Karpokrates und Epiphanius vgl. Altaner-Stuiber, aO. lol.

[30] Altaner-Stuiber, aO. 197-208 u. 589f.

[31] H. Lietzmann, Geschichte der Alten Kirche, Berlin, ³1961, 306.

[32] Altaner-Stuiber, aO. 315-318 u. 614f.

[33] Epiphanius, Panarion 26.4f.; vgl. dazu C. Schmidt, Gnostische Schriften in koptischer Sprache aus dem Codex Brucianus (TU 8), Leipzig, 1892, 571ff.

interpretierten.[34] Die Gnostiker waren — wie wir wissen — die ersten Exegeten des Alten und Neuen Testamentes: Basilides[35] erklärte das Evangelium in 24 Büchern, Ptolemäus[36] exegesierte das Alte Testament, Herakleon[37] kommentierte das Johannesevangelium, um nur einige Beispiele zu nennen. Sie fanden dabei ihre Anschauungen in den Bibeltexten wieder.

Sie konnten sich auf das Neue Testament berufen, denn Lukas 24, 45 lesen wir, daß der Auferstandene seinen Jüngern "das Verständnis öffnete, daß sie die Schrift verstanden". Entscheidend war das richtige Verständnis, die ἑρμηνεία,[38] des Bibeltextes.

Das beste Beispiel für eine allegorische Exegese aus der Nag Hammadi Bibliothek ist m. E. die "*Exegese* über die Seele".[39] Ihr Verfasser versucht nachzuweisen, daß die Lehre vom Fall der Seele und ihrer Rettung bereits im biblischen Schrifttum bezeugt ist. Etwa ein Drittel des ganzen Textes sind Zitate aus dem Alten und Neuen Testament. Auch Homer wird zitiert und allegorisch gedeutet. Nach der "Exegese über die Seele" ist die Seele — solange sie bei Gott ist — jungfräulich und mannweiblich. Bei ihrem Fall in den Körper findet wohl eine Trennung der Seele in ihren männlichen und weiblichen Teil statt, und es fällt anscheinend nur der weibliche Teil, der seine Jungfräulichkeit verliert. Wenn die Seele zu Gott ruft, erbarmt er sich ihrer. Es heißt: "Über die *Hurerei der Seele* nun weissagt der *Heilige Geist* an vielen Stellen. Er sagte nämlich beim Propheten Jeremias."[40] Es folgt ein Zitat von Jeremias, 3, 1-4 (LXX), dann: "Wiederum ist geschrieben beim Propheten Hosea" — es folgt Hosea 2, 4-9 — dann: "Wiederum sagte er bei Ezechiel" — es folgt Ezechiel 16, 23-26 a (LXX) — danach Zitate aus dem Neuen Testament: Apg. 21, 25; 1. Kor. 5, 9f. und Eph. 6, 12. Dabei werden auch biblische Begriffe und Sakramente gnostisch uminterpretiert. Das Reinigen der Seele wird danach als Taufe[41] beschrieben: Gott sendet der Seele vom

---

[34] Vgl. R. McL. Wilson, Gnosis und Neues Testament, Stuttgart, 1971, 60ff. Die ältere Literatur wird bei Wilson, aO. 63ff. besprochen; vgl. auch E. Pagels, The Johannine Gospel in Gnostic Exegesis, Nashville, 1973 und dies., Paul the Gnostic: Gnostic Exegesis of the Pauline Letters, Philadelphia, 1975.

[35] Vgl. A. 25.

[36] Zu Ptolemäus vgl. Rudolph, aO. 345f.; G. Quispel, Lettre à Flora (SChr 24), ²1966; Altaner-Stuiber, aO. lol u. 563.

[37] Rudolph, aO. 346; Altaner-Stuiber, aO. lol u. 563 und B. Aland, "Erwählungstheologie und Menschenklassenlehre. Die Theologie des Herakleon als Schlüssel zum Verständnis der christlichen Gnosis?" NHS VIII, Leiden, 1977, 148-181.

[38] Vgl. J. Behm, ThWB NT II, Stuttgart, 1935, 662 u. X, 1, 1979, 1086.

[39] II, 6: 127, 18-137, 27.

[40] II, 6: 129, 7ff.

[41] II, 6: 132, 3.

Himmel ihren Bruder, d.h. den männlichen Teil der Seele, der als Bräutigam zur Seele, der Braut, herabkommt. Beide vereinigen sich im Brautgemach, stellen den alten Zustand vor dem Fall der Seele in den Körper wieder her. Das findet der Gnostiker bereits beim Propheten[42]: "Sie werden ein einziges Fleisch werden" und Genesis 3, 16 b: "Der Herr der Frau ist ihr Gatte" prophezeit. Die Rückkehr zu Gott findet der Verfasser in Genesis 12, 1 vorhergesagt: "Komme heraus aus deinem Land und deiner Verwandtschaft und aus dem Hause deines Vaters." Diese Rückkehr zum Vater ist für ihn die Auferstehung von den Toten, die Errettung aus der Gefangenschaft, das Heraufsteigen zum Himmel (= die Himmelfahrt). Es ist die Rettung durch die Wiedergeburt, die durch die Gnade Gottes geschieht, was schon Psalm 103 (102), 1-5 und Joh. 6, 44 geschrieben steht: "Keiner wird zu mir kommen, es sei denn, mein Vater zieht ihn und bringt ihn zu mir, und ich selbst werde ihn erwecken am letzten Tage." Sie geschieht durch Buße und Trauer, daher wird Mt. 5, 4.6 (Par) zitiert: "Selig sind die, die trauern, denn ihrer wird man sich erbarmen. Selig sind die Hungrigen, denn sie werden gesättigt werden" und Lk. 14, 26: "Wer nicht seine Seele haßt, wird mir nicht nachfolgen können." Der Verf. erinnert an Johannes den Täufer, der die Taufe der Buße predigte (Mk. 1, 4 par.) und schließt Zitate aus dem Ezechielapokryphon[43]; Jesaja 30, 15 u. 19f.; Jer. 17, 10; aus Homer und Ps. 6, 7-10 an. Nur selten werden alttestamentliche Texte polemisch allegorisiert.[44]

3. Neben die allegorische Exegese tritt die Anfertigung neuer christlich-gnostischer Schriften, die auf Jesus zurückgeführt wurden. Die Gnostiker konnten sich auch dabei wieder auf Aussagen des Neuen Testamentes stützen. In Apostelgeschichte 1, 3 lesen wir, daß Jesus nach seiner Auferstehung 40 Tage lang unter seinen Jüngern weilte und mit ihnen vom Reiche Gottes sprach. Aus 1, 12 ergibt sich, daß die Belehrung auf dem Ölberg stattfand. Sonderbelehrungen Jesu konnten auch aus verschiedenen Schriftstellen am Ende der Evangelien herausgelesen

---

[42] Gemeint ist Gen. 2, 24b.

[43] A. Guillaumont, "Une citation de l'apocryphe d'Ezéchiel dans l'Exégèse au sujet de l'âme Nag Hammadi II, 6" NHS VI, Leiden 1975, 35-39.

[44] Ich verweise auf das "Apokryphon des Johannes" BG 45, 8ff. u. Par.: "Glaubst du, daß es so ist, wie Moses sagte: 'über den Wassern?' Nein, sondern sie sah...''; BG 58, 16ff. u. Par. Auf die Frage: "Was ist das Vergessen?"..."Nicht so wie Moses sagte: 'Er ließ ihn einschlafen', sondern er umhüllte seine Sinne mit einem Schleier..."; BG 59, 17 u. Par.: "Nicht so wie Moses sagte: 'Er nahm eine Rippe und schuf das Weib bei ihm' "; BG 73, 4ff. u. Par.: "Nicht so wie Moses sagte: 'Er verbarg sich in einer Arche', sondern er verhüllte sich an einem Ort".

werden, bei Johannes 21, 25 lesen wir: "Es sind auch viele andere Dinge, die Jesus getan hat; so sie aber sollten eins nach dem anderen
geschrieben werden, achte ich, die Welt würde die Bücher nicht fassen,
die zu schreiben wären" (vgl. auch 20, 30), bei Markus 16, 19: "Und der
Herr, nachdem er mit ihnen *geredet* hatte, ward er aufgehoben gen
Himmel." Die Kirchenväter berichten, daß christliche Gnostiker ihre
Lehren auf Sondertraditionen von Aposteln[45] Jesu zurückführten: Basilides will seine Lehren sowohl von Glaukias, dem Dolmetscher des
Petrus[46], als auch mit seinem Sohn Isidor vom Apostel Matthias[47] erhalten haben. Die christlich-gnostischen Texte gehen einen Schritt weiter
und führen ihre Lehren auf Christus selbst zurück. Sie geben — meist in
ihren Rahmenhandlungen — auch Auskunft über die angeblichen Empfänger der Sonderoffenbarungen. Ferner nennen sie oft den Ort und
Zeitpunkt der Offenbarung.

Wohl in Anlehnung an Acta 1, 3 und 12 verkündet am häufigsten der
Auferstandene seinen Jüngern seine Lehren auf einem Berg, meist dem
Ölberg. Im "Brief des Petrus an Philippus" erscheint der Auferstandene den Jüngern auf dem Ölberg "dem Ort, an dem sie sich mit dem seli-
gen Christus, als er im Leib war, gewöhnlich versammelten".[48] In der
"Pistis Sophia"[49] sitzt er mit den Jüngern mehrfach auf dem Ölberg.
Im "Apokryphon des Johannes"[50] erscheint er dem Johannes an einem
öden Ort auf dem Wege zum Ölberg, in der "Paulusapokalypse"[51] auf
dem Wege nach Jerusalem und dem Berg von Jericho. Im 2. Teil der "1.
Jakobusapokalypse"[52] findet ein Gespräch des Auferstandenen mit Jakobus bzw. den Jüngern auf dem Berge Gaugelan[53] wenige Tage nach
Ostern statt. In der "Sophia Jesu Christi" erscheint der Auferstandene
seinen 12 Jüngern und 7 Frauen, die ihm als Jünger gefolgt waren, auf

---

[45] Vgl. W. Schneemelcher, Hennecke-Schneemelcher, Neutestamentliche Apokryphen,
Bd. 2, Tübingen, ²1964, 17 u. 19ff. Selbst Clemens Alexandrinus (Hypotyp. bei Euseb II,
1) meint, der Herr habe nach seiner Auferstehung die Gnosis dem gerechten Jakobus,
Johannes und Petrus gegeben. Diese gaben sie an die anderen Apostel, diese den 70, von
denen einer Barnabas war; vgl. A. v. Harnack, Dogmengeschichte, Tübingen, 1922, 144.
[46] Nach Clemens Alex. VII 17, 106, 4; vgl. dazu H.-Ch. Puech, E. Hennecke, Neutestamentliche Apokryphen in deutscher Übersetzung, 3. völlig neubearb. Aufl. hrsg. von W.
Schneemelcher, Bd. I, Tübingen, 1959, 257.
[47] Nach Hippolyt, Ref VII 20, 1; S. 195, 19-24 Wendland, vgl. dazu Puech, aO. 226f.
[48] VIII, 2: 133, 13ff.
[49] Pistis Sophia 3, 9; 6, 6.17; 9, 25; 110, 14 u.ö.; 111, 23.
[50] BG 20, 5f. u. Par.
[51] V, 2: 19, 12f.
[52] V, 3: 30, 13-44, 8.
[53] V, 3: 30, 20f.

dem Berg in Galiläa, der "Ort von Reifezeit und Freude"[54] genannt wird. Kein Ort der Offenbarung wird im "Dialog des Soter"[55] und im "Jakobusapokryphon" genannt, wo der Empfang einer Vielzahl von Geheimlehren berichtet wird: zuerst eine dem *Petrus und Jakobus* geoffenbarte Sonderbelehrung[56], die — wie ausdrücklich[57] betont wird — *der Herr nicht einmal allen seinen 12 Jüngern mitteilen wollte.* Sie ist erhalten im "Apokryphon des Jakobus". Eine weitere, nur dem *Jakobus allein geoffenbarte Belehrung, will dieser bereits 10 Monate früher an den Empfänger des Briefes gesandt haben.*[58] Dann[59] wird berichtet, daß alle 12 Jünger dasaßen und jeder einzelne sich an das erinnerte, was der Soter jedem einzelnen von ihnen — sei es geheim, sei es offenbar — gesagt hatte und sie diese Sonderbelehrungen in Buchform brachten. Also war jeder Jünger einer Offenbarung gewürdigt worden. Das "Thomasbuch" in Codex II, 7 will eine geheime Lehre sein, die der Soter dem *Judas Thomas* mitgeteilt hat und die Matthäus mitgehört und aufgeschrieben haben will. Ein Ort wird nicht genannt. Aus der Formulierung ⲚⲈⲈⲒⲘⲞⲞⲰⲈ ⲈⲈⲒⲤⲰⲦⲘ̄ ⲈⲢⲞⲞⲨ "als ich wandelte, hörte ich sie"[60] kann ich nur schließen, daß die Offenbarung nicht an *einem* Ort, etwa auf einem Berg stattfand, sondern an mehreren. Aus II 138, 23 geht hervor, daß das Gespräch *vor* der Himmelfahrt stattfand. Die im "Evangelium der Maria" der Maria zuteil gewordene Sonderlehre will Maria in einem Gesicht erlebt haben.[61] Sie wird also wohl auf den auferstandenen Jesus zurückgeführt.

Neben den Offenbarungsreden des Auferstandenen finden wir — wenn auch weniger häufig — Lehren, die Jesus früher, bei seinem Erdenwandel, verkündet haben soll "als er noch im Körper war" (ⲈⲊ2Ⲙ̄ ⲠⲤⲰⲘⲀ), wie es z. B. im "Petrusbrief an Philippus" mehrfach[62] heißt.

Hierher gehören vor allem das "Thomasevangelium", das geheime Worte Jesu bieten will, die Didymos Judas Thomas aufgeschrieben

---

[54] BG 77, 9ff. u. Par.; im "Philippusevangelium" Spr. 26 (II, 3: 57, 28ff.) erscheint Jesus den Jüngern auf einem Berge, dessen Name nicht genannt wird.

[55] III, 5.

[56] I, 2: 1, 10ff.

[57] I, 2: 1, 22ff.

[58] I, 2: 1, 28ff.

[59] I, 2: 2, 7ff.

[60] II, 7: 138, 3.

[61] BG 10, 10f.: ⲀⲒⲚⲀⲨ ⲈⲠⲬⲤ 2Ⲛ ⲞⲨ2ⲞⲢⲞⲘⲀ.

[62] VIII, 2: 133, 17 u. 139, 10; vgl. auch 138, 3: "als ich im Körper war" und II, 7: 143, 6f.: "am Tage, als er im Körper war."

hat.[63] Bekanntlich werden in 13 Logia[64] die Jünger oder "seine" Jünger[65] insgesamt als Redende oder ihn Fragende genannt, außerdem einzelne Jünger namentlich: Simon Petrus,[66] Matthäus,[67] Thomas,[68] und Maria.[69] Für einen frühen Zeitpunkt dieser Verkündigung sprechen die Parallelen zu den Evangelien, z. B. die Nennung einer Frau aus der Menge in Log. 97,[70] die Zinsgroschenperikope in Log. 100[71] und der Samariter auf dem Wege nach Judäa in Log. 60. In Logion 13 wird außerdem noch eine aus drei Worten Jesu bestehende Sonderoffenbarung an Thomas bezeugt.

In der "Petrusapokalypse"[72] besitzen wir eine Schrift, in der der Soter dem Petrus die Leidensgeschichte Jesu als ein zukünftiges Ereignis gnostisch interpretiert. Der erste Teil der "1. Jakobusapokalypse"[73] schildert Geschehnisse am Dienstag der Karwoche in Jerusalem; in der "2. Jakobusapokalypse"[74] teilt Jakobus vor seinem Märtyrertode frühere Gespräche mit Jesu mit.

Die Zeit zwischen Auferstehung und Himmelfahrt, in der der Auferstandene nach dem Neuen Testament einzelnen oder allen Jüngern erscheint,[75] und in der er mit ihnen vom Reiche Gottes spricht, betrug nach Apostelgeschichte 1, 3 40 Tage. Dieser Zeitraum wird in den gnostischen Texten immer weiter ausgedehnt, wohl um genügend Zeit für die Verkündigung der neuen Lehren zu gewinnen, die — je jünger die Texte sind — umso länger werden. Im "Apokryphon des Jakobus" verweilt Jesus 540 Tage bei den Jüngern: "Nach den vierzig Tagen habt ihr mich gezwungen, noch achtzehn Monate bei euch zu bleiben"[76] und er erscheint 550 Tage nach seiner Auferstehung noch einmal den Jüngern,[77] in der "Pistis Sophia" 11 Jahre lang![78]

---

[63] II, 2: 32, 10ff.
[64] Log. 6. 12. 18. 20. 22. 24. 37. 43. 51. 52. 53. 99. 113.
[65] Log. 22.
[66] Log. 13. 114.
[67] Log. 13.
[68] Log. 13.
[69] Log. 21. 114.
[70] Vgl. Lk. 11, 27f.; 23, 29.
[71] Vgl. Mk. 12. 13ff. u. Par.
[72] VII, 3.
[73] V, 3: 24, 11-30, 13.
[74] V, 4.
[75] Vgl. Mk. 16, 9ff. (Maria Magdalena); Mk. 16, 12f. (zwei Apostel); Mk. 16, 14ff. (allen 11 Jüngern).
[76] I, 2: 8, 1ff.
[77] I, 2: 2, 19ff.
[78] PS 1, 1ff. Nach Irenäus, adv. haer. I 3, 2 verbrachte Jesus mit den Jüngern nach seiner Auferstehung 18 Monate, nach der Ascensio Jesaiae (9, 16) sollen es 545 Tage sein.

Gegen diese von den Gnostikern erfundenen Sonderoffenbarungen Jesu werden sich die "katholischen Christen" gewandt haben, da die christlichen Gnostiker in ihnen ihre Sonderlehren auf den Soter zurückführten. Eine solche Kritik an den Sonderlehren finde ich im "Evangelium der Maria."[79] Dort bittet kein Geringerer als Petrus die Maria, die ihr zuteil gewordene Sonderoffenbarung auch den Jüngern bekanntzugeben: "Schwester, wir wissen, daß der Erlöser dich mehr liebte als die übrigen Frauen. Sage uns die Worte des Erlösers, deren du dich erinnerst, die du kennst, nicht (aber) wir, die wir auch nicht gehört haben."[80] Danach teilt Maria den Jüngern mit, was Jesus nur ihr offenbart hat. Andreas meldet Zweifel an. Er spricht: "Sagt, was ihr meint betreffs dessen, was sie sagte. Ich wenigstens glaube nicht, daß der Erlöser das gesagt hat. Denn sicherlich sind diese Lehren andere Meinungen."[81] Petrus stimmt dem Andreas bei und fragt: "Hat Christus sich einer Frau heimlich vor uns und nicht offen offenbart? Sollen auch wir umkehren und alle auf sie hören? Hat er sie uns gegenüber bevorzugt?"[82] Maria weint und antwortet Petrus: "Mein Bruder Petrus, was glaubst du denn? Glaubst du, ich habe das selbst ersonnen in meinem Herzen oder ich lüge über den Erlöser?"[83] Lewi verteidigt daraufhin Maria und spricht zu Petrus: "Petrus, du bist immer heißblütig. Jetzt sehe ich, daß du die Frau wie die Widersacher bekämpfst. Wenn aber der Heiland sie würdig gemacht hat, wer bist du, um sie zu verwerfen? Sicher kennt der Heiland sie sehr gut. Daher liebte er sie mehr als uns. Wir sollen uns vielmehr schämen, den vollkommenen Menschen anziehen, weggehen, wie er uns befohlen hat, und das Evangelium verkündigen, wobei wir kein anderes Gebot oder Gesetz erlassen außer dem, was der Erlöser gesagt hat."[84] In diesen Passagen sehe ich den Versuch christlicher Gnostiker, die Kritik katholischer Christen an diesen Geheimlehren als nicht authentische Lehren Jesu vorweg zu nehmen.

Leider wissen wir nicht, in welchem zeitlichen Verhältnis die Sonderlehren einzelner Jünger zu den allen Jüngern zuteil gewordenen Lehren stehen.[85] Ich vermute aber, daß aufgrund der Kritik an den Sonderleh-

---

[79] Ich meine nicht, daß der Text sich nur gegen Frauen richtet.

[80] BG 10, 1ff.

[81] BG 17, 11ff.

[82] BG 17, 18ff.

[83] BG 18, 2ff.

[84] BG 18, 7ff.

[85] Wenn ich Kretzschmar (aO. 1658) richtig verstehe, setzt er folgende Reihenfolge voraus: zuerst Berufung auf das AT, dabei Umwertung der Aussagen, die dem "Auferstande-

ren einzelner versucht wird, durch Hinzuziehung weiterer Personen, die
die Authentizität dieser Lehren bezeugen sollen, Zeugen für die Echtheit
dieser Tradition zu gewinnen. *So* verstehe ich die Nennung des Matthäus als Schreiber des "Thomasbuches", der ein Ohrenzeuge des Ge-
spräches zwischen Jesus und Judas Thomas sein will.[86] In der "Pistis
Sophia" wird die Anzahl der Jünger, die Jesu Reden niederschreiben,
wohl in Anlehnung an Deuteronomium 19, 15,[87] sogar auf drei gesteigert: "Es geschah nun, als Jesus Philippus gehört hatte, sprach er zu
ihm: 'Höre, Philippus, Du Seliger, damit ich mit Dir rede, denn Du und
Thomas und Matthäus sind es, welchen durch das erste Mysterium auf-
getragen ist, alle Reden zu schreiben, die ich sagen und tun werde, und
alle Dinge, die ihr sehen werdet. Was Dich aber betrifft, so ist bis jetzt
noch nicht die Zahl der Reden, welche Du schreiben sollst, vollendet;
wenn sie nun vollendet, sollst Du vortreten und verkünden, was Dir ge-
fällt. Jetzt nun sollt ihr drei alle Reden niederschreiben, die ich sage
und tun werde und < alle Dinge >, die ihr sehen werdet, auf daß ihr be-
zeuget alle Dinge des Himmelreiches'."[88] In der "Sophia Jesu Christi"
sind die 12 Jünger und 7 Frauen Zeugen der Offenbarung Jesu,[89] im "2.
Buch des Jeu" seine 12 Jünger und die Jüngerinnen,[90] in der "2. Jakobusapokalypse" werden die Reden des Jakobus — auch die ihm mitge-
teilten Worte Jesu — von allen Menschen im Tempel von Jerusalem[91]
gehört. Sie werden außerdem von Marim niedergeschrieben.[92] Als Ohrenzeuge wird sogar einer der Priester genannt, der sie Theudas, dem
Vater des Jakobus, berichtet haben soll.[93] Eine weitere Steigerung liegt
m. E. im "Brief des Petrus an Philippus" vor, wo mehrfach betont
wird, daß zwischen dem, was Jesus den Jüngern jetzt auf dem Ölberg
sagt und dem, was er vor bereits seinem Tode verkündet hat, kein Unterschied besteht: "Ihr selbst seid Zeugen, daß ich das alles (schon) gesagt habe, aber wegen Eures Unglaubens will ich es *noch einmal*

---

nen in den Mund gelegt" werden. "Später sind auch Gnostiker an der Produktion von
Evangelien und Apostelschriften beteiligt. Schließlich übernahm die Gnosis weithin die
kanonischen Evangelien, exegesierte sie aber nach ihren Methoden."

[86] II, 7: 138, 2ff.

[87] "In dem Mund zweier oder dreier Zeugen soll die Sache bestehen".

[88] PS 71, 18ff. nach der Übersetzung von C. Schmidt, Koptisch-gnostische Schriften,
Bd. I, 3. Aufl. bearb. von W. Till, Berlin, 1959, 44f.

[89] BG 77, 12ff. u. Par.

[90] C. Schmidt, Gnostische Schriften (vgl. A. 33), 99; Schmidt-Till, aO. 303.

[91] V, 4: 44, 13ff.

[92] V, 4: 44, 16.

[93] V, 4: 44, 16ff.

sagen."⁹⁴ "Ich habe euch viele Male gesagt......"⁹⁵. "Unser Herr Jesus hat uns, als er im Leibe war, *über alles* Weisung gegeben."⁹⁶ Mit diesen Aussagen soll wohl Kritikern, die auf Unterschiede zwischen Neuem Testament und den Lehren der Gnostiker hinwiesen, begegnet werden.

Diese christlich-gnostischen Werke werden einesteils als Geheimlehren bezeichnet, die nur den Vollkommenen bekannt werden sollen, andererseits enthalten sie die Aussage, daß die Jünger, nachdem sie diese Lehren gehört haben, zur Mission aufbrechen, also Mission treiben. Ich zitiere nur einige Beispiele: im "Apokryphon des Johannes" soll Johannes die Lehren aufschreiben und den Gleichgeistern im Verborgenen weitergeben, weil dieses Geheimnis dem nicht wankenden Geschlecht gehört.⁹⁷ Das "Thomasbuch"⁹⁸ und "Thomasevangelium"⁹⁹ wollen nach der Rahmenhandlung "geheime" Lehren Jesu enthalten. Auch die Logia 23¹⁰⁰ und 62¹⁰¹ betonen, daß nur wenige Würdige diese Geheimnisse kennenlernen sollen. Die "1. Jakobusapokalypse"¹⁰² soll geheim gehalten und nur dem Addaios offenbart werden, in der "Petrusapokalypse" soll Petrus das, was er gesehen hat, den ἀλλόγενης, die nicht aus dem Äon stammen, überliefern.¹⁰³ Log. 33¹⁰⁴ des "Thomasevangeliums" ruft den Gnostiker zur Mission auf, ebenso das "Evangelium der Maria."¹⁰⁵ Drei christlich-gnostische Evangelien, das "Evangelium der Maria",¹⁰⁶ die "Sophia Jesu Christi"¹⁰⁷ und der "Brief des Petrus an Philippus"¹⁰⁸ enden mit der Aussage, daß die Jünger nach der Verkün-

---

⁹⁴ VIII, 2: 135, 5ff.

⁹⁵ VIII, 2: 138, 22ff.

⁹⁶ VIII, 2: 139, 10f.

⁹⁷ BG 75, 17ff. u. Par.

⁹⁸ II, 7: 138, 1.

⁹⁹ II, 2: 32, 10.

¹⁰⁰ II, 2: 38, 1f.: "Ich will euch auswählen, einen aus tausend und zwei aus zehntausend...".

¹⁰¹ II, 2: 43, 34f.: "Ich sage meine Geheimnisse denen, die [meiner] Geheimnisse würdig sind...".

¹⁰² V, 3: 36, 13ff., 20ff.

¹⁰³ VII, 3: 83, 13ff.

¹⁰⁴ II, 2: 39, 10ff.: "Das, was du mit deinem einen Ohr und dem anderen hören wirst, verkündigt auf euren Dächern; denn keiner zündet eine Lampe an und stellt sie unter einen Scheffel noch stellt er sie an einen verborgenen Ort, sondern er stellt sie auf den Leuchter, damit alle, die hereinkommen und hinausgehen werden, ihr Licht sehen werden!"

¹⁰⁵ BG 8, 21f.: "Geht nun und verkündigt das Evangelium von Reich!"

¹⁰⁶ BG 18, 21ff.: "Als aber Levi das gesagt hatte, begannen sie zu gehen, um zu verkündigen und zu predigen."

¹⁰⁷ BG 127, 4ff. u. Par.: "Von jenem Tage an begannen seine Jünger, das Evangelium Gottes, des ewigen, bis in Ewigkeit unvergänglichen Vaters, zu verkündigen."

¹⁰⁸ VIII, 2: 140, 23ff.: "Da trennten sich die Apostel nach den vier Himmelsrichtungen, um zu verkündigen. Und sie gingen in der Kraft Jesu in Frieden."

digung der gnostischen Sonderlehren durch Jesus zur Verkündigung
aufbrechen. Die "Akten des Petrus und der 12 Apostel"[109] enthalten
einen Missionsbefehl. Auch das "Thomasbuch" enthält Aussagen über
die Mission und unterscheidet drei verschiedene Menschenklassen:
1. blinde Menschen,[110] 2. "Lehrlinge" oder Kleine,[111] die noch nicht die
3. Gruppe, den Status der Vollkommenen, die Vollkommenheit, erlangt
haben.[112] Es dürfte sich um die Gruppen der Hyliker, Psychiker und
Pneumatiker handeln. Auf Thomas' Frage, was den blinden Menschen
gelehrt werden soll,[113] erhält er die überraschende Antwort,[114] sich nicht
um sie zu kümmern, weil sie von der Wahrheit ausgeschlossen seien. Als
Thomas danach nach dem "*Wie*" der Verkündigung fragt,[115] wird seine
Frage nicht beantwortet. Diesen Menschen wird nur Bestrafung in
Aussicht gestellt, auch in Weherufen über die Hyliker.[116] Die
Seligpreisungen[117] gelten den Psychikern, die Pneumatiker werden.

4. Die Gnostiker übernahmen nicht nur die heiligen Schriften der
Großkirche, in denen sie allerdings ihre Lehren wiederfanden, wie wir
sahen, sondern sie übernahmen auch die *Sakramente der Kirche*,[118] um
sich der Großkirche anzupassen und Christen für ihre Lehren zu
gewinnen. Dabei bedarf der Gnostiker zu seiner Rettung keiner
Sakramente.[119] Er trägt in sich den in den Körper gefallenen göttlichen
Funken, in der "Exegese über die Seele" war es der in den Körper gefallene weibliche Teil der Seele.[120] Dieser göttliche Funke vergißt im Körper und in der ihm feindlichen Welt seine göttliche Herkunft. Der Ruf

---

[109] VI, 1: 10, 1ff.: "Geht in die Stadt, aus der ihr gekommen seid, die man 'Gorg'
nennt. Bleibt ausdauernd dabei, alle zu belehren, die zum Glauben an meinen Namen
gekommen sind."

[110] II, 7: 141, 20f.

[111] II, 7: ⲤⲂⲞⲨⲒ 138, 35f.; ⲔⲞⲨⲈⲒ 139, 11f.

[112] II, 7: 138, 35f.; 139, 11f.; 140, 10f.

[113] II, 7: 141, 19ff.

[114] II, 7: 141, 25ff.

[115] II, 7: 142, 24ff.

[116] II, 7: 142, 27ff.

[117] II, 7: 145, 1ff.

[118] Zu den Sakramenten bei den Gnostikern vgl. H.-G. Gaffron, Studien zum koptischen Philippusevangelium unter besonderer Berücksichtigung der Sakramente, Diss.
Bonn, 1969; M. Krause, "Die Sakramente in der Exegese über die Seele", NHS VII, Leiden, 1975, 47-55.

[119] Vgl. z. B. Kretzschmar, aO. 1658: "Der Mensch hat nicht eigentlich auf Grund von
Kulthandlungen am Schicksal des Erlösers teil, sondern das Selbst des Gnostikers findet
durch die vom Erlöser verliehene Gnosis aus eigener Kraft den Weg." W. Foerster, "Das
Wesen der Gnosis", Die Welt als Geschichte, 1955, 100-114, 107f.; ders., Die Gnosis, Bd.
1, Zürich, ²1979, 13ff. Zum Problem eines gnostischen Ursystems vgl. Rudolph, aO. 328f.

[120] II, 6: 127, 19ff.

aus der Höhe *erinnert* den göttlichen Funken an seine Herkunft und
errettet ihn. Die Erlösung ist in der Gnosis ein *Wieder-Gott-Werden* des
Menschen. Die Rückkehr zum Ursprung wird durch das Erinnern möglich, bedarf keiner Hilfe, außer dem Ruf, dem Aufwecken aus dem
Schlafe, der Selbsterkenntnis.[121] Es bedarf also keiner Sakramente, die
in den Mysterienreligionen der Spätantike die Aufgabe der *Ver*gottung
des Menschen haben.[122]

Ganz folgerichtig haben nach dem Zeugnis des Irenäus (I 21, 4) einige
Valentinianer Sakramente abgelehnt, weil "man das Mysterium der un-
aussprechbaren und unsichtbaren Macht nicht durch sichtbare und ver-
gängliche Geschöpfe, noch das der unausdenkbaren und unkörperlichen
Wesen durch sinnliche und materielle Dinge darstellen dürfe."[123] Sie
weisen darauf hin, daß die wahre Erlösung nicht durch Körperliches erlangt werden könne, weil der Körper vergänglich sei, noch durch etwas
Seelisches, weil auch die Seele aus der Verfehlung stamme und keinen
Anteil am Geist habe, also auch nichts Geistiges bewirken könne.[124]

Der größere Teil der Valentinianer übernahm dagegen die Sakramente der Kirche. In den excerpta e Theodoto haben wir bekanntlich in den
§§ 66-86 Belege für eine stark christianisierte Form der Gnosis, ebenso
bei Irenäus I, 21.[125]

Aber auch Nag Hammadi-Schriften beweisen die Übernahme der
christlichen Sakramente durch die Gnostiker. In der "Exegese über die
Seele" sandte der Vater der Seele ihren männlichen Teil[126] bzw. das
Licht als Rettung,[127] was nicht in das System paßt. In anderen gnostischen Systemen wird der männliche Paargenosse[128] zur Rettung gesandt, ein Mensch "Adamas" u. a.,[129] im Irenäusbericht über Basilides
war Christus der Retter.[130]

---

[121] Aus der Vielzahl der Aussagen zur Selbsterkenntnis in den gnostischen Texten verweise ich auf eine Passage aus dem "Dialog des Soter" III, 5: 133, 21-134, 34, die in NHS
VII, Leiden, 1977, 30 übersetzt ist.

[122] Vgl. H.-M. Schenke, "Hauptprobleme der Gnosis. Gesichtspunkte zu einer neuen
Darstellung des Gesamtphänomens", Kairos 7 (1965), 114-123, 117f.

[123] Übersetzung von Gaffron, aO. 95.

[124] Gaffron, aO. 95.

[125] Vgl. Gaffron, aO. 97f.

[126] II, 6: 132, 7.

[127] II, 6: 135, 26ff.

[128] Z.B. im "Apokryphon des Johannes" BG 47, 3ff. Hier sind mehrere Quellen zu-
sammengearbeitet, vgl. z.B. Rudolph, aO. 142f.; S. Arai, "Zur Definition der Gnosis in
Rücksicht auf die Frage nach ihrem Ursprung", The Origins of Gnosticism (Supplements
to Numen XII), Leiden, 1967, 182f.

[129] Vgl. Rudolph, aO. 141f. mit Belegen.

[130] Irenäus, adv. haer. I 24, 4: "Der erstgeborene Nus — das sei der, der Christus
heißt."

Besonders viele Aussagen über Sakramente enthält das "Philippusevangelium." Hans-Georg Gaffron[131] hat das Material — soweit es ihm
zugänglich war — gesammelt und ausgewertet. Die ihm 1969 nicht zugänglich gewesenen Texte aus Nag Hammadi mit Aussagen über gnostische Sakramente erfordern einige Korrekturen an den Ergebnissen seiner Arbeit.[132]

Gaffron[133] meinte *5 Sakramente* wegen "Philippusevangelium"
Spruch 68 feststellen zu müssen: "Der Herr hat alles in einem Mysterium gemacht, eine Taufe und eine Salbung und eine Eucharistie und
eine Erlösung und ein Brautgemach",[134] was aber nicht sicher ist, wie
wir noch sehen werden. Diese Reihenfolge entspricht aber ihrem Wert:
die Taufe zählt wenig, das Sakrament des Brautgemaches ist das Wert-
vollste.[135]

Darüber, daß die Taufe[136] ein christliches Sakrament ist, brauchen
wir uns nicht zu unterhalten. Wie Jesus von Johannes dem Täufer getauft wurde (Mt. 3, 13-17 u. Par.), sollen alle Christen getauft werden
(Mt. 28, 19). Im "Philippusevangelium" sprechen viele Stellen von der
Taufe.[137] Sie zeigen, daß Taufe und Salbung[138] eng zusammengehören,
wobei der Salbung der höhere Wert zukommt: "Niemand wird sich
sehen können, weder im Wasser noch im Spiegel ohne Licht. Wiederum
wirst du dich auch nicht im Licht ohne Spiegel sehen können. Daher
ziemt es sich, mit den beiden zu taufen, mit dem Licht und dem Wasser.
Das Licht aber ist die Salbung."[139]

Schon nach Aussage des Neuen Testamentes (2. Kor. 1, 21) erfolgt bei
der Taufe die Salbung des Christen durch Gott (vgl. auch 1. Joh. 2, 20-
27). Mit der Taufe und Salbung übernahmen die Gnostiker offensichtlich eine Praxis der Großkirche,[140] wobei sie aber die Salbung als das
Wichtigere ansahen.

---

[131] Vgl. A. 118.

[132] Es sind vor allem die "Exegese über die Seele" (II, 6), der "Dialog des Soter" (III,
5), der "Authentikos Logos" (VI, 3), der "2. Logos des großen Seth" (VII, 2), in denen
unter den Sakramenten das Sakrament des Brautgemaches bezeugt ist.

[133] Gaffron, aO. 108.

[134] II, 3: 67, 27ff. = Spr. 68. Die zitierten Übersetzungen des "Philippusevangeliums"
entstammen der Arbeit: Die Gnosis, Bd. 2, Koptische und mandäische Quellen, Zürich
und Stuttgart, 1971, 95ff.

[135] II, 3: 69, 14 = Spr. 76.

[136] Zur Taufe vgl. Gaffron, aO. 117-140.

[137] Spr. 59. 68. 75. 76. 90. 95. 101. 109.

[138] Zur Salbung vgl. Gaffron, aO. 140-171.

[139] II, 3: 69, 8ff. = Spr. 75; vgl. auch Spr. 76 und vor allem 95: "die Salbung herrscht
über die Taufe" (74, 12f.).

[140] So auch Gaffron, aO. 170.

Auch über die Eucharistie[141] als christliches Sakrament brauchen wir nicht zu sprechen. Aussagen über die Eucharistie in der Gnosis haben wir wenige,[142] lediglich im "Philippusevangelium" gibt es Hinweise[143] auf sie. Sie zeigen die Übereinstimmung mit dem Sakrament der Großkirche: "Der Kelch des Gebetes enthält Wein, enthält Wasser; er dient als 'Typos' des Blutes, über dem gedankt wird, und ist gefüllt mit dem Heiligen Geist. Und der zum ganz vollkommenen Menschen gehörende ist er (sc. der Heilige Geist). Wenn wir diesen (= Kelch) trinken, werden wir uns den vollkommenen Menschen nehmen."[144] Gaffron[145] urteilt mit Recht: "Dieser Text könnte ebensogut in einer katholischen Schrift des 2. Jh.s stehen." Die wenigen Zitate machen aber deutlich, daß es keine wichtige Rolle spielt. Ich bezweifle, daß die *Erlösung* (gr. ἀπολύτρωσις, kopt. ⲥⲱⲧⲉ)[146] ein Sakrament der Gnostiker war. Auch Gaffron[147] muß eingestehen: "Über das Sakrament der Erlösung läßt sich wenig Sicheres sagen. Vermutlich stellte es den äußeren Akt dar, der die Brautgemachzeremonie einleitete, u. zw. in Form einer Salbung, die den Sinn hatte, überirdische Kraft zu verleihen und den Aufgang ins Pleroma zu garantieren." Darüber sagt das "Philippusevangelium" aber nichts aus: in 3 Sprüchen[148] wird es genannt. Spruch 76[149] zeigt, daß die Erlösung eine Folge der Salbung ist, und daß die Erlösung im Brautgemach stattfindet.

Eindeutig ist dagegen das Sakrament des Brautgemaches[150] ein Sakrament. Im Gegensatz zu den genannten Sakramenten wird es nicht von der Großkirche gefeiert, sondern ist ein neues Sakrament. Bezeichnend ist der Versuch der Gnostiker, ihr Sakrament im Neuen Testament wiederzufinden. Gaffron[151] urteilt: "Man spürt auf Schritt und Tritt, wie krampfhaft sich die Valentinianer bemühen, ihre Gedanken in das NT hineinzuinterpretieren, wozu Ir. I 3, 1-5; 8, 2-6 und die Fragmente des Herakleon hinreichend Beispiele bieten."

Das Sakrament des Brautgemaches ist das wichtigste Sakrament und nimmt daher auch einen großen Raum im "Philippusevangelium" und

---

[141] Zur Eucharistie vgl. Gaffron, aO. 171-185.
[142] Vgl. Gaffron, aO. 171f.
[143] Spr. 53. 68. 98. 100. 108.
[144] II, 3: 75, 14ff. = Spr. 100.
[145] Gaffron, aO. 174.
[146] Gaffron, aO. 185-191.
[147] Gaffron, aO. 222.
[148] Spr. 47. 68 u. 76.
[149] II, 3: 69, 14ff. = Spr. 76.
[150] Zum Sakrament des Brautgemaches vgl. Gaffron, aO. 191-219.
[151] Gaffron, aO. 196.

auch anderen gnostischen Texten ein.[152] Wie es vollzogen wurde, wird im "Philippusevangelium" nicht gesagt. H. M. Schenke[153] meinte, es habe in einem heiligen Kuß bestanden, den der Myste von dem Mystagogen erhielt. Gaffron[154] glaubt, es sei das Sterbesakrament der Gnostiker gewesen, "das den Sterbenden nach seinem Tode für die feindlichen Mächte des Zwischenreiches unangreifbar machen und ihn seiner endgültigen Rettung versichern sollte. Der Ritus selbst ist nicht mehr rekonstruierbar." Letzterer Aussage stimme ich zu: das Wie des Vollzuges wird nicht beschrieben. Dagegen glaube ich nicht, daß es ein Sterbesakrament war, sondern schon zu Lebzeiten vollzogen wurde. Nach den Aussagen des "Philippusevangeliums"[155] und der "Exegese über die Seele"[156] ist es die Wiedervereinigung der Seele mit ihrem himmlischen Paargenossen als Zeichen für die gewonnene Selbsterkenntnis, die dem Gnostiker die Rückkehr in den Himmel, ins Pleroma, in den Zustand vor dem Fall — oder wie man es noch ausdrücken will — ermöglicht.

Ich habe schon oben darauf hingewiesen, daß in der ursprünglichen Gnosis keine Sakramente zur Rettung erforderlich sind, daß die Einführung der Sakramente in die Gnosis eine Anpassung an die Riten der Großkirche war. Diese Bewegung wird in den späten gnostischen Texten, in der "Pistis Sophia" und den "Büchern Jeû"[157] so weit gesteigert, daß nicht mehr die *Gnosis* für die Rettung entscheidend ist, sondern der *Vollzug der Sakramente.*[158] Jeder Gnostiker muß sich ihnen unterziehen, da seine Seele nur an den Ort im Lichtreich gelangen kann, dem das empfangene Sakrament entspricht.[159] Die ersten drei Weihegrade sind Taufen,[160] die sündenvergebende Kraft haben.[161] Auch eine geistige Salbung ist belegt.[162] Die Entwicklung geht so weit, daß auch der

---

[152] Spr. 61. 66-68. 73. 76. 78-80. 82. 95. 102. 124-127; vgl. auch A. 132.

[153] H.-M. Schenke, J. Leipoldt u. H.-M. Schenke, Koptisch-gnostische Schriften aus den Papyruscodices von Nag-Hamadi, Hamburg-Bergstedt, 1960, 38.

[154] Gaffron, aO. 222.

[155] Vgl. Spr. 78/79.

[156] II, 6: 132, 10ff.

[157] C. Schmidt (Koptisch-gnostische Schriften, aO. 1. Bd., XXXIV) setzt sie in die 1. Hälfte des 3. Jh.s.

[158] Vgl. die bei Gaffron, aO. 306 (= A. 92) genannte umfangreiche alte Literatur.

[159] Vgl. z.B. PS 90 (NHS IX, 203 f.); 2. Buch Jeu 52 (NHS XIII, 137).

[160] 2. Buch Jeu 43 (NHS XIII, 102): die Wasser-, Feuertaufe und die Taufe des hl. Geistes; vgl. auch die NHS XIII, 102 A. 2 genannte Literatur.

[161] Nach 2. Buch Jeu 44 (NHS XIII, 104) bewirkt der einmalige Vollzug des Mysteriums der Sündenvergebung die Vergebung aller wissentlich und unwissentlich begangenen Sünden von Kindheit "bis zum heutigen Tage", vgl. auch 2. Buch Jeu 51 (NHS XIII, 126f.).

[162] 2. Buch Jeu (NHS XIII, 102) und die in NHS XIII, 102 A. 3 genannten weiteren Quellen und Lit.

ganz Sündlose keinen Einlaß im Lichtreich findet, falls er keiner Mysterien, keiner Sakramente, teilhaftig wurde.[163] Andererseits kann sogar
ein reuelos verstorbener Sünder noch gerettet werden, falls ein Gerechter ein bestimmtes Mysterium stellvertretend für ihn vollzieht.[164] Angesichts solcher Aussagen wird man fragen müssen, was — bei dieser Anpassung an das Christentum — noch an gnostischen Gedanken erhalten
geblieben ist.

Letztlich siegte aber in Ägypten die Großkirche über diese verchristlichte Gnosis, nachdem die Glaubensregel ausgebildet, der Kanon fest-
gelegt — und damit die christlich-gnostischen Werke indiziert — und die
Stellung des Bischofs gestärkt worden war. Spuren finden wir auch in
den Texten von Nag Hammadi: im "Thomasbuch" (II 140, 11ff.) sollen
die τέλειοι oder "Klugen" nicht mit den "Dummen" zusammen sein,
hier wird also eine Abtrennung der Gnostiker geboten. Die Stärkung der
Stellung der Bischöfe und Kleriker führte in der "Apokalypse des Petrus" und anderen Schriften zur Polemik der Gnostiker gegen das kirchliche Christentum, vor allem seine Hierarchie, darüber will ich nicht
sprechen. Ich darf Sie daher auf die Arbeiten von Herrn Koschorke ver-
weisen, vor allem auf seine in NHS 12 erschienene Dissertation.[165]

---

[163] PS 133 (NHS IX, 346f.): "Ohne Mysterien wird niemand in das Lichtreich eingehen,
sei es ein Gerechter, sei es ein Sünder"; aO. 347: "Ohne Mysterien können sie nicht in das
Licht aufgenommen werden."

[164] PS 108 (NHS IX, 276f.) und PS 128 (NHS IX, 322ff.).

[165] Vgl. A. 8
Nach Abschluß des Aufsatzes sandte mir Frau Kollegin Elaine Pagels ihr Buch The Gnostic Gospels, New York, 1979, zu dem ich leider nicht mehr Stellung nehmen konnte.

THE EPISTLE OF EUGNOSTOS AND VALENTINIANISM

BY

ALASTAIR H. B. LOGAN

Jean Doresse, who was the first to make known, translate and comment on the Epistle of Eugnostos or "Eugnostos the Blessed" in the version in Nag Hammadi Codex III, argued that the Sophia of Jesus Christ which followed it in the Codex was dependent on Eugnostos.[1] The author of the Sophia had transformed Eugnostos into a dialogue between the Saviour and his disciples, adding fresh material at the end in answer to questions from Mary. But in addition to his various literary and doctrinal arguments in support of this hypothesis, Doresse also drew attention to the similarity of the preamble and *explicit* of Eugnostos to those of the letter of the Valentinian Ptolemy to Flora.[2] The resemblances are not as striking as Doresse seems to think, but he was unwittingly pointing in the right direction. Hans-Martin Schenke, who attempted to reverse Doresse's thesis and argue for the priority of

---

[1] J. Doresse, "Trois livres gnostiques inédits: Évangile des Égyptiens — Épître d'Eugnoste — Sagesse de Jésus Christ", *Vig. Chr.* 2 (1948), 137-60, esp. 143-6, 150-6; *The Secret Books of the Egyptian Gnostics* (trans. P. Mairet), London 1960, 192-6. There is also a much less well preserved version of Eugnostos (abbreviated Eug) in N(ag) H(ammadi) C(odex) V and a complete version of the Sophia of Jesus Christ (abbreviated SJC) in the Berlin Coptic Gnostic Codex (BG 8502, 3) which has been edited and translated into German by W. C. Till, *Die gnostischen Schriften des koptischen Papyrus Berolinensis 8502* (Texte und Untersuchungen 60, V Reihe, Band 5), Berlin 1955, second revised and enlarged edition ed. H.-M. Schenke, Berlin 1972. There is also a Greek fragment of SJC in POxy 1081 edited with conjectural restorations by A. S. Hunt, *The Oxyrhynchus Papyri VIII*, London 1911, 16-19, and C. Wessely, "Les plus anciens Monuments du Christianisme", *Patrologia Orientalis* XVIII, Paris 1924, 493-5. See on this H.-C. Puech, "Gnostic Gospels and Related Documents", E. Hennecke — W. Schneemelcher (eds.), *New Testament Apocrypha* I (Eng. trans. ed. R. McL. Wilson), London 1963, 243-8; H. W. Attridge, "P. Oxy 1081 and the Sophia Jesu Christi", *Enchoria* 5 (1975), 1-8. An English translation by R. McL. Wilson of the German by M. Krause (*Die Gnosis* II, ed. W. Foerster, Zürich 1971) based on the Codex III version supplemented by that in Codex V can be found in *Gnosis* vol. II (Eng. trans. ed. R. McL. Wilson) Oxford 1974, 24-39, and one by D. M. Parrott, also based on Codex III supplemented by Codex V (alongside SJC based on the Codex III version supplemented by BG), in *The Nag Hammadi Library in English*, Leiden 1977, 206-28.

[2] Ibid., 154f.; *Secret Books*, 192f.

the Sophia,[3] came even nearer the mark. Although his arguments were convincingly dealt with by Martin Krause, whose case for the priority of Eugnostos has been generally accepted,[4] he also compared Eugnostos, as a cosmogonic treatise, with another Valentinian epistle, the doctrinal letter preserved in Epiphanius *Panarion* XXXI 5f.[5] But, apart from noting that the latter was generally held to be a late product of Valentinianism, Schenke went no further. However, as we shall see, his suggested comparison is much more fruitful than that of Doresse, although Doresse may well be nearer the truth as regards the priority of Eugnostos to the Sophia.

Thus careful analysis reveals a striking number of parallels between Eugnostos (and the Sophia) and the doctrinal letter, which appear to have gone unnoticed and which raise the question of what the precise relationship of the texts is: are Eugnostos and the Sophia borrowing from the supposedly late Valentinian letter, or is it borrowing from them, and if so, from which? If the former hypothesis were true, this would appear fatally to weaken the contention that Eugnostos is pre-Christian. If, on the other hand, the doctrinal letter borrowed from Eugnostos, this might suggest that the dividing lines between Valentinianism and non-Christian forms of Gnosticism were much less firm than had previously been supposed. The purpose of this paper is therefore to examine the similarities on the basis of Eugnostos (and the parallel passages in the Sophia) in an attempt to answer the question about the precise relationship of these texts, to ascertain which text is the borrower and which the source.

The first point of resemblance between Eugnostos and the Valentinian doctrinal letter is of course the epistolary form of both, which does not apply to the Sophia. Thus both open with the customary greeting on

---

[3] H.-M. Schenke, "Nag-Hamadi Studien II: Das System der Sophia Jesu Christi", *ZRGG* 14 (1962), 263-78, esp. 263-7.

[4] M. Krause, "Das literarische Verhältnis des Eugnostosbriefes zur Sophia Jesu Christi: zur Auseinandersetzung der Gnosis mit dem Christentum", *Mullus: Festschrift Theodor Klauser* (Jahrbuch für Antike und Christentum, Ergänzungsband 1), Münster 1964, 215-23. See also on this R. McL. Wilson, *Gnosis and the New Testament*, Oxford 1968, 111-117; E. M. Yamauchi, *Pre-Christian Gnosticism*, London 1973, 104-7.

[5] K. Holl, Epiphanius Band 1, *Ancoratus* and *Panarion Haer.* I-XXXIII, *GCS* 25, Leipzig 1915, 390.5-395.14. Against the opinion of O. Dibelius (*ZNW* 9 (1908), 329ff.) who holds it to be late, Holl sees the letter as one of the oldest pieces of information on Valentinianism, reflecting the monistic basis of original Valentinianism as found in Hippolytus *Ref.* VI 37, 7 (Wendland 167. 17ff.).

the part of the writer (Eugnostos)[6] or subject (νοῦς ἀκατάργητος).[7] If the doctrinal letter were the borrower this would already suggest that its source was Eugnostos in its present epistolary form rather than in either what Krause supposes to be its original form, that of a tractate,[8] or its Christianised dialogue form as the Sophia. Then, as regards content, while Eugnostos and the Sophia insist that the supreme being is ineffable,[9] the doctrinal letter has the writer assert that he is making mention of nameless, ineffable and supraheavenly things.[10] But the continuation betrays a much closer parallel, particularly in the Codex V version of Eugnostos. Thus it relates that neither rulers (ἀρχή) and authorities (ἐξουσία) nor (οὔτε) subordinations nor (οὔτε) every nature ([φ] ὐ [σ] ις) know him (the supreme being) except himself alone,[11] while the doctrinal letter describes the ineffable mysteries as incapable of being conceived (περινοεῖν) either (οὔτε) by rulers (ἀρχή) or (οὔτε) authorities (ἐξουσία) or (οὔτε) subordinations (ὑποταγή) or every confusion (σύγχυσις) but revealed only to the thought (ἔννοια) of the Unchangeable (ἄτρεπτος).[12] The Codex III versions of Eugnostos and the Sophia obscure the fact that the entities are plural and add "from the foundation (καταβόλη) of the cosmos (κόσμος)" to "every nature",[13] while the BG version of the Sophia generally corresponds to the NHC III version but adds "power" to the list of entities involved.[14] That the doctrinal

---

[6] Eug NHC III 70, 1f. (ⲣⲁ ⲩ̣ ⲉ) ; NHC V 1, 3 (χαῖρε). For the proper understanding and translation of this epistolary introduction see P. Bellet, "The Colophon of the *Gospel of the Egyptians*: Concessus and Macarius of Nag Hammadi", *Nag Hammadi and Gnosis*, ed. R. McL. Wilson (Nag Hammadi Studies vol. XIV), Leiden 1978, 56-8.

[7] Epiph. *Pan.* XXXI 5, 1 (Holl 390. 5f.: χαίρειν).

[8] Ibid., 222.

[9] Eug NHC III 71, 13f.; NHC V 2, 8-10; SJC NHC III 94, 5; BG 83, 5f.

[10] *Pan.* XXXI 5, 2 (Holl 390. 7f.).

[11] Eug NHC V 2, 10-13. "Subordinations" is read from NHC III 71, 16 (ὑποταγή) instead of the ⲚⲎⲈⲦⲦⲱ [   ] of NHC V 2, 11, which might be translated "those which are theirs (or "belong to them")", in the sense of being subordinate to the aforementioned rulers etc.

[12] *Pan.* XXXI 5, 2 (Holl 390. 8-10). σύγχυσις is certainly the more difficult reading and may refer to the mixed nature of the non-spiritual. However it might mark an attempt to make sense of the φύσις of Eug and SJC.

[13] Eug NHC III 71, 14-18; SJC NHC III 94, 6-10. The latter adds "till now" to "from the foundation...". Since the phrase "from the foundation ... till now" occurs in Eug NHC III 70, 4f.; SJC NHC III 92, 9f.; BG 80, 7-9 (cf. AJ NHC II 30, 6f.; NHC IV 46, 15), its occurrence at this point in Eug NHC III and SJC NHC III is probably an addition. The first part of the phrase echoes the New Testament usage ἀπὸ καταβολῆς κόσμου (cf. Matt. 25:34; Luke 11:50; Heb. 4:3; 9:26; Rev. 13:8; 17:8).

[14] SJC BG 83, 7-14. It also omits the "every (ⲚⲒⲘ)" of "every nature", cf. Eug NHC III 71, 17 and SJC NHC III 94, 8. NT influence may account for the addition of "power", cf. I Cor. 15:24; Eph. 1:21.

letter has the Thought ("Εννοια) of the Unchangeable as the recipient of revelation or knower rather than the supreme being himself, as in Eugnostos and the Sophia, is due to the particular theological scheme of the former which gives Thought/Ennoia a major role.[15]

Both Eugnostos (and the Sophia) and the doctrinal letter agree over certain aspects of the supreme being, although the former gives a much more detailed description. Thus both present him in terms of negative, apophatic theology as unbegotten (ἀγέννητος), Eugnostos and the Sophia directly,[16] the doctrinal letter more obliquely in that it describes Man ("Ανθρωπος), the first product of the supreme being and his Ennoia, as the antitype of the pre-existing Unbegotten ('Αγέννητος).[17] For Eugnostos and the Sophia the Father has no name,[18] while the doctrinal letter claims to speak of nameless (ἀνονόμαστος) mysteries.[19] For the former he is also described as "unchanging good",[20] while the doctrinal letter designates him "the Unchangeable ("Ατρεπτος)".[21] The former texts also appear to describe him as "the Greatness (ⲘⲚⲦⲚⲞ6) with the authorities in him embracing the All (or "the totalities") of the totalities while nothing embraces him",[22] while the doctrinal letter designates the supreme being as "the Greatness (Μέγεθος)"[23] and describes him as embracing (περιέχειν) the totalities (τὰ πάντα) and not being embraced (ἐνπεριέχεσθαι).[24] Now in Valentinianism "greatness (μέγεθος/magnitudo)" appears to have become virtually a technical term used either to signify the ineffable unsearchable character of the

---

[15] Cf. e.g. the views of some followers of Ptolemy on the primary role of Thought/Ennoia in Iren. *adv. haer.* I 12, 1f. (Harvey I 109-112).

[16] Eug NHC III 71, 22; SJC NHC III 94, 18f. (ἀγέννητος); BG 84, 6 (ⲀⲦⲬⲠⲞ).

[17] *Pan.* XXXI 5, 5 (Holl 391.7).

[18] Eug NHC III 72, 1; SJC NHC III 94, 22; BG 84, 10f.

[19] *Pan.* XXXI 5, 2 (Holl 390.7).

[20] Eug NHC III 72, 17 (ⲀⲦ6ⲒⲂⲈ): SJC NHC III 95, 10 (ⲘⲈϥ6ⲒⲂⲈ); BG 85, 14f. (ⲘⲈϥ6ⲒⲂⲈ).

[21] *Pan.* XXXI 5, 2 (Holl 390.9). The Coptic forms of 6ⲒⲂⲈ are translations of ἄτρεπτος, cf. W. E. Crum, *A Coptic Dictionary*, Oxford 1939, 552a.

[22] Eug NHC III 73, 4-8; NHC V 3, 6-10; SJC NHC III 95, 23-96, 3; BG 86, 11-16. However, Eug NHC V 3, 6 reads "greatness (ⲐⲈⲚⲘⲚⲦⲚⲞ6)", which might suggest that "greatness(es) and authorities" are both entities in the Father rather than the former being a designation of the Father.

[23] *Pan* XXXI 5, 1 (Holl 390.6); 5, 4f. (ibid., 391.2.4.5) etc. ⲘⲚⲦⲚⲞ6 is the usual Coptic translation of μέγεθος, cf. Crum, *Dictionary* 251a s.v. ⲚⲞ6.

[24] *Pan* XXXI 5, 3 (Holl 390.10-13: αὐτὸς ἐν ἑαυτῷ περιεῖχε τὰ πάντα ὄντα ἐν ἑαυτῶ ἐν ἀγνωσίᾳ...ὃς πάντοτε περιέχει τὰ πάντα καὶ οὐκ ἐνπεριέχεται). Cf. also 5, 8 (Holl 392.6); 5, 9 (Holl 392.16); 6, 2 (Holl 393.2), and Iren. *adv. haer.* II 4, 1 (Harvey I 259: everything is contained by the inexpressible Greatness (*magnitudo*)).

supreme Father or to designate the Father himself.²⁵ However it is surely significant that in Eugnostos and the Sophia the term "greatness" does not appear to designate the supreme being and is employed in a much less circumscribed way as the attribute or designation of various heavenly beings.²⁶

Again, in Eugnostos and the Sophia the supreme figure is described as being complete intellect (νοῦς), thought (ἔννοια), reflection (ἐνθύμησις), thinking (φρόνησις), rationality (λογισμός) and power (δύναμις),²⁷ and although there is no list corresponding to this in the doctrinal letter, the first four occur, Nous (νοῦς) as the author of the letter,²⁸ Ennoia ("Εννοια) as his hypostatised thought,²⁹ reflection (ἐνθύμησις) as the means by which the Greatness completed everything,³⁰ and thinking (φρόνησις) as that which the later heavenly light-beings, the children of the Middle, are without along with Thought ("Εννοια).³¹ That all these intellectual powers are in the foreknowledge of the Unbegotten until the end, according to Eugnostos,³² recalls the statement in the doctrinal letter that everything was in the supreme being (i.e. the Unbegotten) in ignorance.³³ Further, just as in the doctrinal letter the Thought ("Εννοια) of the Greatness is responsible for his self-revelation through his emanations,³⁴ so for Eugnostos if anyone wishes to believe his message they must investigate from what is hidden to the completion of what is revealed and this thought (ἔννοια!) will instruct him how belief in the hid-

---

²⁵ On its use by Valentinians to describe the Father's nature, cf. Iren. *adv. haer.* I 1, 1 (Harvey I 9); 2, 1 (Harvey I 13); 2, 2f. (Harvey I 15); Tripartite Tractate NHC I 52, 26; 53, 1; 54, 19f.; 55, 2 etc. (ⲙⲚⲦⲚⲟϬ); on its use as a designation of the Father, cf. Iren. *adv. haer.* I 19, 2 (Harvey I 176); 21, 4 (Harvey I 186); GTr NHC I 42, 13f. (ⲙⲚⲦⲚⲁϬ).

²⁶ Cf. e.g. Eug NHC III 77, 17; NHC V 6, 23; SJC NHC III 102, 5; BG 95, 13f. (Man creates a great aeon according to his greatness); Eug NHC III 86, 5f.; SJC BG 109, 16 (Man revealed all the greatnesses); Eug NHC III 88, 17; SJC NHC III 112, 17; BG 114, 9 (the imperishables create according to their greatness(es)).

²⁷ Eug NHC III 73, 8-11; NHC V 3, 10-13; SJC NHC III 96, 3-7; BG 86, 16-87, 1. Eug NHC V 3, 11f. has Coptic equivalents for the last four and adds to rationality "what is superior to rationality", while SJC NHC III 96, 5f. has φρόνησις third and a Coptic equivalent for δύναμις (ϬⲟⲘ), and SJC BG 86, 19f. has Coptic equivalents for the last three.

²⁸ *Pan.* XXXI 5, 1 (Holl 390.6).

²⁹ 5, 2ff. (Holl 390.9.13f.).

³⁰ 5, 4 (Holl 391.3).

³¹ 6, 5 (Holl 394.5f.).

³² Eug NHC III 73, 14-16. Cf. SJC NHC III 96, 10-14; BG 87, 4-8.

³³ *Pan.* XXXI 5, 3 (Holl 390.11).

³⁴ 5, 2-6 (Holl 390.7-392.1).

den was found in what was revealed.[35] Finally, with regard to the designations of the supreme being, we should note that both Eugnostos and the doctrinal letter use the term "Self-Father (Αὐτοπάτωρ)" of him, although the former applies it to his self-projection.[36]

Eugnostos then relates how the Self-Father, who is full of light, caused the beginning of that light to be revealed as an immortal androgynous man.[37] The versions differ, however, over the male and female names of this being. Thus the version in Codex III appears to give the male name as "the [Begetting] of the Perfect One" and the female as "Pansophos Begettress (γενέτειρα) Sophia", relating that she is like her brother and consort, a truth uncontested above, but not here below.[38] The version in Codex V gives the male name as "the begetter Nous (νοῦς) per[fect] in himself" and the female as "the Ennoia (ἔννοια), she of all the Sophias, the begetter of the Sophias whom they call 'the Truth'."[39] The doctrinal letter relates how the imperishable Ennoia united with the Greatness and revealed (ἀναδείκνυναι) the Father of Truth whom the perfect named "Man ("Ανθρωπος)" because he was the antitype of the pre-existing Unbegotten. Sigē/Ennoia then effected a natural union of Light (Φῶς) and the Man (their union being will) and revealed Truth ('Αλήθεια). She was called "Truth", the letter continues, by the perfect, appropriately enough since she was truly like her mother Sigē (Silence), this being part of Sigē's plan to ensure that the division of lights (or human beings, a play on φῶς/φώς?) of both male and female should be equal to reveal the (unity?) in them to those separated into sense-perceptible lights (or human beings?).[40]

Reference to other accounts of Valentinianism may help to cast some light on the obscurity of these texts. Thus we should note that the Father

---

[35] Eug NHC III 74, 12-19; NHC V 4, 1-7; SJC NHC III 98, 13-20; BG 90, 4-13; POxy 1081 ll. 27-34 (ed. Wessely, PO XVIII, 494). The Sophia speaks of "she, the ἀπόρροια of the ἔννοια" and adds "of the unbegotten Father" at the end. Thus the Sophia makes clear what is not clear in Eugnostos, that some sort of divine revealer-figure is involved here.

[36] Cf. Eug NHC III 75, 5f.; Pan. XXXI 5, 3 (Holl 390.10). In the Sophia the title Αὐτοπάτωρ does not occur in any of the parallel passages at this point, including POxy 1081 which appears to read [προπάτ]ωρ in l. 46 (Wessely, ibid.), a reading confirmed by SJC NHC III 91, 9, although it does occur later applied to the Father, the Man, cf. SJC NHC III 102, 1f.; BG 95, 9f. and Eug NHC III 77, 14f.

[37] Eug NHC III 76, 14-24. Cf. SJC NHC III 100, 21-101, 8; BG 93, 18-94, 11. The Sophia has a soteriological addition not present in Eugnostos.

[38] Eug NHC III 76, 24-77, 9. There is a trace of the first letter of ΧΠΟ in 77, 2. The Sophia omits this passage on the names, but cf. SJC NHC III 104, 6-11; BG 98, 16-99, 3.

[39] Eug NHC V 6, 4-10. Cf. SJC NHC III 104, 8f. which speaks of "the Begetter Nous (νοῦς) perfect in himself".

[40] Pan. XXXI 5, 6 (Holl 391.8-392.1).

of Truth of the doctrinal letter is elsewhere called "Nous (Νοῦς)", "Only-Begotten (Μονογένης)", "Father" and "Beginning ('Αρχή) of all".⁴¹ Moreover, some accounts (like Eugnostos and the Sophia) do not distinguish Nous and Truth as separate hypostases,⁴² and according to some Valentinians the supreme being is called "Man".⁴³ Thus the doctrinal letter can be seen to be presenting its own interpretation of the origin of the first Valentinian syzygy produced by the supreme being, Father of Truth (i.e. Nous) and Truth, which derives the latter from the former and sees them as representing the archetype of the origin, equality and unity of male and female, a unity and equality obscured by the division of the sexes in this world. This may also be what the version of Eugnostos in Codex III is alluding to with its reference to the truth of the equality of Sophia and her brother which is opposed here below. But perhaps the most striking feature is that the whole motif of the light in the doctrinal letter; its abrupt appearance and natural union with the man, the designation of the aeons of the Pleroma as "lights", and the evident play on light (φῶς) and man (φώς), all of which are missing in other accounts of Valentinianism, would appear to derive from Eugnostos. Not only does the latter refer to the Father as full of light, and Man as the Beginning of that light or Adam the man or eye of light,⁴⁴ but later, as we shall see, talks of the multitude of lights (or men?) revealed by Immortal Man, who form the "Assembly", the archetype of the earthly church.⁴⁵

Further, the pattern and terminology of emanation in Eugnostos and the doctrinal letter appear similar. Thus the various divine beings are revealed (ΟΥ ω Ν Ϩ ΕΒΟΛ/ἀναδείκνυναι) in both rather than being emitted (προβάλλειν) as is usual in Valentinianism.⁴⁶ Again, just as in Eugnostos the offspring of the Son of Man, the Saviour, harmonises with his consort, Pistis Sophia, and reveals six androgynous spiritual

---

⁴¹ Cf. Iren. *adv. haer.* I 1, 1 (Harvey I 9). In the account of Hippolytus, *Ref.* VI 29, 6 (Wendland 156. 15-18), the Father emanates Nous and Truth as the ἀρχή of all the aeons. Cf. also Iren. *adv. haer.* I 11, 1 (Harvey I 99f.); 12, 2 (Harvey I 111f.); *Exc. ex Theod.* 6, 2-3 (Sagnard 64).

⁴² Cf. Hipp. *Ref.* VI 29, 6 (Wendland 156. 16f.); *Exc. ex Theod.* 6, 3 (Sagnard 64); Iren. *adv. haer.* I 12, 2 (Harvey I 111f.).

⁴³ Cf. Iren. *adv. haer.* I 12, 3 (Harvey I 113f.).

⁴⁴ Cf. Eug NHC III 76, 17-24; 81, 10-12 and the parallels in SJC.

⁴⁵ Cf. Eug NHC III 85, 21-86, 24 and parr.

⁴⁶ Cf. e.g. Eug NHC III 81, 23f.; 82, 9f.; 86, 5f.; and par. (ΟΥ ω Ν Ϩ ΕΒΟΛ); Epiph. *Pan.* XXXI 5, 5 (Holl 391.6); 5, 6 (Holl 391.9); 5, 7 (Holl 392.3); 5, 8 (Holl 392.8) etc. (ἀναδείκνυναι) and Iren. *adv. haer.* I 1, 1f. (Harvey I 9f.); *Exc. ex Theod.* 7, 1 (Sagnard 66); Hipp. *Ref.* VI 29, 6f. (Wendland 156. 15-22) (προβάλλειν).

(πνευματικός) beings, i.e. six male and six female, in the type (τύπος) of those who preceded them (a passage absent in the Sophia),[47] so in the doctrinal letter the Father and Truth unite and reveal an androgynous spiritual (πνευματικός) tetrad (male plus female, male plus female), the antitype (ἀντίτυπος) of the pre-existing tetrad, and the first pair of this latter tetrad, Man and Church, unite and reveal a duodecad of androgynous beings, i.e. six male and six female.[48] However, since neither the tetrad nor the duodecad of the doctrinal letter are androgynous in the strict sense, i.e. individuals who are both male and female, as are the six in Eugnostos, and since the duodecad of Man and Church is produced before the decad of Logos and Life, reversing the usual order of events in Valentinianism,[49] it would appear that the doctrinal letter is the borrower here and has adjusted its Valentinian scheme to accommodate ideas derived from Eugnostos. Conversely, Eugnostos' account makes perfect sense and it also appears to cast some light on an obscure gloss in the doctrinal letter. Thus, summing up the series of powers produced by the harmonising of the twelve, Eugnostos asserts that the union of them all is the will (ογωϣ).[50] Now the doctrinal letter says both of the conjunction of Light and Man and of Logos and Life that their union was the will.[51]

Later Eugnostos and the Sophia recount how Immortal Man allowed all those revealed by him to do what they wished and how they harmonised with each other and revealed a multitude of lights which are glorious and without number, named the first, the middle, the perfect, that is the first, second and third aeons. The first was called "Oneness" and "Rest" and each one has his own name.[52] This passage seems to be echoed in garbled fashion by the doctrinal letter which once again ap-

---

[47] Eug NHC III 82, 7-11; NHC V 10, 13-17.

[48] *Pan.* XXXI 5, 7f. (Holl 392. 1-11).

[49] Cf. Iren. *adv. haer.* I 1, 1f. (Harvey I 10f.: Logos and Life, who produce Man and Church, emit ten aeons, Man and Church then emit twelve); 11, 1 (Harvey I 100: Logos and Life produce ten powers, then Man and Church twelve); Hipp. *Ref.* VI 29, 7-30, 2 (Wendland 156. 22-157. 10: Nous and Truth produce ten, Logos and Life twelve); Val Exp NHC XI 29, 25-37; 30, 30-8 (Ten from Logos and Life, twelve from Man and Church). However, according to Iren. *adv. haer.* I 12, 2 (Harvey I 111f.), some Valentinians argued that Man and Church were responsible for Logos and Life.

[50] Eug NHC III 83, 19f. This passage also is not present in the Sophia. ογωϣ clearly means "will" (cf. Crum, *Dictionary* 501a, θέλημα), as Krause translates it (*Gnosis* vol. II, 32), and not "interval" (cf. Crum, ibid., 501ab), as Parrott renders it (*The Nag Hammadi Library*, 219).

[51] Cf. *Pan.* XXXI 5, 6 (Holl 391.9: ἦν δὲ αὐτῶν ἡ συνέλευσις τὸ θέλειν); 5, 9 (Holl 392.12f.: ἦν δὲ ἡ κοινωνία αὐτῶν τὸ θέλημα).

[52] Eug NHC III 85, 21-86, 16; NHC V 13, 18-14, 10; SJC BG 109, 4-110, 9.

pears to combine Valentinian ideas with those derived from Eugnostos. Thus it speaks of the Thirty (aeons of the Pleroma) perfecting marriage among the imperishables and revealing imperishable lights (φῶς) called "children of the unity ('Ενότης)", of how they came into being, the multitude of which need not be expressed numerically but one ought to recognise it, and how each (light) has allotted to it its own particular name.[53]

Finally, Eugnostos and the Sophia describe how Sophia, the consort of Immortal Man, was called "Silence (σιγή)" because in reflection (ἐνθύμησις) without a word she perfected her (whole) greatness (ⲘⲚⲦⲚⲟϬ).[54] Now the doctrinal letter has an almost identical statement which it puts near the beginning when it is enumerating the titles of Ennoia. Some call her "Thought ("Εννοια)", some "Grace (Χάρις)" and appropriately because she dispensed the treasures of Greatness (Μέγεθος) to those from him, but those who spoke the truth have named her "Silence (Σιγή)" because through reflection (ἐνθύμησις) without a word (λόγος) the Greatness (τὸ Μέγεθος) completed everything (τὰ ἄπαντα).[55] The key to understanding the relationship of the texts here lies in the term "greatness (μέγεθος/ⲘⲚⲦⲚⲟϬ)". The doctrinal letter has evidently taken the term in its almost technical Valentinian sense to signify the supreme being: he is made the subject. But this destroys the point of the gloss which was to supply the reason for the title of his consort. This further confirms the priority of Eugnostos. The explanation of the title "Grace" with its reference to "Greatness" has prompted the author of the doctrinal letter to transfer the passage about Silence from its original position at the end of Eugnostos to the beginning of the doctrinal letter.

In conclusion, our analysis of the parallels between Eugnostos the Blessed (and the Sophia of Jesus Christ) and the Valentinian doctrinal letter would suggest: (1) that the parallels are not merely accidental but that the two texts are undoubtedly very closely related; (2) that it is Eugnostos in its present epistolary form rather than the Sophia to which the doctrinal letter is closest, since the Sophia omits or obscures a number of parallels; (3) that it is more often the version of Eugnostos in

---

[53] *Pan.* XXXI 6, 5f. (Holl 394. 3-9). Holl reads Μεσότητος in 394.4 for the 'Ενότητος of the MSS. Equivalents to both occur in Eugnostos and the Sophia.

[54] Eug NHC III 88, 6-11; NHC V 15, 20ff.; SJC NHC III 112, 7-11; BG 113, 15-114, 2. The Sophia, by making the Immortal Man the subject, obscures the sense and the parallel with the doctrinal letter, and thus cannot be the source of this passage.

[55] *Pan.* XXXI 5, 4 (Holl 390.13-391.4).

Codex V which the doctrinal letter most resembles, and (4) that the doctrinal letter is the borrower rather than vice versa. Thus it has clearly incorporated motifs and terminology from Eugnostos into its existing Valentinian scheme, adapting the latter to accommodate them. Eugnostos, of course, is not the only source employed by the letter for its obscure speculations on the Pleroma, but it does appear to explain features peculiar to the letter such as the monistic base structure which Holl took to be a sign of the archaic character of the letter,[56] the references to the names ("Silence", "Man", "Truth") given by those who spoke the truth or are perfect,[57] and the developed speculation on light/man (φῶς/φώς). The willingness of the author of the letter to modify his own tradition to accommodate material from Eugnostos may suggest not only the high regard in which the latter was held but also the readiness of Valentinians, who were avowedly Christian Gnostics, to make use of apparently non-Christian Gnostic documents to develop their views. The former point might indicate the antiquity of Eugnostos, although if it were pre-Christian one might have expected evidence of its influence on Valentinian works and systems earlier than the plainly late and developed form found in the doctrinal letter.[58] The latter point should make us more cautious about attempting to classify either Valentinianism or Eugnostos too strictly. That proponents of the former felt able to use texts like Eugnostos in their non-Christian rather than their Christianised form might suggest not only openness on their part to external influences, but also perhaps that Eugnostos was not felt to be entirely alien and totally free of Christian influence.[59]

---

[56] On p. 390 of his edition in the note on line 5ff.

[57] Cf. *Pan.* XXXI 5, 4-6 (Holl 391.2-10).

[58] See, however, notes 41-3 for parallels with Eugnostos in other Valentinian systems. There are also close similarities between Eugnostos and the "Ophite" system described by Irenaeus in *adv. haer.* I 30, which Irenaeus believed represented the source (or one of the sources) of Valentinianism (cf. *adv. haer.* I 30, 14: Harvey I 241; 31, 3: ibid., 243).

[59] See Wilson, *Gnosis*, 114-7, for a similar conclusion based on signs of possible NT influence on Eugnostos.

THE CONCEPT OF PLEROMA IN GNOSTICISM

BY

VIOLET MACDERMOT

The word Pleroma in Greek literature has a number of meanings connected with ideas of filling up or completing. It means that which fills, and also the fulness of a container, or the fill. Thus it means the complement of the crew on a ship or the sum of a series of numbers. In the New Testament it is used to mean fulfilment of the law, as in Romans 13.10, and also fulness as in Ephesians 1.23 and Colossians 2.9, when it relates to the Godhead. These same meanings are given a wider connotation when the word is used by gnostic writers.

In Gnosticism, the concept of pleroma is mainly found in the literature relating to the Valentinian school, but it also occurs in writings connected with other sects. The various meanings of the word are confirmed by its use in different contexts in the anti-heretical writings of Irenaeus, Hippolytus and Clement of Alexandria. As a gnostic concept, pleroma is perhaps most useful for the understanding of that aspect of gnostic teaching which deals with self-knowledge. This knowledge is essentially the knowledge of man's divine origin, of his fall in which he lost or forgot his divine status, and finally of the means by which ti is self-knowledge can be regained in order to achieve salvation or redemption.

The concept of pleroma as fulness is applied generally in gnosticism to the totality of unmanifest qualities of the Godhead, and also at times to those which are manifest in the universe or in man. In contemporary Hellenistic thought there is a currently found notion that soul qualities in the human world are paralleled by corresponding qualities in the world of the heavens. In the myth of the fall of Sophia from the pleroma, gnosticism elaborates and systematises this idea to show how the human world and the created universe have lost their connection with the divine fulness, and have thus become "deficient". In gnosticism, deficiency has to be seen as the polar opposite of the fulness of pleroma. The concept of pleroma denoting the fulness of all soul qualities or faculties is thus of great importance for conveying the notion of selfhood as both a multiplicity and also a unity. The fall from pleroma, according to this gnostic doctrine, is from a state of fulness to one of deficiency; that is to say, for man, from a state of self-knowledge to one of ignorance, from consciousness of his divine origin and nature to unconsciousness.

Pleroma differs in meaning from the somewhat similar gnostic concept "All" (τό πᾶν or ⲡⲧⲏⲣϥ), in that pleroma usually means more than merely totality. As fullness, pleroma implies an ordered system centred round an unknown, ineffable Godhead, usually called the Father. The imagery of the year, subdivided into 12 months and 365 days, is sometimes used to convey the concept of pleroma as an ordered whole.[1] The zodiacal circle with a circumference of 360 degrees and 12 signs, each of 30 degrees, is another symbol of pleroma.[2] The subdivisions of pleroma or aeons, usually 30 or 28 in number, correspond to the number of days in the solar or lunar month; they are given the names of various virtues and qualities. In the account of the Valentinians by Irenaeus, the invisible and spiritual pleroma is divided into three: an ogdoad, a decad and a duodecad of aeons.[3] Sophia, or wisdom, is the last and youngest aeon of the duodecad.[4] According to Hippolytus, there is a system of 28 aeons, consisting of three primary dyads, a decad and a duodecad. Here also Sophia is said to be the twelfth of the twelve aeons.[5] In this account the aeons bring forth other aeons so that the total finally reaches the perfect number.[6] The ordered fulness of pleroma thus denotes perfection, and in contrast to this concept is the notion of the unordered universe after the fall as deficiency or shapelessness.[7]

As well as being an expression of order, pleroma also means the conscious unity and identity of its constituent parts. In the *Tripartite Tractate*, pleroma is the system of aeons brought forth for the sole purpose of giving glory to the Father. This pleromic congregation which is both unity and multiplicity is a self-revelation of the Father, while he himself remains unknown. The begetting of the aeons is described as a process of extension from the Father, so that those who come forth from him

---

[1] *A Valentinian Exposition* NHL XI.2.30, *The Untitled Text in the Bruce Codex* (NHS Volume XIII) 246.

[2] Irenaeus *Adv. Haer.* I 17.1.

[3] Irenaeus *Adv. Haer.* I 1.3.

[4] Irenaeus *Adv. Haer.* I 2.2.

[5] Hippolytus *Ref.* VI 30.3, 6.

[6] Hippolytus *Ref.* VI 29.7, 8.

[7] Irenaeus *Adv. Haer.* I 4.1; Hippolytus *Ref.* VI 31.1-6; Clement of Alexandria *Exc. ex Theod.* 31.4.

can become him as well. The aeons are said to have a love and longing
for a full and perfect discovery of the Father, and for their full and
perfect union with him.[8] The unity of the aeons with one another is
expressed as conjugal union in Hippolytus.[9]

If pleroma itself originates from within the Godhead, the visible
universe is said to be the result of an act of apostasy by one of the aeons.
The gnostic accounts of the creation vary, and in the *Tripartite Tractate*
it is not Sophia but the Logos which is the aeon that falls by attempting
to grasp the incomprehensibility of the Father. This aeon with his own
arrogant thought begets images of the pleroma, but these images lack
reason and light. They have no knowledge of their ultimate origin, and
therefore exist in disobedience and rebellion.[10] Salvation for the Logos
comes as a result of a revelation of the Father to his mind. The Logos
separates himself from the images which he has created, and casts them
out from himself. When his mind is illumined his pleroma is said to
begin. Henceforth he acts with wisdom and knowledge.[11]

This account differs from the mainstream of Valentinian teaching in
which the aeon which breaks the unity of pleroma is Sophia, which, as
the female aspect of the soul, is tempted to act without her male partner,
and by so doing falls into the chaos, matter, or under the domination of
passions. From thence she is saved by the descent from pleroma of the
male, logoic soul function. It is only possible here to paraphrase briefly
the various gnostic accounts, but it seems that creation was considered
to occur on three levels, or in three stages. In the universe, the giving of
form to chaotic matter is the work of the cosmic Logos or Christ. In the
world of mankind, human salvation and the creation of the church are
effected by the incarnation in human form of Jesus as perfect Man. On
the individual level, the detachment of the soul from its involvement
with the material world and the recollection and restoration of pleroma
are the function of the logoic Spirit within man which is evoked, in the
first instance, by the Saviour himself. A number of gnostic writings
occur in the form of a dialogue between the Saviour and his disciples.

In the gnostic creation myth, the aeons of pleroma are finally revealed
to be the constituents of man. The Saviour who is the Son of the Father
represents and contains the whole pleroma. This is expressed in some

---

[8] *The Tripartite Tractate* NHL I.5.68-73; see also *The Gospel of Truth* NHL I.3.41;
The Sophia of Jesus Christ NHL III.4.98-100; Irenaeus *Adv. Haer.* I 1.2.
[9] Hippolytus *Ref.* VI. 32.1.
[10] *The Tripartite Tractate* NHL I.5.75-78.
[11] *The Tripartite Tractate* NHL I.5.85-91.

accounts as the wearing, by the Son, of all the aeons of pleroma in the form of a garment.[12] In this way the Son reveals the nature of the Father,[13] and conveys the notion that both the material universe and humanity are manifestation of the divine qualities of pleroma. A similar notion is contained in the accounts of the Son, or Jesus, as the Fruit of the Pleroma. In the account by Irenaeus of Valentinian doctrines, Jesus is described as the Perfect Fruit of the Pleroma;[14] in that of Hippolytus, the single aeon brought forth by all 30 aeons as proof of their unity, agreement and peace is called the Joint Fruit of the Pleroma;[15] in the *Tripartite Tractate* it is said that the aeons brought forth the Fruit revealing the countenance of the Father.[16]

In some gnostic writings, Jesus in person declares himself to be the pleroma.[17] In the *Letter of Peter to Philip*, Jesus is reported as saying: "Concerning the pleroma, it is I. ... And I spoke with him who belongs to me, and he hearkened to me just as you who hearken today. And I gave him authority that he might enter the inheritance of his fatherhood. ... And since he was a deficiency, for this reason he became a pleroma."[18] In *Pistis Sophia*, Jesus declares himself to be the mystery of the Ineffable.[19] *The Gospel of Truth* is said to be the gospel of the discovery of the pleroma for those who await salvation.[20] In other places pleroma appears as that which fills up the deficiency, man's ignorance of his own nature.[21] The knowledge of pleroma enables man himself to become a pleroma. The disciples of Jesus are spoken of as being pleromas, or partaking in the nature of pleroma, or as Sons of the Pleroma.[22] Pleroma as self-knowledge is said to be a mystery, not to be

---

[12] *Pistis Sophia* (NHS Volume IX) 15, 16; *The Untitled Text in the Bruce Codex* (NHS Volume XIII) 226, 250; Hippolytus *Ref.* VIII 10.5.

[13] Hippolytus *Ref.* VIII 10.9; Clement of Alexandria *Exc. ex. Theod.* 31.1.

[14] Irenaeus *Adv. Haer.* I 2.6.

[15] Hippolytus *Ref.* VI 32.1-2.

[16] *The Tripartite Tractate* NHL I.5.86.

[17] C.f. *The Gospel of Thomas* NHL II.2.46 (Log. 77); *The Sophia of Jesus Christ* NHL III.4.96; *The Second Treatise of the Great Seth* NHL VII.2.49ff.; *Apocalypse of Peter* NHL VII.3.83.

[18] *The Letter of Peter to Philip* NHL VIII.2.136-137.

[19] *Pistis Sophia* (NHS Volume IX) 208.

[20] *The Gospel of Truth* NHL I.3.34, 35.

[21] *The Gospel of Truth* NHL I.3.35; *The Tripartite Tractate* NHL I.5.90; *The Treatise on Resurrection* NHL I.4.49.

[22] *The Dialogue of the Saviour* NHL III.5.139; *A Valentinian Exposition* NHL XI.2.39; *Pistis Sophia* (NHS Volume IX) 56; *The Second Book of Jeu* (NHS Volume XIII) 105.

spoken of lightly.[23] Fulfilment or perfection are the result of receiving and understanding this mystery knowledge.[24]

The ignorance of fallen mankind about their divine origin and nature is variously described as imprisonment in matter, darkness or purgatory, or else as sleep or forgetfulness. To them the revelation of pleroma may occur as either release from prison, awakening from sleep, or recollection of a previous state. In the *Apocryphon of John*, the body is the place of imprisonment, and the Saviour says: "I ... am the remembrance of the pleroma ... I am the light which exists in the light ... I went that I might enter into the middle of the darkness and the inside of Hades ... and I entered into the middle of their prison which is the prison of the body. And I said: 'He who hears, let him get up from the deep sleep.' And he wept and shed tears ... And he said: 'Who is it who calls my name?' "[25] Both the *Exegesis of the Soul* and *Pistis Sophia* depict the release of the female part of the soul from its imprisonment in matter. In both accounts salvation is preceded by repentance. In Pistis Sophia, this takes the form of hymns of praise and prayer addressed to the Light, asking for enlightenment and for restoration to her rightful place within the pleroma.

The entry of the resurrected soul into pleroma or the restoration of pleroma as a whole is seen as a re-creation of the original state of unity. This is depicted in two main ways. In the first, that portion of mankind which is saved is manifested as one body. Spiritual mankind appear as the members of the body of the Church, which is the body of the perfect man. When mankind has been manifested thus as the "sound body", this is the restoration into pleroma.[26] The coming together of spiritual mankind to form one body is also likened to a bridal chamber where the Saviour unites with his bride who is the Church.[27] This event is prefigured in some accounts by the marriage which unites the form-creating Logos with the material universe or Sophia. Thus in Irenaeus this first bridal chamber is said to be the entire pleroma, and the pair are the Saviour who originated from all the aeons and Sophia, the aeon that

---

[23] *The Apocryphon of John* NHL II.1.31, 32; *Pistis Sophia* (NHS Volume IX) 4; *The Second Book of Jeu* (NHS Volume XIII) 105; Hippolytus *Ref.* V 8.26.

[24] *Pistis Sophia* (NHS Volume IX) 15, 16, 60, 77; *The Second Book of Jeu* (NHS Volume XIII) 105, 125; Hippolytus *Ref.* V 8.26.

[25] *The Apocryphon of John* NHL II.1.30, 31.

[26] *The Tripartite Tractate* NHL I.5.123; Clement of Alexandria *Exc. ex Theod.* 36.1, 2.

[27] *The Tripartite Tractate* NHL I.5.122; *The Gospel of Philip* NHL II.3.85, 86; Clement of Alexandria *Exc. ex Theod.* 63.1-65.1.

fell.[28] According to Hippolytus, Sophia, the mother of all living creatures, is saved by her marriage partner, the Joint Fruit of the Pleroma.[29] On the individual level, the salvation of the female part of the soul by the male part is described in the *Exegesis of the Soul*.[30] The female soul in the material body is depicted as a prostitute who has been seduced from her previous life of virginity with the Father. Her recollection of her own true nature and her desire for restoration are portrayed when she awaits as a bride her bridegroom who is the representative of the Father. Only after her repentance does the marriage take place.

The state of those who have been restored to pleroma is described in the *Gospel of Truth*: "They rest in him who is at rest, not striving or being involved in the search for truth. But they themselves are the truth, and the Father is in them, and they are in the Father, being perfect, being undivided in the good one, being in no way deficient in anything."[31]

To conclude: the theme in relation to which the concept of pleroma particularly applies is that of the human soul and the stages of its development. Gnosticism sees the soul as an entity with innumerable facets and potentialities, at the centre of which is the unknown self, the Father. For man's soul, from its divine centre to its ultimate manifestation in matter, the concept of pleroma provides the notion of unity and multiplicity. The opposite of the fulness of pleroma is not emptiness, but deficiency, the notion of something lacking which has to be replaced in order that the whole be restored. Thus the concept of pleroma also provides the idea of both the individual man and the church of mankind as indivisible wholes, related to one another in their innermost being. In a prescientific age, knowledge about the soul was imparted in religion, and self-knowledge in gnosticism is essentially an understanding of the soul and its workings.

---

[28] Irenaeus *Adv. Haer.* I.7.1.

[29] Hippolytus *Ref.* VI 32.2.-34.4.

[30] *The Exegesis on the Soul* NHL II.6.132-134; see also *Authoritative Teaching* NHL VI.3.31-35.

[31] *The Gospel of Truth* NHL I.3.42.

THE APOCALYPSE OF ADAM:
EVIDENCE FOR A
CHRISTIAN GNOSTIC PROVENANCE

BY

G. M. SHELLRUDE

The *Apocalypse of Adam*[1] has aroused considerable interest because of the claim by its first editors, which has been supported by other scholars, that it is a document of a non-Christian and perhaps pre-Christian Gnostic sect.[2] The significance of this claim lies in the Redeemer myth in the *Apoc. Adam*. According to the myth a heavenly Redeemer enters history by means of a docetic union with an historical person. His purpose is to create a redeemed community by the proclamation of Gnosis. When the Demiurge tries to destroy this enigmatic figure, the heavenly Redeemer departs into the heavenly world while the fleshly vehicle of his manifestation suffers. If this text represents a non-Christian and temporally pre-Christian Gnosticism, then it is the first concrete evidence for a pre-Christian Redeemer myth of this type. The conclusion of this communication is that the *Apoc. Adam* cannot be admitted as evidence for a pre-Christian Redeemer myth because of the clear evidence that it is a document of Christian Gnosticism.

---

[1] I am using the Coptic text and English translation prepared by G. W. MacRae in *Nag Hammadi Codices, V, 2-5 and VI with Papyrus Berolinensis 8502, 1 and 4*, ed. D. M. Parrot, Leiden, 1979, 154-195. I have consulted the Coptic text and German translation prepared by A. Böhlig and P. Labib, *Koptisch-gnostische Apokalypsen aus Codex V von Nag Hammadi*, Halle-Wittenberg, 1963, 96-117, and the translation of M. Krause, "The Apocalypse of Adam", in *Gnosis: A Selection of Gnostic Texts*, II, ed. W. Foerster, Oxford, 1974, 13-23.

[2] Böhlig, *Koptisch-gnostische Apokalypsen*, 86-95. He has elaborated his views in two subsequent articles: "Die Adamapokalypse aus Codex V von Nag Hammadi als Zeugnis jüdisch-iranischer Gnosis", *OrChr* 48 (1964), 44-49, and "Jüdisches und Iranisches in der Adamapokalypse des Codex V von Nag Hammadi", in *Mysterion und Wahrheit*, Leiden, 1968, 149-161. The non-Christian nature of the text has been supported by G. W. MacRae, "The Coptic Gnostic Apocalypse of Adam", *Heythrop Journal* VI (1965), 27-35, and "The Apocalypse of Adam Reconsidered", *SBL Seminar Papers*, Missoula, 1972, 573-579. K. Rudolph has adopted this position in a number of articles: his review of Böhlig and Labib's work in *TLZ* 90 (1965) 361-362, in "Gnosis und Gnostizismus, ein Forschungsbericht", *ThR* 34 (1969), 160-169, and in *Die Gnosis: Wesen und Geschichte einer spätantiken Religion*, Göttingen, 1977, 148-149.

A number of scholars have argued that the *Apoc. Adam* is a Christian Gnostic text.[3] The evidence they have adduced falls into two categories:[4] evidence that the author was acquainted with the literature of the canonical New Testament, the correspondence of motifs in the *Apoc. Adam* to demonstrably Christian Gnostic motifs. While it is impossible to review all this evidence, I would like to make a few observations about the debate.

It is admitted on all sides that the *Apoc. Adam* contains motifs and expressions that could be interpreted as evidence for an acquaintance with the New Testament.[5] However the supporters of the pre-Christian hypothesis object to inferring Christian influence from these parallels on the ground that the allusions are not sufficiently explicit. Professors MacRae and Böhlig have argued that Gnostic literature is explicitly syncretistic and invariably makes some clear references to the religious traditions employed.[6] The obvious response to this is that the *Apoc. Adam* veils its allusions to Jesus and the early Church because of its apocalyptic character. In a later article Professor MacRae had to take this counter argument seriously in light of the Nag Hammadi text *The Concept of Our Great Power* (VI, 4). In this text there is a veiled prophecy of the coming Redeemer which is an *ex eventu* interpretation of the historical Jesus (40.24-42.21). Professor MacRae's response is that this text differs from the *Apoc. Adam* in that "...the very effectiveness of the revelatory vision depends on its evoking known New Testament

---

[3] The first arguments were contained in reviews of Böhlig and Labib's work: Schenke, *OLZ* 61 (1966), 31-34; J. Daniélou, "Bulletin d'histoire des origines chrétiennes", *RechSR* 54 (1966), 291-292; R. Haardt, *WZKM* 61 (1967), 153-159. R. McL. Wilson, *Gnosis and the New Testament*, Oxford, 1968, 135-139, tentatively argued for the presence of Christian influence. A. F. J. Klijn, *Seth in Jewish, Christian and Gnostic Literature*, Leiden, 1977, 90-96, thinks that a Christian background is obvious although he does not defend his position. For further lists of opinions on both sides see the notes in Klijn and in F. T. Fallon, *The Enthronement of Sabaoth*, Leiden, 1978, 69-70, note 146.

[4] E. Yamauchi, "The Apocalypse of Adam, Mithraism, and Pre-Christian Gnosticism", *Textes et Memoires*, 4, *Etudes Mithriaques*, Leiden, 1979, 537-563, has argued that the *Apoc. Adam* cannot be dated before the second century A.D. because of the allusion to Mitha's rock birth in 80.21-26.

[5] Professor MacRae, *Coptic Gnostic Apoc. Adam*, 32, has noted the following motifs: the Redeemer is a man of supra-historical origins, the community he creates are metaphorically called 'fruit-bearing trees', the hostile powers are angry with him, he suffers in the flesh, and his followers 'receive his name upon the water', i.e. by baptism. One could also add the reference to the Holy Spirit's descent on the fleshly vehicle of the Redeemer's manifestation, the use of the designation 'Name' for the Redeemer, the statement that he works 'signs and wonders', and the apparent allusion to Revelation 12.1-6 in 78.18ff.

[6] MacRae, *Ibid.*, 32, and Böhlig, *Jüdisches und Iranisches*, 154.

circumstances.'''[7] This statement clearly begs the question, for *if* the *Apoc. Adam* is a Christian Gnostic text then its allusions to the New Testament would have had the desired effect on the reader precisely because they evoked known New Testament circumstances and motifs. Professors Böhlig and MacRae's attempt to dismiss the apparent New Testament allusions in the *Apoc. Adam* is not convincing, and full weight must be given to these allusions unless other arguments can be advanced to disqualify them as evidence of Christian influence.

The correspondence of motifs in the *Apoc. Adam* to those in demonstrably Christian Gnostic texts has also been used to support a Christian Gnostic background for the text.[8] This approach must be used with care, but it can yield positive results. Surprisingly, it is the Redeemer myth which provides one of the most promising lines of investigation. According to Professor Colpe's classification of types of Redeemer myths, the myth in the *Apoc. Adam* belongs to the Christian Gnostic type.[9] The question, of course, is whether this myth is a characteristicly Gnostic interpretation of Jesus, or whether it is a pre-Christian construction. It is impossible to explore this question in detail, but it is worth pointing out that a number of scholars who continue to argue for the existence of a pre-Christian Redeemer myth (e.g. Professors Schenke, Schmithals and Rudolph) are reconstructing the myth in such a way that it bears no resemblance to the Illuminator myth in the *Apoc. Adam*.[10] According to the reconstruction of each of these scholars, the Illuminator myth in the *Apoc. Adam* belongs to the Christian Gnostic type.[11] Those who wish to argue that this myth is in fact pre-Christian must be prepared to relate this particular myth to a com-

---

[7] MacRae, *Apoc. Adam Reconsidered*, 574-575.

[8] Schenke, *OLZ*, 32, cites evidence for a dependence on the N.T. and then adds: "...hinzu kommt auch noch die weitgehende sachliche Übereinstimmung mit eindeutig christlich-gnostischen Schriften."

[9] C. Colpe, *Die religionsgeschichtliche Schule*, Göttingen, 1961, 198. It is quite possible that the Illuminator in the *Apoc. Adam* is the heavenly Seth (65.6-9; 72.6-7; 77.1). If this is the case then the *Gospel of the Egyptians* (III. 2) provides a close parallel to this redeemer myth. In both cases the redeemer would be the heavenly Seth who manifests himself through an historical figure in the third epoch of salvation history. The *Gos. Eg.* explicitly identifies this historical person as Jesus (64.1-3).

[10] H.-M. Schenke, "Die neutestamentliche Christologie und der gnostische Erlöser", in *Gnosis und Neues Testament*, ed. K.-W. Tröger, Gerd Mohn, 1973, 205-218. W. Schmithals, "Gnosis und Neues Testament", *VF* 21 (1976), 38-41. K. Rudolph, *Die Gnosis*, 130-162, cf. his statements on pp. 163-165.

[11] There appears to be an inconsistency in Professor Rudolph's treatment of the *Apoc. Adam*. In his recent book, *Die Gnosis*, he characterizes the *Apoc. Adam* as a non-Christian Gnostic document (148f.), and then on p. 163 summarizes his view of the

prehensive account of pre-Christian Redeemer mythologies. It seems highly probable that the Redeemer myth itself is primary evidence that the *Apoc. Adam* is a Christian Gnostic work.[12]

In summary, the presence of New Testament allusions and striking parallels with Christian Gnostic literature strongly suggests that the *Apoc. Adam* is a document of Christian Gnosticism. In this communication I would like to advance three new arguments in support of a Christian Gnostic provenance for the *Apoc. Adam*.

First, I would like to argue that the Illuminator pericope (76.8-77.18) is an *ex eventu* prophecy which interprets an historical person as the Gnostic Redeemer. If this conclusion is correct then Jesus must be the historical person in question.

The *Apoc. Adam* has a tri-partite division of salvation history, and for the sake of convenience the major periods can be designated as 'Acts': Act I covers the period from Adam to the flood; Act II reaches its climax in the rescue of the Gnostic community from the conflagration; Act III commences with the manifestation of the Illuminator. Those who argue that the *Apoc. Adam* is a non-Christian Gnostic text place the transition from *ex eventu* to genuine prophecy at the beginning of Act III, i.e. with the prophecy of the Illuminator (76.8).[13] This interpretation has never been defended and one suspects that it arises from a need to avoid coming to terms with the possibility that the Illuminator pericope interprets past history.

The following evidence suggests that the Illuminator pericope is an *ex eventu* prophecy. In interpreting historical surveys written in an apocalyptic style it is relatively easy to locate the time in which the author is writing in that he moves from an interpretation of past and

---

modifications which the pre-Christian Redeemer myth underwent when Jesus was interpreted as the Gnostic Redeemer. He writes that: "Die Einführung der christlichen Erlösergestalt in die gnostische Soteriologie hat in erster Linie zu drei charakteristischen Erscheinungen geführt, die wir (1.) als 'Historisierung' oder Vergeschichtlichung' des gnostischen Erlösers, (2.) als 'Aufspaltung' der Christusgestalt und (3.) als 'Doketismus' oder 'Scheinleibvorstellung' bezeichnen wollen." The problem for Professor Rudolph is that each of these points characterizes the Redeemer myth in the *Apoc. Adam*!

[12] In the *Apoc. Adam* the departure of the Redeemer is followed by the Demiurge's attempt to nullify the effect of his work. This is a recurrent motif in Christian Gnostic texts which try to account for the existence of the orthodox Church (e.g. *Apocalypse of Peter*, VII. 3, 73.23-79.31; *The Second Treatise of the Great Seth*, VII, 2, 59.19-60.3, 60.13-35; *The Concept of Our Great Power*, VI. 4, 42.31-43.2).

[13] MacRae, *Coptic Gnostic Apoc. Adam*, 30, states that "The final era in this apocalyptic distortion of salvation history will be inaugurated when the Illuminator of Gnosis will come..." cf. P. Perkins, "The Apocalypse of Adam: The Genre and Function of a Gnostic Apocalypse", *CBQ* 39 (1978), 389-391.

present history to a projection of the future. In doing this he inadvertently provides an historical context for himself. Two things become clear when one tries to locate the real author within his own framework for salvation history. First, the author's understanding of Gnostic salvation history explicitly rules out the possibility that the author could have written prior to the Illuminator's appearance. From the author's point of view no Gnostic community existed in the world between the conflagration and the Illuminator's manifestation. When the Gnostics were rescued from the conflagration they were taken into the Pleroma and became the companions of angels (75.17-76.7). Now after the Gnostics' deliverance from the flood they were returned to the earth (71.8-15), but there is no mention of a similar return after the conflagration. One might argue that the author assumed that such a return took place. However the fact that the Illuminator does not come to a flourishing community of Seth's natural posterity renders this assumption highly unlikely. The impression is conveyed that the original Sethian community remained in the Pleroma and that the world lacked a Gnostic witness until the Illuminator's appearance. Thus one cannot place the time of writing in a period when, from the author's point of view, there were no Gnostics in the world. Second, the radical discontinuity between Acts I and II on the one hand and Act III on the other points to the conclusion that the Illuminator pericope interprets past history. In the first two acts redemption involves deliverance from physical danger, in the third it means the proclamation of saving Gnosis. In the first two acts angels rescue a flourishing Gnostic community, in the third the Illuminator creates a community *de novo*. In the former case it is Seth's natural posterity who are rescued, in the latter case the Illuminator creates a community from the Sethian's former enemies, i.e. 'the seed of Noah and the sons of Ham and Japheth.' This last point is especially significant if this is a veiled reference to Jews and Gentiles. The accounts of the flood and conflagration are accounts of Biblical events according to the same artificial model. To some extent this model is employed in the construction of the genuine eschatological prophecy in 83.4ff. The Illuminator pericope does not fall into this pattern, and the best explanation is that the author is interpreting past history which constitutes the *raison d'être* of his community's existence.[14]

---

[14] The difficulty of maintaining that the author belonged to a Gnostic community for whom everything from 76.7ff was the object of future expectation becomes evident when

I would thus argue that the author's view of salvation history excludes the possibility that the real author could have written prior to the Illuminator's appearance and that the best explanation for the radical discontinuity between Acts I/II and Act III is that the Illuminator pericope interprets past history.

If these arguments are sound, then it follows that the Illuminator pericope is an *ex eventu* interpretation of an historical figure as the Gnostic Redeemer. The only plausible candidate for this *ex eventu* prophecy is the historical Jesus as he is the only known historical figure who was interpreted as a Gnostic Redeemer *in the way* that the *Apoc. Adam* interprets the person and work of the Illuminator.

The second and third arguments are based on interpretations of the *dramatis personae* in the historical survey. The first of these two arguments is that when the author says at 76.12-13 that the Illuminator's redemption embraced 'the seed of Noah and the sons of Ham and Japheth', he is referring to Jews and Gentiles. The following evidence points to the conclusion that the author identified 'the seed of Noah' with Shem's posterity who are the Jews and 'the sons of Ham and Japheth' with the Gentiles. First, it is clear from 74.17-19 that 'the seed of Noah' is distinguished from 'the sons of Ham and Japheth.'' These lines occur within the context of an accusation made against the Gnostics before the Demiurge. The accusers state that in contrast to the 400,000 from Ham and Japheth's posterity who have joined the Sethians, 'the seed of Noah' has remained faithful to the Demiurge. They claim that ''…the seed of Noah through his son has done all your will'' (ⲁⲡⲉ ⲥⲡⲉⲣⲙⲁ ⲛⲧⲉ ⲛⲱ̄ⲏⲉ ⲉⲃⲟⲗ ⳅ̄ⲙ ⲡⲉϥϣⲏⲣⲉ ⲁϥⲉⲓⲣⲉ ⲙ̄ⲡⲉⲕⲟⲩⲱϣ ⲧⲏⲣϥ̄). The singular form of 'son' means that only one of Noah's sons is in view. The phrase must refer to Shem's posterity who are distinguished from that of Ham and Japheth. Second, the identification of 'the seed of Noah' or Shem's posterity with the Jews is required by their special relationship with the Demiurge who is the God of the Old Testament. This is reflected in the passage just quoted. It is confirmed by the attribution of the prayer of 73.1b-12 to Shem. The introduction to this prayer is fragmentary, but it is clear that Shem is the speaker.[15] In the prayer Shem commits his posterity to the Demiurge's service and prays that the Demiurge will act to preserve his descendants'

---

one tries to answer the question of the origins, beliefs and life of this hypothetical Gnostic community. It is much easier to answer these questions if the Illuminator pericope is viewed as the *raison d'être* for the Gnostic community to which the author belonged.

[15] Schenke, *OLZ*, 32, and Klijn, *Seth*, 94.

faithfulness. Shem's posterity are thus identified with the Jews. Third, the conclusion that 'the sons of Ham and Japheth' refers to the Gentiles is an inference drawn from the identification of Shem's posterity with the Jews, but readily intelligible as a simplistic interpretation of Genesis 10.[16]

This evidence that the author believed that the Illuminator's redemption embraced Jew and Gentile is an important clue to the provenance of the work. It is possible that a theology of redemption that embraced Jew and Gentile could have arisen in a Diaspora synagogue context. However the combination of this motif in the *Apoc. Adam* with a Redeemer myth that is so similar to a Christian Gnostic interpretation of Jesus makes it unlikely that the work originated in a Jewish context. It is far more natural to see this motif as the result of Christian influence. The frequently expressed belief that Christ's redemption embraced Jew and Gentile, together with the historical reality of mixed Jewish-Gentile congregations forms the most plausible background to this motif in the *Apoc. Adam*.

The second of these two arguments is based on the interpretation of the *dramatis personae* in the genuine eschatological prophecy. The prophecy begins at 83.4b and lines 4-8 are relevant. The author writes (Professor MacRae's translation): "Then the seed, those who will receive his name upon the water and (that) of them all, will fight against the power." There are a number of difficult textual and interpretive questions in these lines. The important questions are who is referred to by the terms 'seed' and 'power', which designations describe the Gnostics and which their opponents, and which group is characterized as 'those who receive his name upon the water.'

The identification of the protagonists from the words 'seed' and 'power' is extremely difficult. Since the linguistic evidence is ambiguous, the context must ultimately guide the interpretations of these terms. The word for 'seed' (ⲥⲡⲟⲣⲁ) is normally used with reference to the Gnostic community,[17] and it is not used absolutely in the case where it is used of the non-Gnostics (71.5). The word for 'power' (ϭⲟⲙ) is normally used with reference to the Demiurge and his demonic forces.[18]

---

[16] This interpretation is not new. It occurred to F. Fallon, *Enthronement*, 72, and P. Perkins, "Apocalyptic Schematization in the Apocalypse of Adam and the Gospel of the Egyptians", *SBL Seminary Papers*, Missoula, 1972, 597, note 20. However they do not seem to have considered the implications of this interpretation.

[17] 65.4, 8; 66.4; 69.12; 76.7; 85.22, 29.

[18] e.g. 64.18; 65.30; 70.9; 71.20.

This linguistic evidence might suggest that the author imagines the Gnostics mounting an attack on the power of the Demiurge reflected in their opposition. However it is more plausible that the eschatological conflict involves an assault on the Gnostics by their opposition. In this case the 'seed' will refer to the opposition while the 'power' would designate the Gnostics. The most difficult problem is to see how the word сπора could be used absolutely for the non-Gnostics.[19] It would be quite natural to refer to the Gnostics as the 'power' in that power is an attribute of both the Gnostic community (73.21; 74.8) and the Illuminator (77.6). It is the context which clearly favors this latter interpretation. In apocalyptic thought eschatological conflict is normally inaugurated by the believing community's opposition. This tendency is present in the first two Acts of the *Apoc. Adam* in which the Gnostic community is the object of attack. Furthermore, the deliverance and vindication of the Gnostics in 83.7ff is more intelligible on this interpretation.

The question whether the 'seed' or the 'power' is modified by the phrase 'those who receive his name upon the water' is impossible to resolve on strictly linguistic grounds. Scholarly opinion is divided with some interpreters relating the phrase to the 'seed' (e.g. Professor MacRae)[20] and others to the 'power' (e.g. Professor Böhlig).[21] However all interpreters seem to agree that the phrase describes the Gnostic community. In my judgment it is more probable that the baptism is practiced by the Gnostics' opponents. The author takes a dim view of water baptism (84.4-26) and goes so far as to equate true baptism with the reception of Gnosis (85.22-26). I would thus conclude that the 'seed' is identified with the Gnostics' opponents who practice baptism and that the 'power' is a reference to the Gnostic community.[22]

If this conclusion is accepted then it is significant that the Gnostic opposition lays claim to the same Redeemer as the Gnostic community[23] and that baptism is associated with their acceptance of the Redeemer. It

---

[19] cf. *The Paraphrase of Shem*, VII, 1, 35.12f., 40.27f., where the Gnostic opposition is referred to as 'the seed of universal darkness'. However the word is сπерма not сπора.

[20] MacRae, *Nag Hammadi Codices V, 2-5*, 188f.

[21] Böhlig, *Koptisch-gnostische Apokalypsen*, 93f., 115.

[22] My argument would still hold if the identification of the *dramatis personae* was reversed and the Gnostics were viewed as the 'seed' and their opposition as the 'power'. The important point is that it is the opposition group which practices baptism.

[23] The existence of an opposition group claiming the Illuminator as their Redeemer is also indicated by the Demiurge's attempt to create misunderstanding about his real nature (77.18-27) and the false views of the thirteen kingdoms.

is difficult to avoid the conclusion that the Gnostics' opponents are orthodox Christians.[24] The identification is supported by the widespread phenomena of Gnostic polemic against orthodox baptismal practice, especially in works with Sethian associations.[25] This identification receives further support from the appropriateness of the phrase 'receive his name upon the water' to describe Christian baptism. In a general sense a number of texts witness to the association of the 'Name' with baptism.[26] In the *Shepherd of Hermas* there are some phrases which closely parallel this expression in vocabulary and meaning.[27] It may even be that the phrase is a technical one designating a Jewish Christian rite of marking an 'X' on the baptismal candidate which stood, not for the Cross as in later usage, but for *X*ristos, that is the name of the Illuminator.[28] In summary, the identification of orthodox Christians as the eschatological opponents of the Gnostic community is indicated by the characterization of the opposition as those who claim the Illuminator for themselves and practice baptism, by the parallels to this polemic in other Gnostic works and by the appropriateness of the phrase 'receive his name upon the water' to describe Christian baptism.

The difficulty of maintaining that the *Apoc. Adam* represents a pre-Christian Gnosticism is evident when one considers what must be attributed to this non-Christian Gnostic community. One must not only argue that they interpreted an historical figure as the Redeemer in the way that Christian Gnostics later interpreted Jesus, but also that they believed that this Redeemer had created a community from Jews and

---

[24] F. Morard, "L'Apocalypse d'Adam de Nag Hammadi: un essai d'interpretation", in *Gnosis and Gnosticism*, ed. M. Krause, Leiden, 1977, 35-42, and "L'Apocalypse d'Adam du Codex V de Nag Hammadi et sa polémique anti-baptismale", *RevSR* 51 (1977), 214-233, argues that the polemic is directed against another Gnostic sect. A number of her arguments are open to question, but even if she is right the *Apoc. Adam* could not be viewed as a pre-Christian document on her interpretation.

[25] cf. K. Koschorke, *Die Polemik der Gnostiker gegen das kirchliche Christentum*, Leiden, 1978, 142-148.

[26] G. W. Lampe, *The Seal of the Spirit*, London, 1951, 284-296.

[27] *Hermas*, Similitude IX.12.8 ὃς ἂν τὸ ὄνομα αὐτοῦ μὴ λάβῃ ...

IX.13.2 ἔαν γάρ τὸ ὄνομα λάβῃς

IX.13.7 οὗτοι, Θησι, πάντες τὸ ὄνομα τοῦ υἱοῦ τοῦ θεοῦ ἔλαβον...

cf. IX.13.3; 14.5f., and *The Gospel of Philip*, II.3, 64.22-31.

[28] This interpretation was suggested to me by Einar Thomassen. While the interpretation is attractive, the tenuous nature of several links in J. Danielou's reconstruction of this hypothetical Jewish Christian baptismal rite makes it impossible to be certain that the author had this specific baptismal rite in view. cf. J. Danielou, *The Theology of Jewish Christianity*, London, 1964, 154f., 329-331, *Primitive Christian Symbols*, London, 1964, 139-142. D. Daube, *The New Testament and Rabbinic Judaism*, London, 1956, 401-403, has some relevant material.

Gentiles, that they were confronted by another group claiming the same Redeemer but also practicing baptism, and that they employed a variety of motifs which fortuitiously found their way into the New Testament and later Christian Gnosticism. Finally one must take into account the complete silence of first century sources with respect to the existence of this Gnostic community. It is much more natural to take this evidence of Christian influence at face value and interpret the work as a document of Christian Gnosticism.

PART II

GNOSTICISM

NAASSENER ODER VALENTINIANER?

VON

JOSEF FRICKEL

Vor 75 Jahren hat Richard Reitzenstein den Naassenerbericht des Hippolyt von Rom literarkritisch analysiert und innerhalb der sogenannten Naassenerpredigt einen ursprünglich heidnischen[1] bzw. hellenistisch-jüdischen Kommentar zum Attishymnus als eine gnostische Grundschrift herauszulösen versucht. Er glaubte, das literarkritische Problem dieser gnostischen Schrift damit ein für alle mal gelöst zu haben.[2] In Wirklichkeit hat Reitzenstein das Problem erst geschaffen, wie die nach wie vor, z.T. diametral entgegengesetzten Meinungen über einen zugrundeliegenden gnostischen Kommentar deutlich machen.[3]

Trotz dieser die literarische und vor allem die doktrinelle Entwicklung unseres Traktates betreffenden Differenzen gelten die Naassener als eine relativ klar bestimmbare gnostische Gruppe synkretistischer Tendenz innerhalb einer größeren gnostischen Gruppe, die man als "die Drei-Prinzipien-Systeme" zu benennen pflegt. Eben diese klare doktrinelle Abgrenzung der Naassener von anderen gnostischen Gruppen oder Schulen ist mir jedoch, je länger je mehr, zweifelhaft geworden. Nicht (nur) in dem Sinne, daß die Naassener zahlreiche Berührungspunkte und Verwandtschaften mit anderen gnostischen Schriften in Hippolyts *Refutatio* aufweisen. Diese Gemeinsamkeiten hat man bekanntlich

---

[1] R. Reitzenstein, *Poimandres*, Studien zur griechisch-ägyptischen und frühchristlichen Literatur, Leipzig[2] 1922, 82.

[2] Reitzenstein hielt den ursprünglichen Kommentar zunächst für ein rein heidnisches Lehrstück, ohne einen jüdischen Einfluß absolut ausschließen zu wollen (Poim. 82, Anm. 2). Später hat er einen hellenistisch-jüdischen Einfluß ausdrücklich eingeräumt (Reitzenstein-Schaeder, Studien zum antiken Synkretismus aus Iran und Griechenland, Leipzig-Berlin 1926, 105-106).

[3] Für die Anhänger der modifizierten Position Reitzensteins mögen stehen: H. Lietzmann (Geschichte der Alten Kirche, Bd. 1, Berlin-Leipzig[3]1953, 291) und W. Bauer (Der Naassenerpsalm, in: Hennecke-Schneemelcher, Neutestamentliche Apokryphen, Bd. II, Tübingen 1964, 575f.); für die gegenteilige, Reitzensteins Rekonstruktion eines älteren gnostischen Kommentars ablehnende Meinung: G. Quispel, Der gnostische Anthropos und die jüdische Tradition, in: Eranos-Jahrb. 22, 1953, 205 A. 17 und H. Schlier, Der Mensch im Gnostizismus, in: Anthropologie Religieuse (Studies in the History of Religions, 2), Leiden 1955, 61 A.2.

schon lange gesehen und diskutiert, wenn auch—wie ich meine—
keineswegs hinreichend erklärt.[4]

Was mir in steigendem Maß aufgefallen ist, sind die zahlreichen neutestamentlichen Exegesen, die Naassener und Valentinianer gemeinsam
haben. Dieselben Schriftworte und Bilder werden ausgewählt, und in
gleicher oder ähnlicher Weise gnostisch gedeutet, sodaß hier eine besondere, noch näher zu klärende Beziehung zwischen Naassenern und
Valentinianern vorzuliegen scheint.

Um die Begriffe nicht zu verwirren, sind zunächst einige Voraussetzungen betreffs des Begriffes "Naassener" zu klären. Der Naassenerbericht (Ref V 6, 4-10, 2) ist ein komplexes Gebilde. Der uns von Hippolyt
überlieferte Text ist in seiner Gesamtheit m.E. jedoch eine so gewollte
gnostische Komposition und nicht eine (mehr oder weniger willkürliche)
Auswahl Hippolyts. Das Kernstück, d.h. der eigentliche Kommentar
zum Attishymnus, hat auch nach meiner Meinung eine literarische und
doktrinelle Entwicklung durchgemacht, meine Beschäftigung mit dem
Text hat mich allerdings zur Überzeugung gebracht, daß die bisher vor-
geschlagenen Quellenscheidungen dem Text nur partiell gerecht werden,
weshalb ich die früheren Lösungversuche um einen weiteren bereichern
möchte.[5] Unserem Text liegt ein nichtchristlicher Kommentar des in
Kap. 9, 8-9 überlieferten Attishymnus zugrunde, dessen Struktur allerdings nur noch rudimentär erhebbar ist. Dieser ursprüngliche Kommentar enthielt noch nicht die Homerexegese (7, 30-41) über den kylleni-
schen Hermes, er war auch nicht gnostisch, sondern das Produkt einer
für die Kaiserzeit typischen Religionstheosophie. Er hat auch mit den
Naassenern zunächst nichts zu tun, sondern war bei Attis-Mysten
zuhause.

---

[4] Auf Grund der zahlreichen Übereinstimmungen und Parallelen in den neuen gnostischen Quellen Hippolyts (Naassener, Peraten, Sethianer, Apophasis, Monoimos u.s.w.)
hat zunächst G. Salmon (The Cross References in the Philosophumena, in: Hermathena
11, 1885, 389-402) die Echtheit dieser gnostischen Schriften in Zweifel gezogen. Dann H.
Staehelin (Die gnostischen Quellen Hippolyts in seiner Hauptschrift gegen die Häretiker,
in: TU 6, 3, 1890, 1-108). Gegen diese These wandte sich W. Anz (Zur Frage nach dem
Ursprung des Gnostizismus. Ein religionsgeschichtlicher Versuch; in: TU 154, 1897, 9 n.
3), dann besonders E. de Faye (Introduction à l'étude du gnosticisme au IIe et au IIIe siè-
le, Paris 1903, 24-32.62-72) und W. Bousset (Die Hauptprobleme der Gnosis, Göttingen
1907, 128). Die These Salmons und Staehelins gilt heute als überholt. Zur Problemge-
schichte siehe J. Frickel, Die Apophasis Megale in Hippolyts Refutatio (VI 8-19): Eine
Paraphrase zur Apophasis Simons. Orientalia Christiana Analecta 182, Rom 1968, 12-25.
[5] Ich nehme dabei das Ergebnis einer größeren Arbeit über "Strukturanalyse und Quellenscheidung in der Naassenerschrift", die ich in diesem Jahr zu veröffentlichen hoffe,
teilweise vorweg.

Dieser Attis-Kommentar hat eine erste gnostische Weiterbildung erfahren, offenbar durch einen synkretistisch orientierten Gnostiker, der einerseits mit den Mysterien, besonders mit dem Attiskult, vertraut war, andererseits einer sich vor allem an alttestamentlichen Texten inspirierenden gnostischen Gruppe angehörte. Dabei mag offen bleiben, inwieweit diese Gruppe bereits verchristlicht war oder nicht. Sie hat jedenfalls die oberste, allen Tempeln und allen Kulten gemeinsame Gottheit als den Naas verehrt, weshalb diese Gnostiker als die eigentlichen Naassener anzusprechen sind. Innerhalb dieser Gruppe hat der nunmehr gnostische Attiskommentar nach einer gewissen Zeit eine zweite gnostische Erweiterung erfahren, eindeutig im Sinn einer verchristlichten Gnosis, und es ist eben diese zweite gnostische Schicht, in der sich die mit den Valentinianern berührenden neutestamentlichen Exegesen finden, um die es hier geht. Hippolyt hat die Schrift global den Naassenern zugeschrieben. Seine Polemik hält sich in Allgemeinplätzen und verrät keine direkte Bekanntschaft mit Naassenern. Da der Text selbst über den Namen ''Naassener'' so gut wie nichts hergibt, muß man annehmen, daß seine Vorlage als ein Dokument der ''Naassener'' bereits bezeichnet war. Dies wiederum scheint den Schluß zu rechtfertigen, daß auch die Gnostiker, welche die uns überlieferte *zweite* gnostische Fassung des Attiskommentars besaßen, sich als Naassener bzw. als Träger des allgemeinen Naas-Kultes verstanden. Dementsprechend unterscheide ich eine ältere und eine jüngere Gruppe von Naassenern, wovon die letztere eindeutig eine christliche Gnosis darstellt, deren Verhältnis zum Valentinianismus genauer zu untersuchen sein wird.

Der Vergleich der neutestamentlichen Exegese dieser Naassener und der Valentinianer ist jedoch unabhängig von der von mir postulierten zweifachen gnostischen Überarbeitung eines ursprünglich heidnischen Attiskommentars. Auch wer diese meine Voraussetzungen nicht oder nur mit Vorbehalt teilt, kann die Naassener global genommen mit den Valentinianern vergleichen. Bei der Quellenscheidung innerhalb der Naassenerschrift geht es in erster Linie darum, hinter unserem jetzigen Kommentar eine frühere gnostische Schrift, eine ältere Gnosis also, zu ertasten, die viel mehr als unsere christlichen Gnostiker sich an alttestamentlichen Texten, an den Psalmen und Isaias beispielsweise, inspiriert hat. Eine Gnosis, die an die Anfänge des zweiten Jahrhunderts zurückgehen könnte, und die es uns vielleicht ermöglicht, die eingangs erwähnten Übereinstimmungen zwischen Naassenern, Peraten, Monoimos, Doketen, Basilides usw. zu verstehen und besser zu erklären, als das bisher möglich war.

Vergleich einiger neutestamentlicher Exegesen

1) *Testimonien für die pneumatische Menschenklasse*

Nach dem Attishymnus nennen die Phrygier den Attis bald Papas, bald den Toten, bald einen Gott. Dieses letzte Epitheton wird im Kommentar so erklärt: Er wird Gott, wenn er von den Toten auferstehen und durch das Himmelstor eingehen wird.[6] Die Erwähnung dieses Himmelstores ist dem Verfasser Gelegenheit, das Thema von der Auferstehung zu verlassen und die in 2 Kor 12, 2-4 geschilderte Himmelsvision des Apostels Paulus als ein Zeugnis für die besondere Erwählung des Paulus darzutun. Er leitet damit ein Lehrstück ein, das sowohl die Erwählung als auch den lebendigen Glauben des Gnostikers als Gnade erweisen soll.[7] Paulus ist, gerade wegen seiner Schau der himmlischen Geheimnisse, für unseren Gnostiker Typus des Pneumatikers, genau wie für bestimmte Valentinianer bei Irenäus.[8] Gnosis ist nicht intellektuelle Erkenntnis, sondern geistige Schau der Mysterien, welche Mysterien umgekehrt eben deshalb wieder nur vom pneumatischen Menschen erkannt werden können. Zeugnis für diese klassische Formulierung von Gnosis ist das Pauluswort 1 Kor 2, 13-14, wonach nur der Pneumatiker diese Geheimnisse zu erkennen vermag und diese nicht nach menschlicher Weisheit, sondern in vom Geist gelehrten Worten redet, "indem wir Geistiges mit Geistigem vergleichen; der psychische Mensch aber faßt nicht, was des Geistes Gottes ist, denn es ist ihm Torheit."[9]

Daß dieses Pauluswort in der christlichen Gnosis bald ein geflügeltes wurde, zeigt Basilides.[10] Zutreffender und dem Naasener näher ist die Anwendung bei den Valentinianern, die nach Irenäus I 8,3 die drei Menschenklassen aus dem 1. Korintherbrief belegten: die Choiker mit 1 Kor

---

[6] Ref. V, 8, 24 (93, 21-23). Ref. Buch V wird im folgenden für die Zitate aus der Naassenerschrift nicht eigens angeführt. Die Refutatio wird nach der Ausgabe von Paul Wendland (GCS 26 = Hippolyt III, Leipzig 1916) zitiert.

[7] 8, 25-30 (93, 23-94, 29).

[8] Iren. haer. III 13, 1 (II 72f. Harvey).

[9] 8, 26 (93, 28-94, 2). Den folgenden Paulussatz, wonach der Pneumatiker "alles erforscht" (1 Kor 2, 15), läßt der Autor aus, weil er diesen Sachverhalt besonders hervorheben will: "Dies sind die unaussprechlichen Geheimnisse des Geistes", sagt er, "die wir allein kennen" (8, 26: 94, 2-3). Der Satz klingt überheblich, ist aber genau besehen nur die Folge der Voraussetzung, daß die göttlichen Geheimnisse nur der Pneumatiker zu schauen vermag.

[10] Nach ihm wurde der große Archon über den Nicht-Seienden, über die Sohnschaft und den Heiligen Geist, also über die Trinität, belehrt. Das ist die Weisheit, die im Geheimnis ausgesprochen wird, von der die Schrift sagt: "nicht in gelehrten Worten menschlicher Weisheit, sondern in gelehrten (Worten) des Geistes" (1 Kor 2, 13) (Hippol. VII 26, 3: 204, 10-12).

15, 18; die Psychiker und Pneumatiker eben durch unsere Stelle: "Ein psychischer Mensch faßt nicht, was des Geistes ist" (1 Kor 2, 14) und: "Ein Pneumatiker erforscht alles" (1 Kor 2, 15).[11] Naassener und Valentinianer benützen also das gleiche Pauluswort als Testimonium für die Pneumatische Menschenklasse.[12]

Die Kenntnis der Geheimnisse des Geistes bezeugt weiterhin das Jesuswort aus dem Johannesevangelium: "Niemand kann zu mir kommen, wenn ihn nicht mein himmlischer Vater zieht."[13] Es ist also Gnade Gottes, die allein den Menschen zu solcher Erkenntnis erwählt und befähigt. Das Johanneswort ist uns in valentinianischer Tradition nicht überliefert. In den Fragmenten Herakleons fehlen uns gerade die Deutungen zu den Kapiteln 5-7. Eine Parallele findet sich in der *Exegese über die Seele.* Nach dem Kontext empfing die Seele das göttliche Wesen vom Vater, das ist die Auferstehung von den Toten — also ähnlich wie bei dem Naassener —, die Errettung aus der Gefangenschaft, das Hinaufsteigen zum Himmel ... Die Seele ist also neugeworden. Das aber kommt nicht durch asketische Worte usw....., sondern es ist die Gnade Gottes.[14] Daher rief der Heiland aus: "Keiner wird zu mir kommen können, es sei denn mein Vater zieht ihn und bringt ihn zu mir und ich selbst werde ihn auferwecken am letzten Tage."[15] Das Jesuswort ist also ein Beleg für die Gnadenhaftigkeit des Neuwerdens der Seele, d.h. für die Auferstehung von den Toten. Das gilt auch für den Naassener, nur daß bei ihm das Neuwerden der Seele genauer als die Neugeburt des Pneumatikers bestimmt wird, der dadurch befähigt wird, die Geheimnisse des Pneumas zu schauen. Das ist gegenüber der ExAn eine Fortentwicklung, die für das Verhältnis der beiden Schriften zueinander aufschlußreich sein könnte. Da aber der gnostische Charakter der ExAn und deren Zuweisung an eine bestimmte gnostische Richtung noch ungeklärt sind,[16] muß diese Schrift zuerst literarkritisch analysiert

---

[11] Iren. I 8, 3 (72 Harvey). Auch hier wird, ähnlich wie bei Basilides, betont, daß das Wort vom Psychiker par excellence, vom Demiurgen, gesagt sein soll. Ähnlich die Valentinianer nach Hippol. Ref. VI 34, 8 (164, 1-6).

[12] Bei den Valentinianern verrät die Begründung aller drei Menschenklassen aus dem 1. Korintherbrief ein hohes Maß von paulinischer Exegese, was jedoch nicht notwendig Zeichen eines späteren Stadiums sein muß. Der Naassener will an unserer Stelle ja nicht explizit über alle drei Klassen, sondern über die Pneumatiker handeln; er könnte daher auch das paulinische Testimonium für die Choiker gekannt haben.

[13] 8, 27 (94, 3-5) = Joh 6, 44 leicht abgewandelt; vgl. A. Resch, Außercanonische Paralleltexte zu den Evangelien: TU X, 4 (1896) S. 106.

[14] NHC II 134, 9-33.

[15] Joh 6, 44 = NHC II 134, 34-135, 4).

[16] F. Wisse (On Exegeting 'the Exegesis on the Soul', in: Les Textes de Nag Hammadi. NHS VII, Leiden 1975, 68-81) bestreitet sogar den gnostischen Charakter von ExAn.

werden,[17] bevor ihr Ort innerhalb der gnostischen Bewegung bestimmt werden kann. Immerhin ist, auch unabhängig von der parallelen Exegese von Joh 6, 44 als Testimonium für das gnadenhafte Neuwerden der Seele, die Ähnlichkeit zwischen dem Geschick der Seele in der ExAn und in dem sog. Naassenerpsalm[18] auffällig und läßt vermuten, daß zwischen ExAn und der Gnosis der Naassener eine enge Verwandtschaft besteht.[19]

Das Johannestestimonium will der Naassener jedoch nicht im Sinne einer bloßen Gnadenhaftigkeit, die dem Libertinismus Vorschub leisten könnte, mißverstanden wissen. Für den Pneumatiker gilt darum zugleich das andere Wort des Erlösers: "Nicht jeder, der zu mir sagt: Herr, Herr, wird in das Himmelreich eingehen, sondern wer den Willen meines Vaters tut, der im Himmel ist."[20]

Die Neuwerdung, der Glaube des Pneumatikers wird sich also dadurch ausweisen, daß er den Willen des Vaters erfüllt. Nicht natürlich in der Gesinnung eines Knechtes, sondern eines Kindes, aus Liebe. Darin sind sich unsere Gnostiker jedenfalls mit den kirchlichen Exegeten, die denselben Vers auslegen, bes. Clemens von Alexandrien, einig,[21] nur ist deren Tun ein "knechtiges", das Tun der Psychiker, wie die Valentinianer der Kirche vorwarfen.[22] Der Schriftbeleg Mt 7, 21 hat in unseren valentinianischen Quellen keine direkte Parallele. Indirekt mag man ihn finden in den Mahnungen zu einem gottgefälligen Leben, wie sie das *Evangelium der Wahrheit* in § 33 vorträgt, besonders in dem Aufruf: "Tut ihr also den Willen des Vaters, denn ihr stammt aus ihm."[23] Als Söhne, aus Liebe also, sollen die Gnostiker den Willen des Vaters tun.

Die drei besprochenen Testimonien lassen eine gewisse Parallele zwischen Naassenern und Valentinianern erkennen. Wirklich frappant wird diese aber erst beim anschließenden Jesuswort, das wie das vorgehende Bedingungen für das Eingehen in das Himmelreich nennt.[24] Wiederum,

---

[17] Der Versuch von W. C. Robinson, jun. (The Exegesis on the Soul, in: NTS 12, 1970, 102-117), einfach alle christlichen Zitate als Zusätze auszuscheiden, ist als gescheitert anzusehen, Vgl. M. Krause, Die Texte von Nag Hammadi, in: Gnosis. Festschrift für Hans Jonas, hrsg. von B. Aland, Göttingen 1978, 237.

[18] 10, 2 (102, 23-104, 3).

[19] ExAn und Naassenerpsalm müssen auch auf eine Verwandtschaft mit der Vorstellung von der irrenden Sophia und mit dem Plané-Mythos überhaupt untersucht werden.

[20] 8, 27 (94, 7-9).

[21] Clemens von Alexandrien, Strom. VII 104, 4; Quis div. salv. 29, 6.

[22] Vgl. Irenäus I 6, 1-2.4 (53-55. 57-59 Harvey).

[23] NHC I 33, 30f.

[24] Himmelreich meint dabei für den Naassener den pneumatischen Samen, den der Gnostiker in sich trägt; Eingehen in das Himmelreich ist darum für ihn gleichbedeutend

fährt der Autor fort, sprach der Erlöser: "Die Zöllner und Dirnen werden vor euch in das Himmelreich eingehen" (Mt 21, 31).[25] Zöllner und Dirnen sind ihm also Typen für den Pneumatiker. Dabei verliert er über die Dirnen hier kein weiteres Wort, offensichtlich nicht, um sie zu unterschlagen. Sonst wäre in dem Kephalaion am Anfang der Schrift sicher nicht ausdrücklich Mariamne, d.h. Maria Magdalena, als Kronzeugin der von Jesus stammenden geheimen Überlieferung genannt worden.[26] Die Dirne als Typus für die gefallene Seele hat in der Gnosis ihren festen Platz. Was der Naassener hier verkünden will, ist die Rolle der Zöllner. Darum führt er das Schriftwort Mt 21, 31 wie folgt weiter: "Die Zöllner nämlich sind diejenigen, die von allen die Abgaben empfangen. Wir aber sind die Zöllner, auf die die Geschenke der Äonen gekommen sind" (1 Kor 10, 11). Und dann gibt er die weitere Erklärung: "Geschenke sind nämlich die (geistigen) Samen, die ... in diese Welt gesät sind, durch welche die ganze Welt zur Vollendung kommt."[27] Es ist hier nicht möglich, den Text im einzelnen zu erklären. Für uns genügt das Selbstzeugnis des Naasseners, der sich als den "Zöllner" schlechthin bekennt. Das heißt aber als den, der in den Augen dieser verderblichen Welt nichts gilt, in den Augen Gottes dagegen zählt.[28]

Wir können von der frühkirchlichen, typologischen Erklärung des Jesuswortes über die Zöllner und Dirnen (Mt. 21, 31) hier absehen.[29] Hier interessiert nur die gnostische Deutung des Zöllners als Typus des Pneumatikers, die uns der Naassener liefert. Dafür bezeugt nun Irenäus, daß Markion und die Valentinianer, welche das Evangelium des Lukas teilweise ablehnen, mehrere Berichte und Gleichnisse Jesu, die wir nur aus Lukas kennen, annehmen und in ihrem Sinne ausdeuten, unter anderem auch die Worte, die der Herr an den Zöllner Zachäus gerichtet hat (Lk 19, 5) und das Gleichnis vom Pharisäer und Zöllner im Tempel (Lk 18, 10ff).[30] Wir können uns hier mit dem Hinweis begnügen, daß beide Lu-

---

mit der Wiedergeburt des Pneumatikers. Diese gnostische Deutung des Himmelreichs wird noch eigens behandelt werden.

[25] 8, 28 (94, 11-12).

[26] 7, 1 (78, 23f.).

[27] 8, 28 (78, 12-16).

[28] Es ist genau das Selbstzeugnis, das der gleiche Gnostiker am Schluß seiner lehrhaften Homilie ablegt, wo er sagt: "Es ist aber jener Mensch (d.h. der Pneumatiker) ungeschätzt in dieser Welt, aber hochgeschätzt von denen, die ihn kennen; von denen, die ihn nicht kennen, beurteilt wie ein Tropfen am Eimer (Js 40, 15) = 9, 21 (102, 8-10). Textrekonstruktion von mir.

[29] Siehe dazu Iren. IV 20, 12 (II 224f. Harvey), vgl. auch J. Frickel, "Die Zöllner, Vorbild der Demut und wahrer Gottesverehrung": Pietas, Festschrift für Bernhard Kötting, JbAC Erg. Bd. 8, Münster 1980. S. 369-380.

[30] Iren. III 14, 3 (II 78 Harvey).

kastexte von Markioniten und Valentinianern ursprünglich dualistisch auf den Guten Gott und den davon verschiedenen Schöpfergott gedeutet wurden.[31] Entscheidend ist, daß diese dualistische Deutung von Zöllner und Pharisäer zwangsläufig auch die Deutung dieser beiden als Typen für zwei Menschenklassen einschließt: der Zöllner wird dabei dem bisher unbekannten Guten Gott zugeordnet, der Pharisäer dagegen dem altbekannten Schöpfergott der Juden. Vielleicht hat diese Deutung ursprünglich nur zwei Menschenklassen anvisiert: Juden und Christen. Daß sie bei den Valentinianern die drei Menschenklassen einschließt und die Zöllner dabei generell die pneumatischen Menschen bedeuten, bezeugt Irenäus ausdrücklich in Buch I 8, 3. Danach haben die Valentinianer ihre drei Menschklassen nicht nur in den bereits erwähnten drei Stellen des 1. Korintherbriefes bezeugt gefunden, sondern auch in drei in Lukas Kap. 9 überlieferten Jesusworten. Die materielle Gattung in Lk 9, 57f., die psychische in Lk 9, 61f., das Geistige in Lk 9, 60: "Laß die Toten ihre Toten begraben, du aber geh und verkünde das Reich Gottes."[32] Die pneumatischen Menschen hat der Erlöser, heißt es dann, außerdem angezeigt, "indem er zu Zachäus, dem Zöllner sprach: "Steig eilends herab, denn heute muß ich in deinem Hause verbleiben" (Lk 19, 5). Und Irenäus fügt erklärend hinzu: "Diese nämlich, d.h. die Zöllner, seien von dem geistigen Geschlecht."[33] Der Zöllner ist also auch bei den Valentinianern Typus für das Geschlecht des pneumatischen Menschen. Damit haben wir eine enge Entsprechung zwischen Naassenern und Valentinianern festgestellt.

Wir folgen weiter der Argumentation des Naasseners über die Berufung und den Glauben des Pneumatikers, wo der vorgenannte, in die Welt gestreute Samen nun durch das Himmelreichgleichnis vom Sämann und dem Samen weiter veranschaulicht wird.[34] Im Unterschied zum kanonischen Text und auch zum Thomasevangelium Spr. 8 (9), die beide vier Beispiele über das Säen und das Geschick des Samens aufzählen, bringt der Naassener aber nur deren drei: der erste Samen fiel neben den Weg und ward zertreten; ein anderer Teil fiel auf steinigen Grund, ging zwar auf, hatte aber keine Tiefe und verdorrte; ein Teil aber fiel auf guten und rechten Boden und brachte Frucht, hundert —, sechzig — und dreißigfach.

---

[31] Iren. IV 36, 8 (II 284 Harvey); Tertullian, Adv. Marc IV, 36, 1-2 (CC I 643 Kroymann).

[32] Irenäus I 8, 3 (70f. Harvey). Im letzten Testimonium ist bereits eine gnostische Terminologie, die Scheidung der Menschen in Tote und Lebende, miteingeschlossen.

[33] Iren. I 8, 3 (71 Harvey).

[34] 8, 29 (94, 17-22). Die Textgestalt läßt Mt 13, 3-9 als direkte Vorlage vermuten.

Wir haben nur einen einzigen Textzeugen für Hippolyts *Refutatio*, doch möchte ich in den drei Samenbeispielen nicht eine beim Abschreiben unterlaufene, sondern eine bewußt gewählte Auslassung sehen. Das Gleichnis veranschaulicht dann zugleich die drei Menschenklassen, wovon eben nur die pneumatische wirklich Frucht bringt.[35] Der Naassener betont, daß es keinen Hörer dieser Geheimnisse gibt außer den vollkommenen Gnostikern. Diese allein sind nämlich die schöne und gute (Erde)", von der Moses sagt: "Ich will euch in das schöne und gute Land führen, in das Land, das von Milch und Honig fließt" (Deut. 31, 20).[36] Aber dann kommt die Erklärung: "Milch und Honig ist das, durch dessen Genuß die Vollkommenen königlos werden und am Pleroma teilhaben."[37] Wir können die einzelnen Aussagen hier nicht analysieren. Es soll nur deutlich werden, daß das exklusive Heil der Pneumatiker auch für den Naassener ein Heil in Gemeinschaft mit dem Pleroma ist, ähnlich wie bei den Valentinianern, und daß daher außerhalb des Pleroma ein Heil für die Psychiker möglich sein kann. Daß dies tatsächlich so ist, kann man wohl aus dem Kephalaion[38] entnehmen, wonach die Naassener drei Kirchen unterschieden: die engelhafte, die psychische und die stoffliche (choische), wobei die erste, also die pneumatische Kirche, die Auserwählte heißt, die psychische Kirche aber "die Berufene", worin man eben auch eine Berufung zum Heil verstehen muß.

Für die Valentinianer bezeugt Irenäus die Unterscheidung von wenigstens zwei Kirchen, der pneumatischen und der psychischen, welche mit der Großkirche identisch sein soll.[39] Für die drei Namen der Kirchen: die Auserwählte, die Berufene und die Gefangene, finden sich Parallelen in den Exzerpten ex Theodot[40] und bei Herakleon.[41] Die Lehre von den

---

[35] Das würde gut zu dem später erklärten Epitheton des Attis als "Akarpos", des Unfruchtbaren, passen, wo alle als unfruchtbar erklärt werden, die fleischlich sind, d.h. der Begierde des Fleisches frönen. Wirklich Frucht bringen nur die vernünftigen, die lebendigen Menschen, die durch das dritte Tor eingehen: 8, 31 (94, 30-95, 3). Das sind aber nur die Pneumatiker, vgl. 9, 22 (102, 14f.). Choiker und Psychiker sind demnach alle Sarkiker (Fleischliche), die keine Frucht bringen und daher auch keinen Anteil am wahren Heil haben können. Diese Interpretation muß jedoch nicht notwendig als Radikalisierung gegenüber der Heilslehre der Valentinianer verstanden werden, die auch den Psychikern eine Möglichkeit des Heils, wenn auch außerhalb des Pleromas, einräumten, vgl. Iren. I 6, 2.4; Exc. Theod. 58, 3-4; Hippolyt, Ref. VI 32, 9.

[36] 8, 29-30 (94, 22-26).

[37] 8, 30 (94, 26-28).

[38] 6, 7 (78, 20f.).

[39] Iren. I, 8, 3 (72f. Harvey).

[40] Exc. Theod. 56,2 über die drei Naturen: "Der Materiellen sind viel, nicht viele der Psychischen, selten aber sind die Pneumatischen."

[41] Vgl. Herakleon Fragm. 37 (zu Joh 13, 51). Das Testimonium Deut 31, 20 von der schönen und guten Erde findet eine eigenartige Deutung bei den Valentinianern (nach Hippol. VI 30, 9; 34, 4), auf die hier nicht eingegangen werden kann.

drei Menschenklassen findet sich ähnlich bei Naassenern und Valentinianern, während das Gleichnis vom Sämann und vom Samen, das sich
auch im Thomasevangelium findet, nur bei den Naassenern als Zeugnis
für die drei Menschklassen gedeutet zu werden scheint.[42] Die Verwen-
dung derselben neutestamentlichen Zitate oder derselben Figuren (z.B.
des Zöllners) zur Erklärung der pneumatischen Menschenklasse legt dabei die Frage nach einer direkten oder indirekten Verbindung zwischen
den beiden Gruppen nahe.

2) *Der pneumatische Same ist das Himmelreich in uns*

Von den vorgenannten Testimonien für die pneumatischen Menschen
sind drei Jesusworte, welche Bedingungen für das Eingehen in das Himmelreich nennen: man muß den Willen des Vaters tun (M 7, 21); man
muß sich (wie die Zöllner und Dirnen) aufrichtig und demütig zu Gott
bekehren (Mt 21, 31); vor allem aber muß Gott den Menschen gnaden-
haft an sich ziehen, damit er zu Jesus kommt (Joh 6, 44). Diese Auswahl
ist nicht zufällig, sondern bedingt durch das Bild vom Himmelreich.
Dieses Himmelreich ist nämlich im Menschen verborgen, ist der eigentliche Mensch im Menschen, der sog. "innere Mensch",[43] der göttliche
Same, der Pneumafunke. Ihn zu erkennen, ist der Anfang der Gottes-
erkenntnis. Dieses in uns verborgene Himmelreich ist so kostbar, daß es
allein gesucht zu werden verdient. Alles Irdische ist nur Werk des Demiurgen, das nichts, das ohne den Logos und ohne das Leben geworden
ist.[44] Dieses Himmelreich erklärt der Naassener zum ersten Mal nach der
Deutung der assyrischen und phrygischen Mysterien. Die zwei Mysterien bezeugen ihm die selige, verborgene und zugleich offenbare göttliche Natur, diese aber ist das im Menschen zu suchende Himmelreich.[45]
Hierüber überliefern sie ausdrücklich in dem nach Thomas genannten
Evangelium (folgenden Spruch): "Wer mich sucht, wird mich finden in
Kindern vom siebten Jahre an, denn dort im vierzehnten Äon verborgen
offenbare ich mich."[46] Das Jesuswort vom "Reich Gottes in euch" (Lk
17, 21) wird hier radikal vergeistigt genommen und auf das im Men-

---

[42] Ich übergehe die Lehre vom Pleroma, weil dieselbe beim Naassener zwar als bekannt
vorausgesetzt, im Text aber nur angedeutet wird und daher mehrere Deutungen zuläßt.
[43] 7, 36 (87, 22). Vgl. die ähnliche, aber subtilere Unterscheidung bei den Valentinianern (Hippol. VI 34, 7: 163, 22f.), welche Indiz für die Weiterbildung einer älteren gnostischen Deutung von Eph. 3, 16 sein könnte.
[44] 8, 5 (90, 1f.), vgl. 9, 2 (98, 7f.).
[45] 7, 20 (83, 9-13).
[46] 7, 20 (83, 13-16). Hippolyt hat den Text der Vorlage mehrfach polemisch unterbro-
chen und dadurch entstellt.

schen verborgene Göttliche, das mit dem Himmelreich gleichgesetzt wird, bezogen. Als Beleg dafür dient ein Jesuswort aus dem Thomasevangelium, das im Unterschied zu den vier kanonischen Evangelien namentlich genannt wird.[47]

Für das Wort "Reich" oder "Königreich der Himmel"[48] als ein Schlüsselwort im Thomas-Evangelium darf hier das zusammenfassende Urteil von Ernst Haenchen genügen: es ist für Thomas "nicht mehr die kommende Gottesherrschaft, welche die ersten Christen herbeisehnten! Es meint vielmehr die jenseits der Welt liegende Lichtsphäre des Göttlichen... und zugleich jenen Teil davon, den der einzelne Gnostiker verborgen in sich trägt. Diese Fassung des Reichsbegriffs ... widerspricht der großkirchlichen, und Thomas weiß das. Denn er bekämpft die Lehre vom dereinst kommenden Reich in Spruch 113."[49] Die Theologie des Naasseners über das "Himmelreich" hängt mit der des Thomasevangeliums eng zusammen.[50] Daß das Thomasevangelium auch von Valentinianern gebraucht worden sei, wird verschiedentlich angenommen,[51] kann aber hier unberücksichtigt bleiben. Was wirklich zählt, ist die Tatsache, daß die Valentinianer, genau wie die Naassener, das Himmelreich in das Innerste des Menschen selbst verlegten und mit dem pneumatischen Samen identifizierten. Das läßt sich bei den einzelnen Himmelreichgleichnissen, die der Naassener an mehreren Stellen dem Text seiner Vorlage zwecks näherer Erklärung anfügt, deutlich zeigen. Erstmals an der vorgenannten Stelle (Kap. 7, 20), wo er die zu suchende verborgene Natur des Göttlichen in den Menschen hineinverlegt. Die nächste Gelegenheit sah er bei der Erklärung des Attis als des himmlischen Mondhorns der Griechen, welches mittels des Trinkbechers des Anakreon, der

---

[47] Der Spruch selbst dürfte sich auf Logion 2 und Logion 3 des koptischen Thom. Ev. beziehen. Vgl. H. C. Puech, in Hennecke-Schneemelcher, Neutestamentl. Apokryphen I 204 Spr. 2 (Zählung nach J. Leipoldt): "...das Königreich ist inwendig in euch und außerhalb von euch...", Spr. 3: "Jesus sprach: Der alte Mann wird nicht zögern, ein kleines Kind von sieben Tagen wegen des Ortes des Lebens zu fragen, und er wird leben..." Den griechischen Text von Logion 3 diskutiert und restauriert D. Mueller, Kingdom of heaven or Kingdom of God? in: VC 27, 1973, 266-276. Dort auch einige Literatur zum Thom. Ev. Vgl. auch den Forschungsbericht von K. Rudolph, Theol. Rundschau, N.F. 34, 1969, 181-194.

[48] So Log. 20 und 113 (114).

[49] E. Haenchen, Die Botschaft des Thomas-Evangeliums (Theologische Bibliothek Töpelmann 6. Heft), Berlin 1961, 44.

[50] Vgl. auch das *Evangelium nach Maria*: "Denn der Sohn des Menschen ist in eurem Innern. Folget ihm nach! Die ihn suchen, werden ihn finden." Deutsch nach Hennecke-Schneemelcher I 252.

[51] Vgl. J. B. Bauer, Echte Jesusworte? in W. C. van Unnik, Evangelien aus dem Nilsand, Frankfurt 1959, 144f.

die Wahrheit erkennen ließ, dem Gnostiker zeigte, was er werden soll.[52]
Wasser und Wein, im Becher vermischt, sind dem Naassener ein Anlaß,
das gnostische Selbstwerden durch die Umwandlung des Wassers in
Wein bei der Hochzeit von Kana (Joh 2, 1-11) zu veranschaulichen.
"Das ist", sagt er, "der große und wahrhaftige Anfang der Zeichen,
den Jesus in Kana von Galiläa machte und (wodurch er) das Himmelreich offenbarte. Das", sagt er, "ist das Himmelreich, das wie ein
Schatz in euch liegt, wie Sauerteig, in drei Scheffel Mehl."[53] Das Wein-
wunder soll also die erste Offenbarung des Himmelreiches sein, das
1) in euch liegt (nach Lk 17, 21) und zwar verborgen 2) wie ein Schatz
(nach Mt 13, 44) oder 3) wie ein Sauerteig in drei Scheffel Mehl (nach
Mt 13, 33). Die Anwendung dieser zwei Himmelreichgleichnisse ist nur
die konsequente Weiterführung der grundlegenden Vorstellung, daß das
Göttliche im Menschen das zu suchende Himmelreich ist. Die konkrete
Anwendung der zwei Bilder ist hier demnach sekundär im Vergleich zur
Grundvorstellung vom Himmelreich im Menschen. Ebenfalls sekundär,
aber ursprünglich in der konkreten Anwendung ist dagegen das Beispiel
des Weinwunders für die Umwandlung des Menschen in Gott. Seine
Wahl ist nicht nur durch das Wasser und den Wein der Anakreonverse
verursacht, wie Reitzenstein meinte,[54] sondern setzt auch die Vorstellung von der Gottwerdung des Menschen als einer wesenhaften inneren
Verwandlung voraus.[55] Die Anakreonverse waren dem Naassener nur
der Anlaß, die gnostische Vorstellung vom Göttlichen als dem im Menschen verborgenen Himmelreich um ein neues Beispiel, eben das Weinwunder von Kana, zu vermehren. Dabei ist ihm aufgegangen, daß Jesus
durch das Weinwunder nicht nur, wie der kanonische Text sagt, "den
Anfang der Zeichen (ἡ ἀρχὴ τῶν σημείων) machte und (dadurch) seine
Herrlichkeit offenbarte" (Joh 2, 11), sondern daß er mit diesem ersten
Zeichen das Himmelreich (τὴν βασιλείαν τῶν οὐρανῶν) offenbarte. Darum
hat er den Johannestext verändert[56] und, was noch interessanter ist, eine
ganz neue Interpretation der johanneischen Semeia geschaffen. Ausdrücklich nennt er darum das Weinwunder "*den großen und wahrhafti-
gen Anfang* der Zeichen, den Jesus machte in Kana von Galiläa und (da-

---

[52] 8, 4-7 (89, 24-90, 16).

[53] 8, 7-8 (90, 17-22).

[54] Poimandres 101 Anm. 4: "Der Christ fügt wegen der Erwähnung von Wein und
Wasser den übel gelungenen Verweis auf die Hochzeit zu Kana ein."

[55] Eine Vorstellung, die uns auch aus dem Apophasisbericht bekannt ist: Hippol. VI 16,
5 (142, 16-19); 17, 5-7 (143, 16-144, 4).

[56] 8, 7 (90, 20).

durch) das Himmelreich offenbarte.''[57] Folglich muß der Naassener auch die anderen Zeichen (Semeia) so erkannt haben: als Offenbarung des im Menschen verborgenen Himmelreiches. Diese Theologie der Semeia hat er im vorgegebenen Rahmen des Attiskommentars nicht durchführen können, sie ist aber notwendig vorausgesetzt.[58]

Damit kommen wir zu den Valentinianern und ihrer Deutung des Göttlichen im Menschen als das Himmelreich. Diese ergibt sich zunächst indirekt aus den Schriftworten, die sie nach dem Zeugnis von Irenäus I 8, 3 für die psychische und die pneumatische Menschenklasse anführen. Die Psychiker hat der Erlöser angezeigt, indem er dem, der ihm sagte: "Ich will dir folgen, gestatte mir erst, Abschied zu nehmen von denen zu Hause", antwortete: "Niemand, der seine Hand an den Pflug legt und zurücksieht, ist geeignet für das Himmelreich" (Lk 9, 61). Der Psychiker geht also nicht ins Himmelreich ein. Die Pneumatiker hat er angezeigt, indem er sagte: "Laß die Toten ihre Toten begraben, du aber geh hin und verkünde das Reich Gottes" (Lk 9, 60).[59] Der Pneumatiker kennt also das Reich Gottes und ist außerdem berufen, dieses weiter zu verkünden. Vielleicht ist nicht sofort einsichtig, daß diesen zwei Testimonien bereits die Vorstellung des Göttlichen als des im Menschen verborgenen Himmelreiches zugrundeliegt. Das wird jedoch durch die weiteren Ausführungen des Irenäus deutlich. Denn: "Auch das Gleichnis von dem Sauerteig, den die Frau unter die drei Scheffel Mehl verbarg, offenbart nach ihnen die drei Arten von Menschen. Das Weib soll die Sophia bedeuten, die drei Scheffel Mehl aber die drei Arten von Menschen: Pneumatiker, Psychiker und Choiker. Der Sauerteig soll der Hei-

---

[57] 7, 7 (90, 19f.). Aus Exc. Theod. 65, 1 wissen wir, daß die Valentinianer das Weinwunder ebenfalls allegorisch deuteten. Die dortigen Spekulationen über den Speisemeister, der nichts wußte (Joh 2, 9), wie auch über den Freund des Bräutigams, der draußen vor dem Brautgemach steht und sich über die Stimme des Bräutigams freut (Joh 3, 29), können wir für den Naassener nicht überprüfen.

[58] Wir wissen nicht, ob der Naassener einen eigenen Traktat verfaßt hat, welcher die johanneischen Semeia als Offenbarungen des im Menschen verborgenen Himmelreiches deutete, doch ist mit dieser Möglichkeit zu rechnen. Die Semeia-Theologie des Naasseners kommt übrigens in seinem Kommentar mehrfach deutlich zum Ausdruck. So das Brotwunder (Joh 6, 1-14) als Zeichen für das Himmelreich, indem das Trinken des Blutes und das Essen des Fleisches Christi als Bedingung für das Eingehen in das Himmelreich umgedeutet wird: 8, 11 (91, 6-8). Die Heilung des Blindgeborenen am Sabbat (Joh 9, 1-41) wird zum Typus des gnostischen Erkennens: 9, 20 (102, 1f.). Auch die von Moses in der Wüste erhöhte Schlange als Zeichen der lebenspendenden Erhöhung des Erlösers am Kreuz (Joh 3, 14) ist wahrscheinlich in dem Passus über die Wiedergeburt (7, 40:88, 23-26) vorausgesetzt.

[59] Irenäus I 8, 3 (71 Harvey).

land selbst sein.''[60] Diese Exegese wird noch weiter ausgedeutet: Sie lehren, ''daß der Heiland von dem, was er retten wollte, die Erstlinge
annahm, habe Paulus gesagt: »Wenn die Erstlinge heilig sind, so ist es
auch die Teigmasse« (Röm 11, 16). Der Erstling bedeutet nach ihnen das
Geistige (Pneumatische), die Teigmasse sind wir, d.h. die psychische
Kirche, von der er die Teigmasse angenommen und mit sich emporgeho-
ben hat, weil er selbst der Sauerteig war.''[61] Die Valentinianer des Irenäus haben also das Himmelreichgleichnis vom Sauerteig zur Erklärung
der drei Menschenklassen benützt und bis in die Einzelheiten ausgedeutet. Die hier überlieferte Exegese weicht von der naassenischen insofern
ab, als sie Christus und die Rettung der Pneumatiker durch diesen erklären will, der Naassener dagegen individuell die Rettung des einzelnen
Menschen im Auge hat. Nach ihm bedeutet der Sauerteig den im Menschen verborgenen göttlichen Samen, nach den Valentinianern des Irenäus ist es der Erlöser selbst. Die drei Scheffel Mehl sind daher nach
ihnen die drei Arten von Menschen, nach dem Naassener dürften sie dagegen die drei Substanzen bedeuten, die jeder Mensch besitzt: das Noeti-
sche (Verständige), das Psychische (Seelische) und das Choische (Stoffliche), ähnlich wie der Erlöser selbst diese drei Substanzen angenommen
hat.[62] Die Valentinianer der *Excerpta aus Theodot* haben ebenfalls ihre
Deutung des Sauerteigs. Nach *Exc. 2, 1-2* erklären sie den Schöpfungsbericht so, daß bei der Bildung des psychischen Leibes ''in die auserwählte Seele, als sie schlief, vom Logos der männliche Same hineinge-
legt worden sei, ... der von den Engeln kommt... Und dieser (Same)
wirkte wie ein Sauerteig (ἐζύμωσεν), indem er, was geteilt zu sein schien,
vereinig e, nämlich die Seele und das Fleisch, die auch geteilt von der
Sophia h rvorgebracht worden waren. Der Same war ein Ausfluß des
Männlichen und Engelhaften. Darum sagt der Heiland: ''Rette dich und
deine Seele (vgl. Gen 19, 17 u. Lk 17, 28-33).[63] Aus dem letzten Zitat
geht hervor, daß der von den Engeln stammende pneumatische Same
was wahre Ich des Menschen ist. Dieser Same wirkte wie ein Sauerteig.
Seine Wirkung erstreckt sich auf die Seele und das Fleisch, die er, da sie
geteilt waren, vereinigte. Wir können den Passus hier nicht analysieren.
Wichtig ist, daß auch diese Valentinianer den pneumatischen Samen mit
dem Sauerteig verglichen, auch wenn das Fragment nicht sagt, ob die
geteilten Substanzen Seele und Leib mit den drei Scheffeln Mehl in Ver-

---

[60] Irenäus I 8, 3 (72 Harvey).
[61] Irenäus I 8, 3 (72f. Harvey).
[62] 6, 7 (78, 15-19).
[63] Exc. Theod. 2, 1-2 (GCS 17 = 3. Clemens, 105f. Staehlin).

bindung gebracht wurden. Aufschlußreich ist auch Excerpt 1,3, das F. Sagnard wegen der Wir-Form des Verbums dem Theodot abgesprochen und dem Klemens selbst zugewiesen hat.[64] Inhalt und Terminologie des Abschnittes sind jedoch typisch gnostisch, was sowohl die Excerpte 2 und 3, wie auch die Naassener deutlich zeigen.[65] Im Kontext geht es um den pneumatischen Samen, das Geschlecht der Auserwählten (vgl. Exc. 1, 1-2), von dem der gnostische Lehrer selbst, nicht Klemens, in der Wir-Form erklärt: "Den auserwählten Samen nennen wir auch den vom Logos[66] zum Leben gebrachten Funken und Pupille des Auges und Senfkorn und Sauerteig, der das, was geteilt zu sein schien, auf den Glauben hin einte."[67] Gehört dieser § 3 wie die vorangehenden §§ 1 und 2 zur Lehre Theodots, — woran ich persönlich nicht zweifle —, so haben wir hier ein klares Zeugnis, daß diese valentinianische Richtung den pneumatischen Samen als das Himmelreich im Menschen verstand und, wie die Naassener, die verschiedenen Symbole der synoptischen Himmelreichgleichnisse in diesem Sinne deutete. Ausdrücklich werden das Senfkorn und der Sauerteig genannt.[68]

---

[64] F. Sagnard, Clément d'Alexandrie, Extraits de Théodote. Texte grec, introduction et notes. SC 23, Paris 1948, S. 9 und 55 Anm. 6. Auch W. Foerster hat in seiner deutschen Übersetzung der Exzerpte den Passus ausgelassen, in: C. Andresen (Hrsg.), Die Gnosis, Bd. I (Zürich-Stuttgart 1969) 288. Sagnard sieht in dem φαμέν, das in Exc. 1, 3 (III 105, 12 Stählin) und am Anfang von Exc. 8, 1 (III 108, 20 Stählin) vorkommt, ein Kriterium für eine persönliche Anmerkung des Klemens. Aber in 8, 1 hebt Klemens die kirchliche Lehre deutlich von der gnostischen ab: ἡμεῖς δὲ ... φαμέν. Nicht so in 1,3, das den letzten Satz von 1, 2 weiterführt bzw. erläutert. Die lateinische Übersetzung von Migne (PG IX 654) hat diesen Zusammenhang richtig erfaßt: (1, 2)'' Sic omne semen spirituale, electos nempe, voce praedicta commendat: (1, 3) electum semen vocamus (φαμέν) scintillam a Verbo vivificandam, et oculi pupillam et senapis granum et fermentum (ζύμην) ...''. Excerpt 1, 1-3 ist ein Zitat aus einer Schrift Theodots.

[65] O. Dibellius, Studien zur Geschichte der Valentinianer (ZNW 9, 1908, 230-247) sieht die Exzerpte 1-3 als eine Einheit, die sich dadurch abheben, "daß sie den himmlischen Erlöser schlechtweg — nicht nur gelegentlich und beiläufig — als Logos bezeichnen" (S. 242).

[66] Vgl. Anm. 65.

[67] Exc. Theod. 1, 3 (III 105, 12-14 Stählin).

[68] Die Vorstellung vom Funken, den der Logos belebt, begegnet ebenso in Exc. 3, 1.2 (III 106, 9f. 12 Stählin) und in der Apophasis (Ref. VI 17, 7: 144, 1-4). Das Bild von der Pupille des Auges (vgl. Deut. 23, 10) verwenden die Doketen analog für den aus dem Pleroma herabkommenden, in dieser Welt verborgenen Erlöser (Hippol., Ref. VIII 10, 4: 230, 4-8). Die Sethianer Hippolyts veranschaulichen durch das gleiche Bild den in der Finsternis der Materie gefangenen Pneumafunken (Hippol., Ref. V 19, 7: 117, 17-19). Diese sethianische Vorstellung, d.h. das von der Lichtwelt erhellte, in der Nacht des Mutterschosses gefangene Pneuma, könnte am ehesten zu dem Vergleich mit der Pupille des Auges geführt haben. Die Anwendung bei den Doketen wäre demgegenüber sekundär, während sie bei Theodot überdies eine Weiterführung der Himmelreichbilder ist.

Von diesen Himmelreichbildern scheint das Gleichnis vom Senfkorn das am besten geeignete zu sein, um das Wachsen des göttlichen Samens im Menschen zu veranschaulichen. Das wird bei der einfachen Erwähnnung des Senfkorns bei Theodot nicht sofort einsichtig, wohl aber bei dem Naassener, der dieses Bild in Kap. 9, 6 ebenfalls verwendet. Im Kontext geht es um die Deutung des Attis als Weltseele, nach der jede Natur gemäß ihrer Eigenart strebt. Sie ist das weltbelebende göttliche Prinzip, das unter vielen Namen von den Menschen verehrt wird.[69] Es ist dies der organische Schluß und Höhepunkt des ursprünglichen Kommentars, der dann jedoch plötzlich umgedeutet und, typisch gnostisch, in die innerste Mitte des Menschen verlagert wird. Dies geschieht mittels eines umfangreichen Zitats aus der gnostischen Offenbarungsschrift, der *Apophasis Megale*, welches das Göttliche Allprinzip, "die große Kraft" (ἡ μεγάλη δύναμις), als Wurzel des Alls offenbart, aus der alles entspringt: Überhimmlisches, Himmlisches, Irdisches; Seiendes, Nichtseiendes u.s.w.[70] Diese göttliche Kraft liegt nach der Apophasis in jedem Menschen als eine unbegrenzte Möglichkeit verborgen. Zunächst liegt sie dort als reine geistige Möglichkeit, real ist sie eigentlich nichts, ähnlich wie der unteilbare Punkt in der Geometrie, von dem aus jedoch das Kleinste anfängt allmählich zu wachsen und zum Körper wird. Wie er, wird auch das Göttliche durch seine eigene Einsicht eine unbegreifliche Größe.[71] Hier nun, bei dem unteilbaren Punkt als Bild für das Göttliche im Menschen, fügt der Naassener hinzu: "Dieser ist das Himmelreich, das Senfkorn, der unteilbare Punkt, der im Körper ist, den niemand kennt als die Pneumatiker allein."[72] Es ist die für ihn und die Valentinianer typische Lehre vom Himmelreich in uns, aber die konkrete Anwendung hier ist einmalig und in höchstem Maße passend: wie der Punkt zunächst das Kleinste ist, aber wächst, bis er eine Größe, ein Körper im Raum wird, so ist auch das Senfkorn nach dem Jesuswort das Kleinste von allen Samenkörnern, aber es wächst und wird größer als alle anderen Kräuter und wird ein Baum, so daß die Vögel des Himmels kommen und in seinen Zweigen wohnen (Mt 13, 32 par.).

Die Entsprechung zwischen dem Punkt der Apophasis und dem synoptischen Himmelreichgleichnis ist so gelungen, daß man sich unwill-

---

[69] 9, 3.4 (98, 8f. 14-16).

[70] 9, 5 (98, 16-22).

[71] 9, 5 (98, 22-24). Vgl. dieselbe Lehre im Apophasisbericht, Ref. VI 14, 6 (140, 4-6). Das Beispiel mit dem unteilbaren Punkt erklärt Hippolyt nach einer neupythagoreischen Vorlage in Buch VI 23, 3 (150, 6-10).

[72] 9, 6 (98, 25-99, 2).

kürlich fragt, ob hier nicht der eigentliche Sitz im Leben für die gnostische Anwendung der Himmelreichgleichnisse ist. Man darf vermuten,
daß das Gleichnis vom Senfkorn das erste war, das in gnostischen Kreisen auf das Göttliche und sein Wachstum im Menschen angewandt wurde, und zwar eben dort, wo das Göttliche im Menschen nach der *Apophasis* durch den unteilbaren Punkt vorgestellt wurde. Mit anderen
Worten: dort, wo simonianisch orientierte Gnosis[73] anfing, christliches
Gedankengut zu adaptieren, dort wurde nach aller Wahrscheinlichkeit
das Bild von Senfkorn erstmals auf das Göttliche im Menschen angewandt und dieses Göttliche damit als das Himmelreich im Menschen
bestimmt. War dieser Schritt einmal getan, dann war es nur folgerichtig,
auch die anderen Bilder vom Himmelreich entsprechend anzuwenden,
so wie es Naassener und Valentinianer bezeugen.

Der hier vorgelegte Versuch, die gnostische Deutung des Himmelreiches genetisch zu erklären, besagt jedoch nicht notwendig, daß der
Naassener als erster den unteilbaren Punkt der Apophasis als das Senfkorn und als das Himmelreich gedeutet hätte. Das von ihm beanspruch-
te exklusive Wissen[74] bezieht sich primär auf die Kenntnis des im Körper
verborgenen Göttlichen und erst sekundär auf die Identität von Punkt
und Himmelreich. Seine Spekulation über die johanneischen Semeia als
Offenbarung des Himmelreiches (Kap 8, 7f.) läßt sich außerdem nur als
Fortbildung einer schon als bekannt vorausgesetzten Spekulation über
die synoptischen Himmelreichgleichnisse verstehen. Die Identifikation
des Punktes mit dem Senfkorn und dem Himmelreich ist also schon vor
ihm gemacht worden, vielleicht in der Gnosis der älteren Naassener,
welche die Apophasis gekannt und weitergedeutet haben. Der letzte
Kommentator hat diese ursprüngliche Anwendung in seinem Zusatz
zum Attiskommentar nur überliefert. Diese Genese ist jedoch
aufschlußreich für das Verhältnis zum Valentinianismus. Sie läßt nämlich vermuten, daß die gnostische Deutung der Himmelreichgleichnisse
relativ alt ist und auch der valentinianischen Gnosis vorauslag. Diese
begründete Vermutung erhält eine Bestätigung durch das Himmelreichgleichnis von der Perle (Mt 13, 45f.), das unser Naassener folgerichtig
ebenfalls auf die Pneumatiker anwendet. Diese sind nach ihm die einzig
wahren Menschen, die von oben stammenden Perlen, die in das irdische

---

[73] Die Apophasis Megale war nach den Informationen Hippolyts in Kreisen der simonianischen Gnosis beheimatet und wurde von dem Exegeten, dessen *Paraphrase zur Apophasis* Hippolyt in Buch VI 9, 3-18, 7 wiedergibt, Simon selbst zugeschrieben; vgl. VI 18, 1
(144, 9f.).

[74] 9, 6 (99, 1f.).

Gebilde herabgeworfenen Früchte.[75] Von ihnen gilt das Wort des Erlösers: "Werfet das Heilige nicht den Hunden und die Perlen nicht den
Schweinen vor" (Mt 7, 6).[76] Nach Epiphanius hat Basilides dieses
Schriftwort ganz ähnlich gebraucht.[77] Sollte das zutreffen — und wir
haben keinen Grund, Epiphanius hier zu mißtrauen —, dann haben wir
hier ein Indiz für die frühe Verbreitung der gnostischen Deutung des
Himmelreiches. Wir dürfen diese Exegese dann so früh ansetzen, daß sie
sowohl Basilides als auch Valentin vorauslag; damit kommen wir an den
Anfang des 2. Jahrhunderts. Die zwischen Naasenern und Valentinianern festgestellte Übereinstimmung in der Himmelreichdeutung braucht
demnach keine direkte Abhängigkeit zwischen beiden Gruppen zu besagen, sondern kann sich so erklären, daß beide Gruppen (und ähnlich
auch Basilides) von einer älteren, bereits verchristlichten Gnosis
beeinflußt wurden.

3. *Einige Parallelen in der Auslegung des Johannesevangeliums*

a) Das göttliche Weltprinzip und die Exegese von Joh 1, 1-4

Auffällig ist zunächst, wie der Naasener die Verse 3 und 4 aus dem
Johannesprolog auf das Weltprinzip anwendet. Zunächst am Beginn
von Kap. 8 bei der Deutung des Attis als himmlisches Mondhorn, das allen alles durcheinandermischte. Dann folgt die zusätzliche Erklärung:
"Denn alles ist durch ihn geworden, und ohne ihn ist nichts geworden.
Was aber *in ihm* geworden ist, ist Leben" (Joh 1, 3-4).[78] Und weiter:
"Dies ist das Leben, das unaussprechliche Geschlecht der vollkommenen Menschen, das den früheren Geschlechtern unbekannt war (vgl.
Eph 3, 5)."[79] Die zweite Deutung erinnert sehr an Herakleon, Fragm.
2 (zu Joh 1, 4): "Was in ihm geworden ist, war Leben", hat er (= Herakleon), "statt »in ihm« auf die pneumatischen Menschen gedeutet,
gleich als ob der Logos und die Pneumatiker dasselbe seien."[80] Ähnlich,

---

[75] 8, 32 (95, 4-6)..

[76] 8, 33 (95, 7-8). Das Perlengleichnis klingt auch in 9, 21 (102, 9) an, wo der pneumatische Mensch als hochgeschätzt oder kostbar (πολύτιμος) charakterisiert wird, vgl. Mt 13,
46.

[77] Epiphanius, Pan. 24, 5, 2 (GCS 25 = I. Epiph. 262, 7-10 Holl): Es sagt der Gaukler
(= Basilides): "Wir", sagt er, "sind die Menschen, die anderen alle sind Schweine und
Hunde." Und darum hat er (= Jesus) gesagt: "Werfet eure Perlen nicht vor die Schweine
und gebt das Heilige nicht den Hunden." Siehe auch die Parabel vom Perlenverkäufer
(Christus) in den Petrusakten (NHC VI, 1 p. 3-4).

[78] 8, 5 (89, 26-27).

[79] 8, 5 (89, 27-90, 1).

[80] Herakleon, Frgm. 2 (64, 28-31 Völker).

wenn auch exakter, ist die von Irènäus I 8, 5 überlieferte Exegese von
Joh 1, 3-4: "Alles ist durch ihn geworden und ohne ihn ist nichts geworden... Was aber in ihm geworden ist, ist Leben. Damit weist er auf die
Paarungsgemeinschaft (συζυγίαν) hin. Denn er sagte, daß alles durch ihn
geworden ist, das Leben aber in ihm... Denn es ist mit ihm zusammen,
und durch ihn bringt es Frucht."[81] Ähnlich auch Excerpt 6, 4 aus Theodot: "Was in ihm, dem Logos, geworden ist, war Leben (Joh 1, 4), (das
meint) die Paargenossin (ἡ σύζυγος); darum sagt der Herr auch: "Ich bin
das Leben" (Joh 11, 25; 14, 6).[82] Es wird hier genauer unterschieden
zwischen dem Leben als Paargenossin des Logos (ἡ ζωή) und dem Leben
als den pneumatischen Menschen, eben den allein Lebendigen. Die
Figur der Zoê wird von den Valentinianern aus dem Johannesprolog ab-
geleitet. Diese Ableitung ist jedoch nicht ursprünglich, denn Zoê ist primär nur der griechische Name für Eva, die nach Gen 3, 20 "die Mutter
aller Lebendigen" ist. Zugrunde liegt der Zoê eine Spekulation über die
ersten Kapitel von Buch Genesis, die am deutlichsten in einem Lehrstück der Peraten sichtbar wird.[83] Zoê ist die Urmutter Eva, die
ursprünglich in Adam, dem ersten Menschen, war und durch diesen die
drei Menschen gebar, von denen alle Menschen abstammen. Diese ältere
Deutung ist eine Hilfe, um die Lehre des Naasseners besser zu verstehen.
In der oben zitierten Deutung des Lebens (Kap 8, 5) findet sich nämlich
weder ein Hinweis auf die Zoê als Paargenossin des Logos noch auf die
Figur der Eva-Zoê. Das erklärt sich aus dem Interesse des Kommenta-
tors, dem es im Kontext primär um die Gottwerdung des Menschen geht
und nicht um die Abstammung von Eva. Daß er die Figur der Mutter
(Eva-Zoê) jedoch kennt und hier voraussetzt, ergibt sich aus Kap. 7, 39,
wo die Gottwerdung nach alttestamentlicher Typologie als Flucht aus
Ägypten und Zug durch das Rote Meer versinnbildlicht wird. Dieser
Weg in die Wüste (εἰς τὸν ἔρημον) bedeutet den Auszug aus den irdischen
Begierden hinauf nach dem Jerusalem oben, welches eben "die Einsa-
me" ist, die zur "Mutter der Lebendigen" wird.[84] Diese Mutter ist niemand anderes als Eva, die hier ähnlich wie Gal 4, 26 als das obere, das
himmlische Jerusalem gedeutet wird, aber nicht mehr als Mutter *aller* le-
benden Wesen überhaupt, sondern gnostisch eingeengt als Mutter nur

---

[81] Iren. haer. I 8, 5 (77f. Harvey). Die Vorliebe der Valentinianer für das Johannesevangelium hat Irenäus (III 11, 7) mit deren Interesse für die Paargemeinschaften zu erklären versucht.

[82] Exc. Theod. 6, 4 (III 107, 24-26 Stählin).

[83] Hippol. Ref. V 16, 12 (113, 11-17).

[84] 7, 39 (88, 16-20); vgl. 8, 36 (95, 23-25).

der *lebendigen* Menschen, welche allein die Pneumatiker sind, genau
wie an der oben zitierten Stelle in Kap. 8, 5.[85] Naassener und Peraten
deuten also Joh 1, 3-4 ähnlich, aber nicht gleich wie die Valentinianer.
Ihre Spekulationen über Eva als Mutter der Lebendigen und über Edem
als Mutter[86] lassen vermuten, daß sie auf einer älteren, der valentinianischen vorausliegenden Gnosis aufbauen.[87] Dieser Eindruck wird bestätigt durch die zweite Stelle, an der unser Naassener Joh 1, 3 zitiert. Im
Kontext geht es um Attis als Sproß des Amygdalos, des Mandelbaumes,
in Kap. 9, 1-2. Dieser Sproß war zunächst im Innern des Allvaters und
wurde dann aus dem Vater als dessen unsichtbarer Sohn (παῖς) erzeugt,[88]
"durch den", heißt es, "das All wurde und ohne den nichts wurde"
(Joh 1, 3).[89] Diese Anwendung ist parallel zu der in Kap. 8, 5 und erinnert zunächst an die valentinianischen Exegesen desselben Verses.[90] Bei
näherer Prüfung zeigen sich jedoch wesentliche Unterschiede. Es ist hier
nicht möglich, auf die valentinianischen Exegesen im einzelnen einzuge-
hen. Typisch für sie ist jedoch, daß sie in den zwei ersten Versen des
Prologs *drei* göttliche Größen unterscheiden: Gott, den Anfang und das
Wort,[91] wobei das Wort ursprünglich im Anfang (d.h. im Sohn) war
und dieser seinerseits im Vater. Diese typisch valentinianische
Unterscheidung[92] fehlt bei den Naassenern. Sie unterscheiden in Kap. 9,
2 und Kap. 8, 5 nur *zwei* göttliche Größen: den Vater des Alls, der auch
der προών, der Vor-Seiende genannt wird,[93] und dessen Sohn, den Unsichtbaren, welcher der in Attis vorgebildete Menschensohn ist, von
dem die Naassenerschrift handelt.[94] Durch diesen Sohn "wurde das All

---

[85] Gegen diese Einengung der universalen Mutterfunktion der Eva scheint sich der Verfasser des oben (Anm. 83) zitierten peratischen Lehrstücks zu wenden, vgl. Hipp. V 16, 13
(113, 15-18). Eine ähnlich universalistische Vorstellung liegt auch der allegorischen Exegese der vier Paradiesflüsse (Gen 2, 10-14) in Kap. 9, 14-20 (101, 1-102, 8) zugrunde. Der
Strom (d.h. die Schlange), der *aus Edem* ausgeht und sich in vier Ursprünge spaltete (9,
15: 101, 5-7), ist das Weltprinzip (der Logos), das allen Dingen Sein und Leben mitteilt.
Wir kommen hier mit einer Genesisspekulation über Edem und Eva in Berührung, welche
unabhängig ist von der valentinianischen Ableitung der Zoê aus dem Johannesprolog,
wohl aber dieser genetisch vorausliegen könnte.

[86] Siehe Anm. 85.

[87] Diese Spekulation ist auch bei dem Gnostiker Justin greifbar: Hippol. V 26, 1-2 (126,
29-127, 5); ebenso im ApokJoh (BG 38, 11f.) und bei den Ophiten (Iren. haer. I 30, 1).

[88] 9, 1-2 (97, 24-98, 3).

[89] 9, 2 (98, 7-8).

[90] Nach Iren. haer. I 8, 5-6 (75-80 Harvey); Exc. Theod. 6 (III Clemens 107f. Stählin)
und Fragm. 1-2 aus Herakleon (63-65 Völker).

[91] Besonders klar bei Iren. haer. I 8, 5 (76f. Harvey).

[92] Zu der als vierte göttliche Größe noch der Mensch (Anthropos) kommt.

[93] 9, 1 (97, 24-26), vgl. X 9, 1 (268, 12f.).

[94] 9, 1 (98, 2f.).

und ohne ihn wurde nichts." Dieser ist in der Sicht des Naasseners demnach der Logos des Johannesprologs.[95] Auch die Peraten haben in den
ersten zwei Versen des Johannesprologs nur zwei göttliche Größen unterschieden: den Vater, den sie als einziges Prinzip, als eine große Quelle
verstanden,[96] und den Sohn, den Logos, die immer sich bewegende
Schlange.[97] Peraten wie Naassener bezeugen damit, daß es im 2. Jh. eine
Exegese der zwei ersten Verse des Johannesprologs gegeben hat, die ein-
facher und weniger subtil als die der Valentinianer gewesen ist. Diese
Exegese läßt sich nicht als naassenische oder peratische Anleihe bei den
Valentinianern verstehen. Die Annahme ist begründet, daß sie der
valentinianischen Exegese zeitlich und vielleicht auch genetisch voraus-
liegt.

b) Das von Jesus verheißene "lebendige Wasser" (Joh 4, 10.14)

Das vierte Kapitel des Johannesevangeliums hat auf die christlichen
Gnostiker eine besondere Anziehung ausgeübt. Besonders das lebendige
Wasser, das Jesus zu geben versprach (Joh 4, 10), hat ihre Spekulation
befruchtet. Der Naassener kommt bei der Allegorie über die vier Paradiesflüsse, genauer bei dem vierten Fluß Euphrat, darauf zu sprechen.
Dieser bedeutet ihm das vierte Sinnesorgan, den Mund, durch den das
Gebet ausgeht und die Nahrung eingeht, die den pneumatischen, den
vollkommenen Menschen erfreut, nährt und kennzeichnet.[98] Dieser die
geistige Nahrung meinende Euphrat hat aber noch eine andere Bedeutung: er ist das im Schöpfungsbericht (Gen 1, 7) genannte Wasser über
dem Firmament, von dem überdies noch gilt, was der Heiland zu der Sa-
mariterin am Jakobsbrunnen gesagt hat: "Wenn du wüßtest, wer der
ist, der dich (um Wasser) bittet, würdest du ihn bitten, und er würde dir
lebendiges Wasser, das sprudelt, zu trinken geben" (Joh 4, 10.14).[99]
Hier sind drei verschiedene Deutungen verschmolzen, was immer

---

[95] Daß er auch den Terminus ἀρχή des Prologs gedeutet und sinngemäß auf den Vorsei-
enden angewandt hat, können wir vermuten. Jedenfalls unterschied er den Anthropos, das
erste Prinzip des Alls (ἡ πρώτη τῶν ὅλων ἀρχή) und den Sohn des Anthropos, den er folglich
als zweites Prinzip des Alls (ἡ δευτέρα ἀρχή) verstanden hat.

[96] V 12, 2 (104, 16-18).

[97] V 17, 1-2 (114, 15-18); vgl. die Deutung von Joh 1, 1-4 (V 16, 12: 113, 8-14). Auch
das koptisch überlieferte, "Unbekannte altgnostische Werk" (Kap 7) bezieht Joh 1, 1.3.4
auf den Eingeborenen, den Nous, welcher der Logos ist. (Koptisch-gnostische Schriften,
Bd. 1 GCS 45 (13), Berlin² 1954, S. 343, 26-31 Schmidt).

[98] 9, 18 (101, 19-21).

[99] 9, 18 (101, 23f.). Mit diesem Mischzitat zieht der Verfasser zwei Eigenschaften des
Wassers, lebendig und sprudelnd, zusammen.

anzeigt, daß eine ältere Allegorie weiterentwickelt wird. Wir können
diesen Sachverhalt bei dem Gnostiker Justin überprüfen, der in seinem
Buch *Baruch* dieselbe Exegese, jedoch mit nur zwei Allegorien liefert.
Auch bei ihm trinkt der Einzuweihende vom lebendigen Wasser, das
Reinigung ist, Quelle lebendigen, sprudelnden Wassers.[100] Auch bei ihm
bedeutet dieses Wasser zugleich das Wasser oberhalb des Firmamentes
(Gen 1, 7), das lebendige Wasser des Guten, in dem sich die pneumatischen, lebendigen Menschen abwaschen.[101] Auch Justin kontaminiert
das lebendige und das sprudelnde Wasser von Joh 4, 10.14, aber er
kennt daneben nur die zweite Allegorie vom Wasser über dem Firmament, das ihm geistiger Trank und zugleich das Wasser für die pneumatische Taufe ist.[102] Reinigungsbad und Trinken des Lebenswassers gehen
in dieser offensichtlich schon traditionellen gnostischen Exegese, die
Joh 4, 10.14 kontaminiert, zusammen,[103] welche von dem Naassener
nur weiter auf den Paradiesfluß Euphrat ausgedehnt wird.[104] Bei den
Valentinianern ist nur die Exegese Herakleons zu Joh 4 erhalten geblieben.[105] Soweit wir aus den Stücken von Fragment 17 (zu Joh 4, 12-15)
ersehen können, hielt sich seine allegorische Deutung nur an den Johannestext, ohne das Wasser über dem Firmament oder das Sondergut des
Naasseners, den Euphratfluß, zu berühren. Wir können diesen negati-
ven Befund bei Herakleon nicht absolut setzen, einmal weil wir nur
weniges über seine Exegese zur Stelle erfahren, dann auch, weil wir die
Exegese anderer Valentinianer nicht kennen. Doch könnte dieser Befund ein Indiz dafür sein, daß keine direkte Verbindung zwischen der
Johannesexegese des Naasseners und der Herakleons bestand, sondern
beide darin in verschiedenen älteren Traditionen standen. Daß diese
Traditionen trotzdem sich sehr nahe standen, zeigt die letzte Exegese,
die hier noch kurz besprochen werden soll.

---

[100] V 27, 2 (133, 6f.).

[101] V 27, 3 (133, 7-12).

[102] Diese baptismale Deutung des Wassers über dem Firmament ist das Echo einer
platonisierenden frühchristlichen Spekulation, die sich auch in den *Eclogae propheticae*
(Eccl. 8, 1-2 = GCS III Clemens 138, 33-139, 7 Stählin) findet; vgl. Exc. Theod. 81, 2-3
(III Clemens 132, 3-9 Stählin).

[103] Auch bei den Sethianern Hippolyts muß der Pneumatiker abgewaschen werden und
den Becher des "lebendigen, sprudelnden Wassers" trinken, wenn er die Knechtsgestalt
ablegen und das himmlische Kleid anziehen will: V 19, 21 (120, 24-121, 2). Ähnlich die
Pistis Sophia, Kap. 141 (242, 35-243, 2 Schmidt).

[104] Die von dem Naassener an den Euphrat angefügte "spirituelle" Ausdeutung erweist
sich damit zugleich als ein Zusatz zu einer Allegorie der vier Paradiesflüsse, die ursprünglich die universale Belebung durch das Allprinzip veranschaulichen sollte.

[105] Herakleon, Fragm. 17 (71f. Völker).

c) Die Anbetung in Geist und Wahrheit (Joh 4, 23)

Die Deutung des Naasseners erscheint bei der Erklärung des bereits genannten letzten Epitheton des Attis als Sohn des Amygdalos. Diesen Sohn nennen die Phrygier Syriktas (Flötenspieler), weil er ein harmonischer Geist (Pneuma) ist.[106] Dann folgt die Erklärung: "Denn »Gott ist Geist; darum werden die wahren Anbeter weder auf diesem Berge noch in Jerusalem anbeten, sondern im Geiste« (Joh 4, 21. 23. 24 kontaminiert). Denn pneumatisch ist die Anbetung der Vollkommenen, nicht fleischlich (πνευματικὴ ... οὐ σαρκική)."[107] In zwei knappen Sätzen faßt der Naassener die ihm wesentlichen Aussagen des Johannestextes zusammen, die den Kern seiner christlichen Gnosis wiedergeben: Gott ist Geist; deshalb sind nur *die* wahre Anbeter Gottes, die ihn im Geiste anbeten. Das heißt: allein die Pneumatiker, kein Psychiker und kein Choiker, denn diese sind alle Fleischliche (Sarkiker), die Gott nicht kennen. Das ist der typisch gnostische Exklusivanspruch, der den Johannestext in die Alternative preßt: entweder Gott im Geiste anbeten, oder im Fleische, d.h. den wahren Gott nicht anbeten.

Diese Exegese stimmt ganz mit der Herakleons überein. Nach Fragm. 20 und Fragm. 21 unterscheidet dieser eine dreifache Gottesverehrung: die der Heiden und die der Juden, die auf dem Berg die Schöpfung bzw. in Jerusalem den Schöpfergott anbeten; sodann die der Pneumatiker, die allein den Vater der Wahrheit ... in Wahrheit anbeten.[108] In Fragm. 24 sagt Herakleon zu dem Wort "Gott ist Geist": "Unbefleckt, rein und unsichtbar ist seine göttliche Natur."[109] Und über die Anbeter in Geist und Wahrheit sagt er: "Entsprechend dem Angebeteten (beten sie) pneumatisch (an), nicht fleischlich" (πνευματικῶς οὐ σαρκικῶς). Denn auch sie selbst, die die gleiche Natur haben wie der Vater, sind Pneuma..."[110] Auch Herakleon setzt also die geistige Anbetung in Gegensatz zur fleischlichen, genau wie der Naassener. Das muß jedoch keine Abhängigkeit besagen, weil Johannes selbst den Gegensatz Pneuma — Sarx besonders hervorhebt.[111] Auch in Qumrân war die gei-

---

[106] 9, 3 (98, 8f.).
[107] 9, 3-4 (98, 9-13).
[108] Frgm. 20f. (73f. Völker).
[109] Frgm. 24 (75, 15-17 Völker).
[110] Frgm. 24 (75, 17-21 Völker).
[111] Besonders klar in Joh 3, 6: "Was geboren ist aus dem Fleische, ist Fleisch, und was geboren ist aus dem Geiste, ist Geist." Dieses Wort zitiert der Naassener (7, 40: 88, 24-26) als Beleg für den Gegensatz von fleischlicher (d.h. irdischer) und pneumatischer Geburt.

stige Anbetung bereits ein Anliegen.[112] Weiter haben beide Exegeten die
Teilung der Menschen in drei Klassen gemeinsam. Nach einer relativ
spät überlieferten Nachricht hat Valentin selbst ein Buch "Über die drei
Naturen" (περὶ τῶν τριῶν φύσεων) verfaßt, woraus aber nicht folgt, daß
die Drei-Naturenlehre erstmals von Valentin entwickelt worden wäre.[113]
Herakleons Dreiteilung in Heiden, Juden und Christen wurde bereits im
Kerygma Petri entwickelt[114] und für die Weiterbildung dieser Gruppen
zu den drei Menschenklassen konnte man sich, wie Irenäus bezeugt,[115]
auf den ersten Korintherbrief berufen. Die den Pneumatikern allein
reservierte wahre Gottesverehrung muß demnach weder Sondergut des
Naaseners noch der Valentinianer sein; jedenfalls gibt sie keine hinrei-
chende Handhabe, eine direkte Verbindung zwischen den beiden Gruppen zu postulieren. Die Annahme liegt also auch bei dieser Exegese
nahe, daß Naasener und Valentinianer zwei verschiedene christlich-
gnostische Exegesen des Johannesevangeliums verkörpern, die sich jedoch sehr nahe stehen. Man darf daher vermuten, daß Naasener und
Valentinianer von einer älteren Gnosis, die schon christlich war, abhän-
gen. Daß diese ältere christliche Gnosis innerhalb der christlichen Gemeinschaften zunächst nicht als heterodox, sondern noch als orthodox
angesehen wurde, ist möglich und sogar wahrscheinlich. Valentin selbst
soll ja wegen seiner Geistesgaben so angesehen gewesen sein, daß er in
Rom Aussicht auf das Episkopat gehabt habe.[116] Richtig scheint auf
jeden Fall die Aussage Tertullians zu sein, daß Valentin als christlicher
Gnostiker bereits Vorgänger hatte, deren Gedanken er in origineller
Weise weitergeführt habe.[117]

Für den Naasener und seine Gruppe gilt analog dasselbe. Zunächst:
sie sind kaum Valentinianer, weil sie nach Ausweis ihrer Exegese weder
in der Nachfolge Valentins[118] noch in der seiner Schüler zu stehen schei-

---

[112] Vgl. R. Schnackenburg, Die "Anbetung in Geist und Wahrheit" (Joh 4, 23) im
Lichte von Qumrân-Texten. in: BZ, N.F. 3, 1959, 88-94.
[113] Valentin, Frgm. 9: bei Anthimus, De sancta ecclesia 9 (60, 7-10 Völker). Dort wird
behauptet, Valentin habe als erster die drei göttlichen Hypostasen und Personen
ausgedacht.
[114] Herakleon, Frgm. 21 (74, 9-11 Völker).
[115] Iren. haer. I 8, 3 (72 Harvey).
[116] Tertullian, adv. valent. 4, 1 (CC II 755 Kroymann).
[117] Tertullian, adv. valent. 4, 2 (CC II 755 Kroymann).
[118] Der Vergleich der Bibelexegesen der Naasener mit Valentin kann nur indirekt, d.h.
mittels der übereinstimmenden Exegesen seiner Schüler erfolgen, weil die wenigen von Valentin erhaltenen Fragmente kein Vergleichsmaterial bieten. Solche Übereinstimmungen,
die auf Valentin selbst zurückweisen (vgl. G. Quispel, The Original Doctrine of Valentine,
in: VC 1, 1947, 43-73), ließen sich bei den Testimonien für die pneumatische Menschenklasse, bei den Himmelreichgleichnissen als Bildern für den im Menschen verborgenen
pneumatischen Samen und bei der Exegese von Joh 1, 1-4 nachweisen.

nen. Gewiß konnte hier nur eine Auswahl einiger neutestamentlichen Exegesen getroffen werden, die beiden Gruppen gemeinsam sind. Der Vergleich dieser Exegesen miteinander scheint jedoch das vorstehende Urteil zu rechtfertigen. Darüber hinaus wird man auf Grund der Ähnlichkeit ihrer Exegesen folgern dürfen, daß Naassener und Valentinianer aus der gemeinsamen Tradition einer älteren christlichen Gnosis hervorgegangen sind. Dieser Sachverhalt würde jedenfalls ihre enge Verwandtschaft am ehesten erklären.

PATRISTISCHE MATERIALEN ZUR SPÄTGESCHICHTE DER VALENTINIANISCHEN GNOSIS

VON

KLAUS KOSCHORKE

Im Folgenden möchte ich weniger fertige Resultate vortragen als vielmehr auf bestimmte Desiderata der Gnosisforschung aufmerksam machen und an einer einzigen Stelle Hinweise zur Lösung der anstehenden Fragen zu geben versuchen. Durch den Fund von Nag Hammadi hat sich unsere Kenntnis der gnostischen Bewegung sprunghaft vermehrt. Insbesondere können wir uns nun erstmals ein genaueres Bild vom Vorgang der Auseinandersetzung zwischen gnostischem und kirchlichen Christentum machen. Denn in Nag Hammadi finden sich zahlreiche Texte aus unterschiedlicher Zeit sowie aus sehr verschiedenen Ecken des gnostischen Lagers, die Stellung beziehen zum katholischen Christentum und damit den Kampf zwischen Kirche und Gnosis, den wir bislang nur durch die Brille der Rechtgläubigkeit studieren konnten, zum erstenmal in gnostischer Perspektive von Augen führen.[1] Trotz dieses sprunghaft angestiegenen Wissens aber sind wir noch weit davon entfernt, so etwas wie eine *Geschichte* der Auseinandersetzung von kirchlichem und gnostischem Christentum schreiben zu können. Eine solche Geschichte hätte die Aufgabe, nicht nur *einzelne* Punkte der wechselseitigen Beeinflussung, der ein- oder beidseitigen Abgrenzung voneinander oder des organisatorischen Verhältnisses zueinander zu beleuchten — was bereits jetzt möglich ist —, sondern die *Entwicklung* durch die einzelnen Phasen der christlichen Konsens- resp. Traditionsbildung sowie durch die unterschiedlichen Stadien der Auseinandersetzung hindurch zu verfolgen.

Ein derartiges Unternehmen ist notwendig und möglich. Zum gegenwärtigen Zeitpunkt fehlen uns aber dafür noch eine Reihe wesentlicher Voraussetzungen. Unter diesen sind — wenn wir hier allein den gnostischen Part ins Auge fassen — vor allem zu nennen:

---

[1] Cf. K. Koschorke, Die Polemik der Gnostiker gegen das kirchliche Christentum. Unter besonderer Berücksichtigung der Nag-Hammadi-Traktate "Apokalypse des Petrus" (NHC VII, 3) und "Testimonium Veritatis" (NHC IX, 3) [NHS XII], Leiden 1978.

1) Eine detaillierte Befragung der einzelnen Nag-Hammadi-Texte auf ihren historischen, religionsgeschichtlichen und traditionsgeschichtlichen Ort. Diese Arbeit ist gegenwärtig im Gang; doch sind wir vom erreichbaren Maß an gesicherten Ergebnissen noch weit entfernt.

2) Eine äußere Geschichte der gnostischen Bewegung bzw. der einzelnen Gruppen. Dazu wäre etwa das zerstreute themarelevante patristische Material zu sammeln und auszuwerten, so wie Harnack dies für die Geschichte der markoniten Kirche getan hat.[2] Diese Aufgabe ist noch überhaupt nicht in Angriff genommen worden.

3) Eine innere Geschichte zumindest einzelner gnostischer Gruppen. Zahlreiche Einzelbeobachtungen vor allem für die valentinianische Gnosis liegen hier bereits vor; eine zusammenhängende Darstellung jedoch bleibt der Zukunft vorhalten.

Desweiteren fehlt völlig eine zusammenhängende Untersuchung der Frage, was eigentlich mit den diversen christlich-gnostischen Gruppen geschah, nachdem sie als wirksamer Rivale des orthodoxen Christentums eliminiert waren. Die Frage nach den Anfängen der gnostischen Bewegung ist bekanntlich intensiv (und im Vergleich zu den erzielbaren Resultaten wohl überintensiv) diskutiert worden; die nach ihrer Spätphase jedoch so gut wie gar nicht. Dabei sind deren vielfältige Entwicklungsformen in dieser Spätzeit von höchstem Interesse: so etwa der Prozeß zunehmender Isolierung oder anpassender Verkirchlichung; die fortdauernde Existenz in eigenen Gemeinschaften trotz sich steigernden äußeren Druckes; wachsende Bedeutungslosigkeit und schließliches Eingehen in die katholische Kirche; Abdrängung an die Peripherie des christlichen Bereiches, Verschmelzung mit der außerchristlichen Gnosis; zunehmende (Re-)Paganisierung sowie der Prozeß der Entchristianisierung; Aufgehen im Manichäismus; Weiterleben in asketischen, monastischen oder enthusiastischen Strömungen; etc. All dies läßt sich im Einzelnen verfolgen;[3] eine systematische Aufarbeitung aber fehlt gänzlich.

Im Folgenden nun möchte ich den zweiten Punkt — Zusammenstellung der verfügbaren Informationen über Verbreitung und Fortdauer der verschiedenen gnostischen Gruppen — an einer einzigen Stelle mit einer sehr begrenzten Zielsetzung aufgreifen: um zu zeigen, daß es sich

---

[2] A. v. Harnack, Marcion. Das Evangelium vom fremden Gott (TU 45), Leipzig, [2]1924, 153ff. Verwiesen sei auch auf Textsammlungen wie die von P. de Labriolle, Les Sources de l'Histoire du Montanisme, Fribourg/Paris 1913; oder M. Kmosko, Antiquorum testimonia de historia et doctrina Messalianorum sectae (Patrologia Syriaca I, 3, 1926, CLXX-CCXCII).

[3] Einige Beispiele bei K. Koschorke, Die Polemik (s. Anm. 1), 250f.

hier zu suchen lohnen würde. Als Beispiel wähle ich die valentinianische
Gnosis und frage also nach externen Daten über Fortbestand, Verbreitung und Geschick dieser Bewegung. Dabei soll unsere Aufmerksamkeit
auf Zeugnisse ab dem Jahr 300 gerichtet sein.

Für das vierte Jahrhundert gilt nun, daß wir hier eine ganze Reihe von
Nachrichten über die valentinianische Gnosis haben. Zunächst verwun-
dert es nicht, daß wir in *Ägypten*, seit alters her eine Hochburg des
Gnostizismus, die Valentinianer noch in der zweiten Hälfte des 4. Jh. s
für das ganze Land bezeugt finden. In seinem zwischen 374 und 377
verfaßten Panarion vermerkt *Epiphanius von Salamis*, daß des Valentinus "Same auch heute noch in Ägypten übriggeblieben ist" (ἔτι ἐν
Αἰγύπτῳ περιλείπεται τούτου ἡ σπορά), und nennt im Einzeln den Bereich
der Küstenstädte Alexandrien und Paralus, das Gebiet von Prosopis
und Attribis im Nildelta, von Arsinoe im Fayum sowie die Thebais [I].
Eine anschauliche Bestätigung erfährt die Auskunft des Epiphanius
durch die Bibliothek von *Nag Hammadi*, die nicht vor Mitte 4. Jh.
entstanden ist und eine Reihe valentinianischer Traktate enthält.[4] Auch
wenn die Besitzer der Bibliothek als solcher keine Valentinianer
waren — es handelt sich hier entweder um nicht näher spezifizierbare
christliche Gnostiker asketischer Prägung oder um pachomianische
Mönche —, so ist doch die Greifbarkeit einer größeren Anzahl valentinianischer Texte, ihre (wahrscheinlich je eigene) Übersetzung ins Koptische (und zwar in verschiedene Dialekte) sowie ihre Reproduktion in der
Sammlung von Nag Hammadi (und in den vorangegangenen Teilsamm-
lungen) ein Indiz für die Bedeutung der valentinianischen Gnosis dieses
Raums. Für die Verbreitung dieser Traktate spricht das Beispiel des
Evangelium Veritatis, das nicht nur in verschiedene Dialekte übersetzt
worden ist,[5] sondern darüber hinaus den beiden Übersetzungen vielleicht bereits in unterschiedlichen Fassungen zugrunde lag.[6] Für Alexandrien ist *Didymus der Blinde* († 398) als Zeuge heranzuziehen, der sich in
seinen Werken nicht selten mit valentinianischen Auffassungen ausein-

---

[4] Als valentinianisch zähle ich: OrPl (NHC I, 1); EvVer (NHC I, 3/XII, 2); TracTrip
(NHC I, 5); EvPh (NHC II, 3); Inter (NHC XI, 1); ExpVal (NHC XI, 2); sowie mit Ein-
schränkung Rheg (NHC I, 4); valentinianische Elemente finden sich in 1ApcJac (NHC V,
3).

[5] Das Evangelium Veritatis findet sich in Codex I in einer subachmimischen, in den
Fragmenten des Textes in Codex XII in einer sahidischen Version.

[6] Für diese Möglichkeit könnten inhaltliche Abweichungen sprechen (cf. C. Colpe,
JAC 17 [1974] 118f. s.u.; W.-P. Funk, OLZ 73 [1978] 153f.). Colpe selber erwägt inzwischen — mir unwahrscheinlich — "neben dem koptischen als Ursprache eine griechische
Parallelversion" (JAC 21 [1978] 134). Die ganze Frage bedarf noch eingehender Diskussion.

andersetzt, gegen ihren Doketismus und Anthropologie polemisiert und beispielsweise erwähnt, daß es "viele" gibt, die den christologischen Auffassungen dieser Gnostiker folgen [II]. Aufschlußreich für die Verhältnisse in Ägypten wie in Syrien dürfte der sog. Tomus ad Antiochenos des *Athanasius* sein, ein Schreiben der von ihm geleiteten alexandrinischen Synode des Jahres 362, das auf die Herstellung kirchlicher Einheit in Antiochien zielt und die Bedingungen für die Zulassung zur Kirchengemeinschaft formuliert. Zu diesen Bedingungen zählt nun nicht nur das Bekenntnis zum Nicaenum und zur Gottheit des Geistes sowie die korrespondierende Verdammung der arianischen Irrlehre, sondern ebenso auch die Anathematisierung dreier gnostischer Häresien: des Valentin, das Basilides und des Mani [III]. Die fließenden Grenzen zwischen Kirche und valentinianischer Gnosis noch im Ägypten des 4. Jh.s werden möglicherweise durch den *Oxford-Papyrus P. Ash. Inv. 3* besonders eindringlich beleuchtet, den C. H. Roberts publiziert und auf den H. Chadwick jüngst aufmerksam gemacht hat. Dieser in den Anfang des 4. Jh. zu datierende Papyrus listet biblische Bücher, den Hirten des Hermas sowie Schriften des Origenes auf und stellt offensichtlich den Katalog einer Gemeindebibliothek dar. Unter diesen Schriften nun findet sich auch das Buch eines Ἄπα Βαλ... [   ], wobei die folgende Lücke von H. Chadwick zu Ἄπα Βαλεντῖ[νος] ergänzt wird. Sollte diese Ergänzung zutreffend sein — das Ἄπα bereitet hier Schwierigkeiten —, so wäre damit das Ansehen demonstriert, dessen sich die Schriften des Valentinos auch in kirchlichen Gemeindekreisen erfreuten, oder aber (was mir die wahrscheinlichere Lösung zu sein scheint) umgekehrt die Bereitschaft der Valentinianer, auch kirchliche Literatur zu übernehmen und gewinnbringend zu studieren [IV].

Auch im Antiochien des *Chrysostomos* stellen die Valentinianer noch eine akute Gefahr dar. In den Genesishomilien von 386 etwa gibt der Goldmund seinen Zuhörern Anweisungen für die Diskussion mit Manichäern, Markioniten und Valentinianern; in dem Traktat De virginitate (vor 392) warnt er vor der verführerischen Askese derselben Häretiker; und in der Programmschrift De sacerdotio (vor 392) rechnet er es zu den erforderlichen Qualitäten eines Priesters, auch den Anhängern des Valentin im Streitgespräch entgegentreten zu können [V]. Sein Landsmann *Severian von Gabala* († nach 406) setzt sich in seinen exegetischen Schriften nicht selten mit Valentinianern auseinander und redet dabei von ihnen wie von Zeitgenossen (zB frgm. in 1 Cor 15, 47-49.50) [VI]. Weiter im Osten ist es *Aphrahat*, der sich in der 336/337 verfaßten Homilie vom Fasten gegen die falsche Askese der Valentinianer wendet

[VII]. Auf die Verhältnisse in Edessa wirft eine Verfügung des Kaisers *Julian* gen. *Apostata* aus dem Jahre 362 ein bezeichnendes Licht. Wir erfahren, daß es wohl unter Konstantius zu schweren Ausschreitungen der Arianer gegen die Valentinianer gekommen war, woraufhin Julian das gesamte Vermögen der reichen arianischen Kirche beschlagnahmen läßt [VIII]. Repressalien waren die Valentinianer auch in Kallinikon, einer wichtigen römischen Festung und reichen Handelsstadt am Euphrat in der Provinz Osroene, ausgesetzt. Dort war es zu zwei Vorfällen gekommen: auf Anstiftung des dortigen Bischof war eine jüdische Synagoge in Schutt und Asche gelegt worden, und Gleiches taten fanatisierte Mönche mit dem Kultgebäude der Valentinianer, nachdem diese ihre Prozession zum Heiligtum der makkabäischen Märtyrer gestört hatten. Das war im Jahr 388. Beide Ereignisse erfahren wir aus zwei Briefen des *Ambrosius* (ep. 40f), dem es durch eine massive Intervention beim Kaiser Theodosius gelingt, diesen zur Rücknahme der von ihm verhängten drastischen Strafen für Bischof und Mönche zu nötigen [IX].

Die Vorfälle in Kallinikon werfen nicht nur ein Licht auf die Situation der dortigen Valentinianer, sondern auch auf die *kaiserliche Religionspolitik*. Zweifellos war das bestimmende Motiv der beabsichtigten Strafaktion des *Theodosius* nicht Eingreifen zugunsten der bedrängten Gnostiker, sondern Einschreiten gegen den Landesfriedensbruch der Mönchshorden ("monachi multa scelera faciunt"); aber dennoch bleibt der Schutz, der den valentinianischen Häretikern zumindest indirekt zuteil werden sollte, bemerkenswert. Denn an und für sich war den Häretikern ja Zusammenkunft und der Besitz eines Kultgebäudes untersagt. Kaiser *Konstantins* Häretikergesetz aus der Zeit um 326, das ausdrücklich die Valentinianer den Häresien zurechnet, deren Versammlungshäuser zu beschlagnahmen sei, gehörte zwar längst der Vergangenheit an [X]; doch hatte Theodosius diesen Grundsatz in allgemeiner Form bestätigt und gegen sämtliche nichtkatholische Glaubensgemeinschaften ein Versammlungsverbot ausgesprochen.[7] Andererseits ist zu berücksichtigen, daß in der Ketzergesetzgebung des Theodosius im wesentlichen nur die Manichäer sowie die im weiteren Sinn am trinitarischen Streit beteiligten Gruppen namentlich genannt werden, jene Häresien also, die als Gefahr für das Reich eingeschätzt wurden[8] oder der

---

[7] S. vor allem den Generalerlaß gegen die Häretiker vom 10-1-381 (CodTheod XVI, 5, 6 = CodJust I, 1, 2; dazu: W. Ensslin, Die Religionspolitik des Kaisers Theodosius d. Gr., München 1953, 28f) sowie das Häretikergesetz vom 26-7-383 (CodTheod XVI, 5, 11; dazu: W. Ensslin a.a.O. 46f).

[8] So die Manichäer; zu den Motiven und Maßnahmen der antimanichäischen Religionspolitik s. E.-H. Kaden, Die Edikte gegen die Manichäer von Diokletian bis Justinian, in:

Einheitspolitik entgegenstanden, während andere Sekten wie die Donatisten oder die älteren Gnostiker nicht eigens erwähnt werden und de facto Toleranz genossen.[9] Unter *Theodosius II* ist das anders; in dem Edikt vom 30-5-428 (CodTheod XVI, 5, 65) werden unter den Häresien, die nusquam in Romano solo conveniendi orandique habeant facultatem, ausdrücklich auch die Valentinianer aufgeführt [XI].

Mit diesem Edikt sind wir im fünften Jahrhundert, für das auch andere Stimmen die Fortexistenz der valentinianischen Gnosis bezeugen. So *Theodor von Mopsuestia* († 428), der neben Manichäern und Markioniten die Valentinianer als diejenigen nennt, in denen die Weissagung von 1 Tim 4, 1-3 sichtlich in Erfüllung gegangen ist [XII]. In seinem 448 verfaßten Brief an den Konsul Nomus beschwert sich *Theodoret*, Bischof des in der Nähe von Antiochien gelegenen Städtchens Cyrus, über das ihm auferlegte Reiseverbot, das im krassen Gegensatz zu der Bewegungsfreiheit steht, deren sich Arianer, Manichäer, Markioniten und Valentinianer erfreuen (ep. 81) [XIII]. In die Zeit um 600 führt der Traktat des konstantinopolitanischen Presbyters *Timotheus* De receptione haereticorum, der das Rekonziliationsverfahren der Kirche gegenüber den verschiedenen Häresien zum Gegenstand hat und dabei auch die Valentinianer behandelt [XIV]. Die jüngste mir bekannte Kunde stammt aus dem Jahr 692. Kanon 95 des *Trullanum II* regelt die Aufnahme von Häretikern, darunter von Valentinianern. Sowohl dieser Kasus (das Aufnahmeverfahren), die Liste der übrigen Häresien, die in diese Zeit passen, sowie weitere Merkmale dürften dafür sprechen, daß hier nicht nur literarische Erwähnung vorliegt, sondern daß die Bestimmungen dieses Kanons auf noch existente Valentinianer abzielen[10] [XV].

Festschr. H. Lewald, Basel 1953, 55-68. Die gesetzgeberischen Maßnahmen gegen streng asketische Sekten wie die Enkratiten, Apotaktiten, Hydroparastraten und Sakkophoren sind nach CodTheod XVI, 7, 3 dadurch mitbedingt, daß sie als Deckname für die manichäische Irrlehre angesehen wurden; doch cf. auch die Bemerkungen von K. Holl, Amphilochius von Ikonium, Tübingen/Leipzig 1904, 36ff.

[9] Hingewiesen sei auch auf die Notiz des Kirchenhistorikers Sozomenos, der Kaiser habe mit seinen Ketzergesetzen die Untertanen nicht bestrafen, sondern nur einschüchtern wollen (h.e. VII, 12, 12). Im Übrigen spricht neben einer Fülle von Einzelnachrichten schon die häufige Wiederholung der gegen die Häretiker gerichteten Erlasse gegen deren Wirksamkeit. Zur Kirchenpolitik des Theodosius cf. die Arbeiten von W. Ensslin, Die Religionspolitik (s. Anm. 7); N. Q. King, The Emperor Theodosius and the Establishment of Christianity, London 1961, 50-59; K.-L. Noethlichs, Die gesetzgeberischen Maßnahmen der christlichen Kaiser des vierten Jahrhunderts gegen Häretiker, Heiden und Juden, Diss. phil. Köln 1971, 128-165; W. K. Boyd, The Ecclesiastical Edicts of the Theodosian Code, New York 1905.

[10] Wie solche spätvalentinianischen Gruppen oder Gemeinden ausgesehen haben könnten, entzieht sich gänzlich unserer Kenntnis. Ebenso unbeantwortbar ist die Frage, ob und

Fragen wir abschließend, welches *Bild von der Verbreitung der valentinianischen Gnosis* sich nun zeichnen läßt, so ist zu sagen: ihre größte Ausdehnung ist Ende des 2. und Anfang des 3. Jh.s zu verzeichnen. In dieser Zeit ist sie — was hier zu demonstrieren nicht der Ort war — nachzuweisen in Rom, Gallien, Nordafrika, Ägypten, Syrien, Kleinasien, Griechenland. Im 4. Jh., dem Zeitpunkt also, wo wir hier einsetzten, ist sie noch recht lebendig in Ägypten und Syrien und wohl auch noch für bestimmte Gebiete Kleinasiens vorauszusetzen (cf. Methodius von Olymp). Einzelne Spuren aber scheinen bis zur Wende vom 7. zum 8. Jh. hinaufzuführen.

Ziel meiner Ausführungen war nicht der Versuch, ein abgerundetes Bild der Verbreitungsgeschichte der Valentinianer zu zeichnen; dazu sind die gegenwärtig zur Verfügung stehenden Informationen zu sporadisch.[11] Vielmehr sollte gezeigt werden, daß es genügend verstreute Hinweise gibt, denen umfassend nachzugehen sich lohnen würde.[12] Die vormanichäische Gnosis pflegt etwa ab dem Jahr 210 aus dem Bewußtsein des Historikers zu schwinden;[13] dabei geht ihre Geschichte sehr viel weiter; und dies ist in ihren vielfältigen Ausläufern nicht nur im Blick auf die interne Entwicklung des Gnostizismus, sondern auch auf die Endphase der Auseinandersetzung zwischen Kirche und Gnosis von großer Bedeutung.

---

in welchem Umfang sachliche Kontinuität gegenüber der früheren valentinianischen Gnosis besteht. Doch könnte man sich vorstellen, daß die Situation der Verfolgung und des äußeren Druckes auch ganz unabhängig von bestimmten verbindenden Überzeugungen oder eines den Zusammenhalt wirkenden kultischen Lebens eine Gruppenidentität und ein Zusammc zehörigkeitsbewußtsein bewirkt haben.

[11] Auch ind, worauf ausdrücklich hingewiesen sei, die gegebenen Hinweise sowohl im Blick auf die herangezogenen Quellen wie auf die aus dem Werk eines bestimmten Autors angegebenen Belegstellen äußerst unvollständig. Die auch nur annähernde Erfassung der Quellenmaterialien für die Geschichte auch nur einer Gruppe bleibt der Zukunft vorbehalten. Sie müßte die Zusammenstellung und sorgfältige Erörterung auch solcher Stellen einschließen, die expressis verbis von der Nicht-Existenz bestimmter Gruppen reden (wie z.B. Bas.ep. 261, 2; Greg. Naz. orat. 25, 8; Optatus Milev. schism. Donat. I 9) einschließen.

[12] Ich möchte diese Gelegenheit gerne dazu nutzen, Kollegen um die Mitteilung relevanter Beobachtungen zu bitten. Wichtige Belege entziehen sich gezielter Suche. Umso mehr wären Informationen gerade auch über Zufallsentdeckungen und Belege an abgelegener Stelle zu begrüßen.

[13] Cf. A. v. Harnack, Lehrbuch der Dogmengeschichte. I, Darmstadt N1964 (= Tübingen ⁴1909), 277 über die gnostischen Schulen: "Sie waren seit c. 210 kein Factor der geschichtlichen Entwickelung mehr, wenn auch erst die konstantinisch-theodosianische Kirche sie wirklich zu unterdrücken vermocht hat".

APPENDIX: MATERIALEN

[I] *Epiphanius, Panarion 31, 7, 1* (GCS 25 395, 16-19). 374/377.

'Εποιήσατο δὲ οὗτος (= Valentin) τὸ κήρυγμα καὶ ἐν Αἰγύπτῳ, ὅθεν δὴ καὶ ὡς λείψανα ἐχίδνης ὀστέων ἔτι ἐν Αἰγύπτῳ περιλείπεται τούτου ἡ σπορά, ἔν τε τῷ 'Αθριβίτῃ καὶ Προσωπίτῃ καὶ 'Αρσινοΐτῃ καὶ Θηβαΐδι καὶ τοῖς κάτω μέρεσι τῆς Παραλίας καὶ 'Αλεξανδρειοπολίτῃ...

Die Angaben des Epiphanius beruhen entweder auf uns nicht näher greifbaren Informationen (so R. A. Lipsius, Zur Quellenkritik des Epiphanios, Wien 1865, 156, der allgemein von einer "mündliche(n) Tradition" spricht) oder auf den Eindrücken, die er während seines Ägyptenaufenthaltes als junger Mann (Epiph. pan. 26, 17, 4; 39, 2; Sozom. h.e. 6, 32, 3) gewann. So berichtet er an anderer Stelle über die gnostische Szenerie Ägyptens unter ausdrücklichem Verweis auf eigenes Erleben (pan. 26, 17, 4ff; cf. pan. 39, 2; cf. 24, 1, 4). Über Valentins Herkunft bringt er in 31, 2, 2f Angaben, die auf mündlicher Tradition beruhen (τὴν μὲν οὖν αὐτοῦ πατρίδα ἢ πόθεν οὗτος γεγέννηται, οἱ πολλοὶ ἀγνοοῦσιν· ... εἰς ἡμᾶς δὲ ὡς ἐνηχήσει φήμη τις ἐλήλυθε· διὸ οὐ παρελευσόμεθα, καὶ ... τὴν εἰς ἡμᾶς ἐλθοῦσαν φάσιν οὐ σιωπήσομεν. ἔφασαν γὰρ αὐτόν τινες γεγενῆσθαι φρεβωνίτην, τῆς Αἰγύπτου παραλιώτην, ἐν 'Αλεξανδρείᾳ δὲ πεπαιδεῦσθαι τὴν τῶν 'Ελλήνων παιδείαν); es ist nicht unwahrscheinlich, daß er diese Überlieferung in Ägypten aus dem Munde dortiger Valentinianer erfahren hat.

[II] *Didymos, Comm. Ps. (PsT 2, 29/3, 1) in ps. 20, 1* (edd. M. Gronewald u.a., Didymos der Blinde. Psalmenkommentar [Tura-Papyrus]. Bd. I, Bonn 1969, p. 61). Wahrscheinlich 370/385.

κα[ὶ διὰ] τοῦτο ἐκ γυναικὸς γέγονεν ὁ σωτήρ, οὐ διὰ γυναικός, εἰ καὶ πολλοὶ ἄλλοι γί[νον]ται λέ[γοντ]ες οὐκ "[ἐ]κ [Μ]αρίας", ἀλλὰ "διὰ Μαρίας". δόκη[σ]ιν οὖν πρεσβεύουσιν πολλοί.

Diese Stelle, auf die mich freundlicherweise Dr. W. Bienert aufmerksam gemacht hat, dürfte sich auf Valentinianer beziehen. Zur Begründung reicht zwar der Hinweis auf die Charakterisierung der Valentinianer durch Irenäus (adv. haer. I, 7, 2: Εἶναι δὲ τοῦτον τὸν διὰ Μαρίας διοδεύσαντα, καθάπερ ὕδωρ διὰ σωλῆνος ὁδεύει; III, 11, 3; 16, 1; 22, 1f; V, 1, 2), Tertullian (carn. Chr. 20, 1: Per virginem dicitis natum, non ex virgine, et in vulva, non ex vulva; adv. Val. 27, 1: per virginem, non ex virgine) u.a. (Ps. Tert. haer. 4, 5) nicht aus, da sich dieses Motiv auch in nichtvalentinianischen Texten findet (zB Testimonium Veritatis [NHC IX, 3]). Doch wird die gleiche "doketistische" Auffassung etwa auch PsT 152, 33ff (Bd. III p. 120/122) bekämpft und dort u.a. ausdrücklich dem Valentin zugeschrieben (PsT 153, 14; zu dieser Stelle cf. auch Didym. trin. III, 42 [MG 39 992B]).

Comm. Ps. (PsT 3, 17-24) in ps. 20, 1 (Bd. I p. 12/14)

... ἐὰν γὰρ δῶμεν, [ὅτι] οὐδεὶς τὴν ἀλήθειαν εἶπεν ἢ [αὐ]τὸς [ὁ Χ(ριστό)ς, δίδ]ομε[ν] εἰς τὴν αἵρεσιν ἀκόνην τὴν ἀ[ν]ώνυμον. ἔνι ἀνώνυμός τις αἵρεσις [ἢ ἐξανα]τ[εῖ]λαι δ[οκ]οῦσα ἢ γεγονέναι ἐκ βιβλίων. κ[αὶ] πολλοὶ βίβλους, συντάξεις, ἔχουσιν καὶ τ[οῦτο λέγουσ]ιν, ὅτι οὐδέποτε ἐν ἀνθρώποις γέγονεν ἡ ἀλήθεια εἰ μὴ ἐπὶ τῇ ἐπιδημίᾳ τοῦ σωτ[ῆρος]· "ἡ χάρ[ι]ς" γὰρ "καὶ ἡ ἀλήθεια διὰ 'Ιησοῦ Χριστοῦ ἐγένετο". καὶ ὅρα ποῦ συνάγει αὐτοῖς ὁ λόγος· ἐπεὶ βούλον[ται τ]ὴν παλαιὰν γραφὴν μὴ ἐκ

θεοῦ εἶναι μη[δ]ὲ τοὺς προφήτας, λέγουσιν, ὅτι οὐδέπ[οτ]ε [ἡ ἀλήθει]α εἰς ἀ[νθ]ρώπους ἐλήλυθεν εἰ
μὴ τῆς ἐπιδημίας γεγενημένης. ταῦτα δὲ λέγ[οντες τὴν μία]ν θεότητ[α] διακό[πτ]ουσιν καὶ ἄλλον
λέγουσιν τὸν πρὸ τῆς ἐπιδημίας τὸν κοσμοπο[ιό]ν, [ἄλλον δ]ὲ ζ[η]το[ῦσιν] π(ατέ)[ρα] Χ(ριστο)ῦ.

Der Zusammenhang mit der oben erörterten Stelle sowie der häufig speziell gegen die Valentinianer gerichtete Vorwurf der "Spaltung" der "Einheit" Gottes und Christi sprechen
über allgemein antignostische Tendenz hinaus für Polemik gegen Valentinianer. Die Berufung auf Joh 1, 17 schließt Markioniten als Gegner aus; umgekehrt spielt der Johannesprolog bei den Valentinianern eine große Rolle (cf. E. Pagels, The Johannine Gospel in
Gnostic Exegesis, Nashville/New York 1973, 23-50; K. Koschorke, Eine gnostische Paraphrase des johanneischen Prologs, VigChr 33 [1979] 383-392, 388 + Anm.).

Comm. Sach. II, 175 in Sach 7, 11f (SourcChrét 84 p. 504). 386/393.

Ἐλεγχέσθωσαν οἱ αἱρετικοί, ἀμαθῶς καὶ ἄγαν ἀπαιδεύτως φύσεις εἰσηγούμενοι
διαφόρους τῶν ἀνθρώπων· δογματίζουσιν γὰρ τοὺς μὲν ἀνεπιδέκτους ἀρετῆς, τοὺς
δὲ πρὸς ἀνάλημψιν κακίας μὴ πεφυκότας· ᾧ ἕπεται μηδὲ νόμον ἀνύειν τι, μὴ νου-
θεσίαν, μὴ ἔλεγχον, μὴ προτροπήν, μηδὲ προσευχὴν πρὸς θεὸν ἀναπεμπομένην.

Mit der Lehre von den verschiedenen Menschennaturen (cf. II, 185: τὴν μυθικὴν ἀσέβειαν
τῶν τὰς φύσεις ἀναπλασαμένων; II, 177: τὸν ἀσεβῆ λόγον τῶν τὰς φύσεις εἰσηγουμένων), die Didymos im folgenden Abschnitt (II, 175-190) wie auch sonst häufig zugunsten der menschlichen Entscheidungsfreiheit bekämpt, dürfte die valentinianische Unterscheidung von Hy-
likern und Pneumatikern attackiert sein; antivalentinianische Ausrichtung ist wahrscheinlicher als antimanichäische (cf. die Bemerkungen zur Stelle bei L. Doutreleau, Didyme
l'aveugle: Sur Zacharie, Bd. I [SourcChrét 83], Paris 1962, 93f). Allgemein zu gnostischen
Gegnern des Didymos cf. auch: J. Leipoldt, Didymus der Blinde von Alexandria (TU 29,
3), Leipzig 1905, 60f.

[III] *Athanasius von Alexandrien, Tomus ad Antiochenos c. 3* (MG 26 797B/800B). 362.

3. Πάντας τοίνυν τοὺς βουλομένους εἰρηνεύειν πρὸς ἡμᾶς, καὶ μάλιστα τοὺς ἐν
τῇ Παλαιᾷ συναγομένους, καὶ τοὺς ἀποτρέχοντας δὲ ἀπὸ τῶν Ἀρειανῶν
προσκαλέσασθε παρ' ἑαυτοῖς, καὶ ὡς μὲν πατέρες υἱοὺς προσλάβεσθε, ὡς δὲ
διδάσκαλοι καὶ κηδεμόνες ἀποδέξασθε, καὶ συνάψαντες αὐτοὺς τοῖς ἀγαπητοῖς
ἡμῶν τοῖς περὶ Παυλῖνον, μηδὲν πλέον ἀπαιτήσητε παρ' αὐτῶν ἢ ἀναθεματίζειν
μὲν τὴν Ἀρειανὴν αἵρεσιν, ὁμολογεῖν δὲ τὴν παρὰ τῶν ἁγίων Πατέρων ὁμολογηθεῖσαν ἐν Νικαίᾳ πίστιν, ἀναθεματίζειν δὲ καὶ τοὺς λέγοντας κτίσμα εἶναι τὸ
Πνεῦμα τὸ ἅγιον, καὶ διῃρημένον ἐκ τῆς οὐσίας τοῦ Χριστοῦ. Τοῦτο γάρ ἐστιν
ἀληθῶς ἀποπηδᾶν ἀπὸ τῆς μυσαρᾶς αἱρέσεως τῶν Ἀρειανῶν, τὸ μὴ διαιρεῖν τὴν
ἁγίαν Τριάδα, καὶ λέγειν τι ταύτης εἶναι κτίσμα. Οἱ γὰρ προσποιούμενοι μὲν ὀ-
νομάζειν τὴν ὁμολογηθεῖσαν ἐν Νικαίᾳ πίστιν, τολμῶντες δὲ κατὰ τοῦ ἁγίου
Πνεύματος βλασφημεῖν, οὐδὲν πλέον ποιοῦσιν, ἢ τὴν Ἀρειανὴν αἵρεσιν τοῖς μὲν
ῥήμασιν ἀρνοῦνται, τῷ δὲ φρονήματι ταύτην κατέχουσιν. Ἀναθεματιζέσθω δὲ
παρὰ πάντων   ἡ Σαβελλίου καὶ Παύλου τοῦ Σαμοσατέως ἀσέβεια, καὶ

Οὐαλεντίνου καὶ Βασιλείδου ἡ μανία, καὶ τῶν Μανιχαίων ἡ παραφροσύνη· τούτων γὰρ οὕτω γινομένων, πᾶσα παρὰ πάντων ὑποψία φαύλη περιαιρεθήσεται, καὶ μόνη τῆς καθολικῆς Ἐκκλησίας ἡ πίστις καθαρὰ δειχθήσεται.

Literatur: M. Tetz, Über nikäische Orthodoxie. Der sog. Tomus ad Antiochenos des Athanasios von Alexandrien, ZNW 66 (1975) 194-222, v.a. 201f. 205. — Die hier geforderte Verdammung von Valentin, Basilides und Mani dient zwar nicht in erster Linie zur Abwehr einer von dort drohenden Gefahr; sie soll vielmehr — wie der oben zitierte Schlußsatz zeigt und c. 5 + 6 näher verdeutlicht — die Vertreter der Drei-Hypostasen-Lehre (die meletianische Partei) vor "Verdächtigung" ihrer Position als einer Drei-Prinzipien-Lehre schützen. Gleichwohl ist die Notwendigkeit dieser Abgrenzung signifikant für die kirchenpolitische Situation. Dies läßt ihr Wegfall bei veränderter Konstellation erkennen (cf. etwa die Bemerkungen von H. Dörries [De Spiritu Sancto, Göttingen 1956, 38f] zum Unionsdokument Basilius ep. 125, wo seiner Meinung nach der Tomus vorausgesetzt ist, aber die Abgrenzung von einer anderen Front als notwendig empfunden wird), sowie des Athanasius' sonstige Bezugnahme auf zeitgenössische Valentinianer (zB Hist. Arian. 66,4 [Opitz II, 219,27f.]; De Synodis 13,4 [II, 241,10-12].

[IV] *Oxford-Papyrus P. Ash. Inv. 3* (ed. C. H. Roberts, Two Oxford Papyri, ZNW 37 [1938] 184-188. Text: p. 187). Anfang 4. Jh.

．．．．．．

δέρμ(α) Ποιμ[ὴν
δέρμ(α) Ὠριγέ[νους
δέρμ(α) εἰς το[
δέρμ(α) Λευιτ[ικὸν
5 δέρμ(α) τῶν ν[
δέρμ(α) τριβακὸν ονο[
    καὶ θειο[
    μαιου .[
δέρμ(α) Ἰὼβ καὶ [
10 δέρμ(α) Πρᾶξις Ἀπ[ο]στόλ(ων) τ..[
δέρμ(α) Ἄπα Βαλ ....[
δέρμ(α) τῶν εἰς τὴν τα[
δέρμ(α) Ἆσμα Ἀσμάτων
δέρμ(α) Ὠριγένους εἰς Ἰω[άννην
15 δέρμ(α) Ἔξοδος Ἀρ[ιθμοὶ?
δέ[ρ]μ(α) Μέγα Βιβλίον ε. ω[
δέ[ρμ(α)] τῶν εἰς πα .[

．．．．．

Dieser Papyrus wird vom Herausgeber C. H. Roberts als "somewhat later" als 312 datiert (a.a.O. p. 185) und von H. Chadwick, der in seiner Vorlesung über The Domestication of Gnosticism auf der International Conference on Gnosticism at Yale 1978 auf diesen Text aufmerksam gemacht hat, als "ca. 300" (Postkarte vom 15-8-1978). Das Katalogfragment zählt nur in Pergament geschriebene Werke auf, und zwar Bücher des AT (Z. 4.9.13.15), des NT (Z. 10.16), des Origenes (Z. 2, wohl auch 3, sowie 14) und — neben unidentifizierbaren Schriften — mit dem Hirten des Hermas ein Lesebuch, das in kirchlich-christlichen Kreisen zeitweilig quasikanonische Autorität genoß (cf. noch Hier. vir. ill. 10: "apud quasdam Graeciae Ecclesias iam publice legitur"). Entscheidend ist nun Z. 11: δέρμ(α) ῎Απα Βαλ …[ ]. Die vom Herausgeber genannte Schwierigkeit (p. 187: "I can find no trace of a Christian writer whose name begins with Bal …") wäre durch die von H. Chadwick vorgeschlagene Ergänzung δέρμ(α) ῎Απα Βαλεντῖ[νος] gelöst (diese Schreibweise ist für das 4. Jh. auch sonst bezeugt). Wie ist aber ἄπα, die nur in Ägypten bezeugte Nebenform zu ἀββᾶς, zu verstehen? ἄπα/ἀπᾶ/ἀββᾶς ist keineswegs nur Ehrentitel kirchlicher Würdenträger, sondern kann auch Märtyrern, geisterfüllten und "rede" befähigten Mönchen und sonstigen Geistträgern beigelegt werden (s. die verschiedenen Lexika sowie: R. Reitzenstein, Historia Monachorum und Historia Lausiaca, Göttingen 1916, 41ff; W. Bousset, Apophthegmata, Tübingen 1923, 79-81; K. Heussi, Der Ursprung des Mönchtums, Tübingen 1936, 164ff, v.a. 165f: "Vermutlich ist die Bezeichnung 'abbas' für den Geistträger von sehr hohem Alter"). Im letzteren, allgemeinen Sinn müßte man ἄπα an der vorliegenden Stelle auffassen. Dann aber ist der dem Valentin gegebene Ehrentitel ἄπα eigentlich nur in einer gnostisch-valentinianischen Gemeinde vorstellbar. Andererseits wäre in diesem Fall das in Z. 11 genannte Opus das einzige erkennbare gnostische Werk in dieser gnostischen Bibliothek (auch in Nag Hammadi findet sich eine Reihe eindeutig außergnostischer Texte, aber doch in deutlicher Minderzahl), und auch die erhebliche Anzahl alttestamentlicher Texte ist der Annahme einer gnostischen Bibliothek nicht günstig.

[V] *Johannes Chrysostomos, Sermo I, 3 in Genesim* (MG 54 584/585). 386.

… Μὴ τοίνυν τὸ στερρὸν ἀφεὶς, τῷ σαθρῷ καὶ ἐπισφαλεῖ τὴν σωτηρίαν ἐγχειρίσῃς τῆς σῆς ψυχῆς· ἀλλά μένε ἐν οἷς ἔμαθες καὶ ἐπιστώθης, καὶ λέγε· Ἐν ἀρχῇ ἐποίησεν ὁ θεὸς τὸν οὐρανὸν καὶ τὴν γῆν. Κἂν Μανιχαῖος προσέλθῃ, κἂν Μαρκίων, κἂν οἱ τὰ Οὐαλεντίνου νοσοῦντες, κἂν ὁστισοῦν ἕτερος, τοῦτο προβάλλου τὸ ῥῆμα· κἂν ἴδῃς γελῶντα, σὺ δάκρυσον αὐτὸν ὡς μαινόμενον. Πύξινον ἔχουσιν ἐκεῖνοι τὸ χρῶμα, καὶ κατεσταλμένην τὴν ὀφρὺν, καὶ ῥημάτων ἐπιείκειαν· ἀλλὰ φύγε τὸ δέλεαρ, καὶ τὸν ἐν τῇ δορᾷ τοῦ προβάτου κρυπτόμενον καταμάνθανε λύκον. Διὰ τοῦτο αὐτὸν μάλιστα μίσησον, ὅτι πρὸς μὲν τὸν ὁμόδουλόν σε προσηνὴς καὶ ἥμερος εἶναι δοκεῖ, πρὸς δὲ τὸν κοινὸν ἡμῶν ἁπάντων Δεσπότην κυνῶν λυττώντων ἐστὶν ἀγριώτερος, ἀκήρυκτον εἰς τὸν οὐρανὸν μάχην εἰσάγων καὶ πόλεμον ἄσπονδον, καὶ δύναμίν τινα ἐξ ἐναντίας ἀντικαθιστῶν τῷ Θεῷ. Φύγε τὸν ἰὸν τῆς πονηρίας, μίσησον τὰ δηλητήρια φάρμακα· καὶ ἣν παρὰ τῶν πατέρων ἐδέξω κληρονομίαν, τὴν ἀπὸ τῶν θείων Γραφῶν πίστιν καὶ διδασκαλίαν, ταύτην κάτεχε μετὰ πολλῆς τῆς ἀσφαλείας. Ἐν ἀρχῇ ἐποίησεν ὁ Θεὸς τὸν οὐρανὸν καὶ τὴν γῆν…

Hervorzuheben ist die Situation des Streitgespräches und die eindringliche Warnung vor der verführerischen Wirkung der gegnerischen Parolen. Auch wenn Chrysostomos nach Ausweis des weiteren Kontextes in erster Linie die manichäische Propaganda im Auge hat, so ist gleichwohl die valentinianische Gnosis als akute Gefahr vorausgesetzt, gegen die es die Hörer zu wappnen gilt.

De virginitate c. 3 (SourcChrét 125, 100/102). Vor 392.

'Αλλ' οὐδὲ Μαρκίων οὐδὲ Οὐαλεντῖνος οὐδὲ Μάνης ταύτης ἠνέσχοντο τῆς συμμετρίας. Οὐ γὰρ εἶχον ἐν ἑαυτοῖς λαλοῦντα τὸν Χριστὸν τὸν τῶν ἰδίων προβάτων φειδόμενον καὶ τὴν ψυχὴν αὐτοῦ τιθέντα ὑπὲρ αὐτῶν ἀλλὰ τὸν ἀνθρωποκτόνον τὸν τοῦ ψεύδους πατέρα. Διά τοι τοῦτο καὶ τοὺς πειθομένους αὐτοῖς πάντας ἀπώλεσαν ἐνταῦθα μὲν αὐτοὺς ἀνονήτοις καὶ ἀφορήτοις βαρύνοντες πόνοις, ἐκεῖ δὲ εἰς τὸ ἡτοιμασμένον ἐκείνοις πῦρ συγκατασπάσαντες ἑαυτοῖς.

c. 1-11 polemisiert gegen die Askese der "Häretiker" und spricht ihr jeglichen Wert ab (5, 1: ἀσελγείας ἁπάσης ἡ τῶν αἱρετικῶν σωφροσύνη χείρων ἐστίν). c. 3 konkretisiert: es handelt sich um die Askese Markions, Valentins und Manis und "ihrer Anhänger" (τοὺς πειθομένους αὐτοῖς). Dabei hat Chrysostomos gegen den Eindruck anzugehen, den die häretischen Jungfrauen machen (cf. die in c. 6, 1 zitierte Stimme: 'Αλλὰ πρόσωπόν μοι δείκνυσι ὠχρὸν καὶ κατισχνωμένα μέλη καὶ στολὴν εὐτελῆ καὶ βλέμμα ἥμερον sowie die Erwiderung in 6, 2: τοῦτο γάρ ἐστι τὸ δεινὸν ὅτι πρὸς μὲν ἀνθρώπους ἐπιείκειαν ἐνδείκνυται πολλήν, πρὸς δὲ τὸν κτίσαντα αὐτὴν Θεὸν πολλῇ κέχρηται τῇ μανίᾳ, καὶ ἡ μηδὲ πρὸς ἄνδρα ἀντιβλέψαι ἀνεχομένη ... πρὸς τὸν τῶν ἀνθρώπων δεσπότην ἀναισχύντοις ὀρθαλμοῖς ὁρᾷ καὶ ἀδικίαν εἰς τὸ ὕφος λαλεῖ).

De sacerdotio IV, 4 (MG 48 666/668). Vor 392.

Διὸ πολλὴν χρὴ ποιεῖσθαι τὴν σπουδήν, ὥστε τὸν λόγον τοῦ Χριστοῦ ἐν ἡμῖν ἐνοικεῖν πλουσίως. Οὐ γὰρ πρὸς ἓν εἶδος ἡμῖν μάχης ἡ παρασκευή, ἀλλὰ ποικίλος οὗτος ὁ πόλεμος, καὶ ἐκ διαφόρων συγκροτούμενος τῶν ἐχθρῶν. Οὔτε γὰρ ὅπλοις ἅπαντες χρῶνται τοῖς αὐτοῖς, οὔτε ἑνὶ προσβάλλειν ἡμῖν μεμελετήκασι τρόπῳ. Καὶ δεῖ τὸν μέλλοντα τὴν πρὸς πάντας ἀναδέχεσθαι μάχην τὰς ἁπάντων εἰδέναι τέχνας... (...) ...καὶ τῷ οἰκείῳ ξίφει περιπαρεὶς ὁ μὴ πολλὴν περὶ ταῦτα τὴν ἐμπειρίαν ἔχων, καὶ τοῖς φίλοις καὶ τοῖς πολεμίοις καταγέλαστος γίνεται. Οἷον (πειράσομαι γάρ σοι καὶ ἐπὶ παραδείγματος ὃ λέγω ποιῆσαι φανερὸν) τὸν ὑπὸ τοῦ Θεοῦ δοθέντα τῷ Μωϋσῇ νόμον οἱ τὴν Οὐαλεντίνου καὶ Μαρκίωνος διαδεξάμενοι φρενοβλάβειαν, καὶ ὅσοι τὰ αὐτὰ νοσοῦσιν ἐκείνοις, τοῦ καταλόγου τῶν θείων ἐκβάλλουσι Γραφῶν· Ἰουδαῖοι δὲ αὐτὸν οὕτω τιμῶσιν, ὡς καὶ τοῦ καιροῦ κωλύοντος φιλονεικεῖν ἅπαντα φυλάττειν, παρὰ τὸ τῷ Θεῷ δοκοῦν. Ἡ δὲ Ἐκκλησία τοῦ Θεοῦ, τὴν ἀμφοτέρων ἀμετρίαν φεύγουσα, μέσην ἐβάδισε, καὶ οὔτε ὑποκεῖσθαι αὐτοῦ τῷ ζυγῷ πείθεται, οὔτε διαβάλλειν αὐτὸν ἀνέχεται, ἀλλὰ καὶ πεπαυμένον ἐπαινεῖ, διὰ τὸ χρησιμεῦσαί ποτε εἰς καιρόν. Δεῖ δὴ τὸν μέλλοντα πρὸς ἀμφοτέρους μάχεσθαι τὴν συμμετρίαν εἰδέναι ταύτην. Ἄν τε γὰρ Ἰουδαίους διδάξαι βουλόμενος, ὡς οὐκ ἐν καιρῷ τῆς παλαιᾶς ἔχονται νομοθεσίας, ἄρξηται κατηγορεῖν αὐτῆς ἀφειδῶς, ἔδωκε τοῖς διασύρειν βουλομένοις τῶν αἱρετικῶν λαβὴν οὐ μικράν· ἄν τε τούτους ἐπιστομίσαι σπουδάζων, ἀμέτρως αὐτὸν ἐπαίρῃ, καὶ ὡς ἀναγκαῖον ἐν τῷ παρόντι τυγχάνοντα θαυμάζῃ, τὰ τῶν Ἰουδαίων ἀνέῳξε στόματα.

[VI] *Severian von Gabala Frgm. in 1 Cor 15, 47-49* (ed. K. Staab, Pauluskommentare aus der griechischen Kirche, Münster 1933, 276 Z. 8ff)

Ἐπιτρέχουσι τούτῳ καὶ οἱ περὶ Οὐαλεντῖνον καὶ Μαρκίωνα καὶ οἱ ἀπὸ Φωτεινοῦ καὶ οἱ Ἀπολιναρίου, πάντας δὲ ἐλέγχει τὸ ῥητόν. ἐρωτῶ γάρ· ὁ ἐκ γῆς χοικὸς εἶχεν ψυχὴν ἢ οὔ; οὐκ ἀρνήσονται. καὶ ὁ ἐξ οὐρανοῦ κύριος εἶχεν σῶμα ἀπὸ γῆς... καὶ πᾶσα ἀνάγκη, εἰ ἀρνοῖντό τινες τὸ σάρκα ἀνειληφέναι τὸν ἐξ οὐρανοῦ κύριον, ἐπειδὴ ἐξ οὐρανοῦ καὶ τοὺς ἐπουρανίους, μὴ συγχωρεῖν ἀνειληφέναι σῶμα, ἐπειδὴ οἷος ὁ χοικός, τοιοῦτοι καὶ οἱ χοικοί, καὶ οὕτως οὐδαμόθεν ἵσταται τοῦτο νοούμενον ἑτέρως ἢ οὕτως...

Angesichts des Zusammenhanges sowie der häufigen Inanspruchnahme von 1 Kor 15, 50 durch die Valentinianer (EvPh [NHC II, 3] § 23; Tert. resurr. 48, 1; Iren. adv. haer. V, 9, 1; Adam. dial. c. 22. 26 [GCS 4 218, 19-23 231, 7-10]) dürfte auch das folgende Fragment zu 1 Kor 15, 50 (Staab 277, 1ff) die Valentinianer einbeziehen.

Κατὰ τῆς ἀναστάσεως τοῦτο ἕλκουσι πολλοὶ τῶν αἱρετικῶν ὑπὸ πολλῆς ἀνοίας· οὐ γὰρ εἶπεν ὅτι σάρξ καὶ αἷμα οὐκ ἀνίσταται, ἀλλὰ βασιλείαν θεοῦ οὐ κληρονομήσει. τῆς βασιλείας τοῦ υἱοῦ τοῦ θεοῦ ἀπέκλεισεν, οὐ τῆς ἀναστάσεως τὴν χάριν.

[VII] *Aphrahat Homilia III, 6* (Übers. von G. Bert, Aphrahat's des persischen Weisen Homilien [TU 3, 3], Leipzig 1888, 46f). 336/337.

Denn siehe, auch die Irrlehrer, die Werkzeuge des Satans, fasten und gedenken ihrer Sünden, aber einen Herrn, der es ihnen lohnt, haben sie nicht. Denn wer wird es dem Marcion lohnen, der unsern Schöpfer nicht als den Gütigen bekennt? Und wer wird dem Valentinus sein Fasten vergelten, der verkündigt, daß es viele Schöpfer gibt, und der sagt, daß der vollkommene Gott mit dem Mund nicht genannt und von der Vernunft nicht erkant wird? Ober wer wird es lohnen den Kindern der Finsternis, der Sekte des verdammten Mani, die im Finstern wohnen wie die Schlangen und Chaldäische Kunst treiben und die Lehre von Babel? Siehe, alle diese fasten und ihr Fasten wird nicht angenommen.

[VIII] *Julian Apostata, ep. 59* (ed. K. Weis, Julian. Briefe, München 1973, 186/188; = ep. 40 Wright = ep. 115 Bidez-Cumont). 362.

Ἰουλιανὸς Ἐδεσσηνοῖς

Ἐγὼ μὲν κέχρημαι τοῖς Γαλιλαίοις ἅπασιν οὕτω πράως καὶ φιλανθρώπως, ὥστε μηδένα μηδαμοῦ βίαν ὑπομένειν μηδὲ εἰς ἱερὸν ἕλκεσθαι μηδὲ εἰς ἄλλο τι τοιοῦτον ἐπηρεάζεσθαι παρὰ τὴν οἰκείαν πρόθεσιν. Οἱ δὲ τῆς Ἀρειανικῆς ἐκκλησίας ὑπὸ τοῦ πλούτου τρυφῶντες ἐπεχείρησαν τοῖς ἀπὸ τοῦ Οὐαλεντίνου, καὶ τετολμήκασι τοσαῦτα κατὰ τὴν ῎Εδεσσαν, ὅσα οὐδέποτε ἐν εὐνομουμένῃ πόλει γένοιτο ἄν. Οὐχοῦν ἐπειδὴ αὐτοῖς ὑπὸ τοῦ θαυμασιωτάτου νόμου προείρηται πωλῆσαι τὰ ὑπάρχοντα , ἵν' εἰς τὴν βασιλείαν τῶν οὐρανῶν εὐοδώτερον πορευθῶσι, πρὸς τοῦτο συναγωνιζόμενοι τοῖς ἀνθρώποις αὐτῶν τὰ χρήματα τῆς ᾿Εδεσσηνῶν ἐκκλησίας ἅπαντα ἐκελεύσαμεν ἀναληφθῆναι δοθησόμενα τοῖς στρατιώταις, καὶ τὰ κτήματα τοῖς ἡμετέροις προστεθῆναι πριβάτοις, ἵνα πενόμενοι σωφρονῶσι καὶ μὴ στερηθῶσιν ἧς ἔτι ἐλπίζουσιν οὐρανίου βασιλείας. Τοῖς οἰκοῦσι δὲ τὴν ῎Εδεσσαν προαγορεύομεν ἀπέχεσθαι πάσης στάσεως καὶ φιλονεικίας, ἵνα μὴ τὴν ἡμετέραν φιλανθρωπίαν κινήσαντες καθ᾿ ὑμῶν αὐτῶν ὑπὲρ τῆς τῶν κοινῶν ἀταξίας δίκην τίσητε, ξίφει καὶ πυρὶ καὶ φυγῇ ζημιωθέντες.

Literatur: H. Lietzmann, Geschichte der Alten Kirche. III, Berlin [3]1961, 282f; J. Leipoldt, Der römische Kaiser Julian in der Religionsgeschichte (Sitz. ber. Sächs. Akad. Wiss. Phil.-hist. Kl. 110, 1), 1964, 18; E. Stein, Geschichte des spätrömischen Reiches. I, Wien 1928, 257. A. H. M. Jones (The Later Roman Empire. I, 1973, 122) verlegt den Vorfall in die Regierungszeit Julians.

[IX] *Ambrosius von Mailand ep. 40f* (ML 16 1148-1169). 388.

Brief 40 ist an Kaiser Theodosius gerichtet und verlangt die Rücknahme der Strafen für Bischof und Mönche; in ep. 41 berichtet Ambrosius seiner Schwester über den Ausgang des Konfliktes.

ep. 40, 6. Relatum est a comite orientis militarium partium incensam esse synagogam, idque auctore factum episcopo. Jussisti vindicari in caeteros, synagogam ab ipso exaedificari episcopo. (...)
(*40, 16*) Vindicabitur etiam Valentinianorum fanum incensum? Quid est enim nisi fanum, in quo est conventus gentilium? Licet gentiles duodecim deos appellent, isti triginta et duos Æonas colant, quos appellant deos. Nam et de ipsis comperi relatum et praeceptum, ut in monachos vindicaretur, qui prohibentibus iter Valentinianis, quo psalmos canentes ex consuetudine usuque veteri pergebant ad celebritatem Machabæorum martyrum moti insolentia incenderunt fanum eorum iniquodam rurali vico tumultuarie conditum.

(*ep. 41, 1*) Nam cum relatum esset synagogam Judæorum incensam a Christianis, auctore episcopo, et Valentinianorum conventiculum; jussum erat, me Aquileiæ posito, ut synagoga ab episcopo reædificaretur, et in monachos vindicaretur, qui incendissent ædificium Valentinianorum. Tum ego, cum sæpius agendo parum proficerem, epistolam dedi imperatori, quam simul misi; et ubi processit ad Ecclesiam, hunc sermonem habui: (es folgt die in Gegenwart des Theodosius gehaltene Predigt über Luk 7, 36-50. Über das sich daran anschließende Gespräch mit dem Kaiser heißt es *41, 27f*:) Ubi descendi, ait mihi: De nobis proposuisti.

Respondi: Hoc tractavi, quod ad ultilitatem tuam pertinerer. Tunc ait: Re vera de Synagoga reparanda ab episcopo durius statueram, sed emendatum est. Monachi multa scelera faciunt. Tunc Timasius magister equitum et peditum cœpit adversum monachos esse vehementior. Respondi ei: Ego cum imperatore ago, ut oportet: quia novi quod habeat Domini timorem: tecum autem aliter agendum, qui tam dura loqueris. Deinde cum aliquandiu starem, dico imperatori: Fac me securum pro te offerre, absolve animum meum. Cum assideret annueretque, non tamen aperte polliceretur, atque ego starem, dixit se emendaturum rescriptum. Statim dicere cœpi, ut omnem cognitionem tolleret, ne occasione cognitionis comes aliqua Christianos attereret injuria. Promisit futurum. Aio illi: Ago fide tua; et repetivi: Ago fide tua. Age, inquit, fide mea. Et ita ad altare accessi, non aliter accessurus, nisi mihi plene promisisset. Et vere tanta oblationis fuit gratia, ut sentirem etiam ipse eam Deo nostro commendatiorem fuisse gratiam, et divinam praesentiam non defuisse. Omnia itaque ex sententia gesta sunt.

Literatur: F. Barth, Ambrosius und die Synagoge zu Callinicum, Theol. Zeitschrift aus der Schweiz 6 (1889) 65-86, v.a. 65-68; G. Rauschen, Jahrbücher der christlichen Kirche unter dem Kaiser Theodosius dem Großen, Freiburg 1897, 292f. 532ff; H. Frh. v. Campenhausen, Ambrosius von Mailand als Kirchenpolitiker (AKG 12), Berlin/Leipzig 1929, 231-234; F. H. Dudden, The Life and Times of St. Ambrose. II, Oxford 1935, 371-379; W. Ensslin, Die Religionspolitik (s. Anm. 7), 60-62; E. Stein, Geschichte des spätrömischen Reiches. I, Wien 1928, 320f.

[X] *Konstantins Häretikererlass* (ap. Eus. Vit. Const. III, 64f [GCS 7 111, 14-113, 3]). Um 326.

(64, 1) Νικητὴς Κωνσταντῖνος Μέγιστος Σεβαστὸς αἱρετικοῖς. Ἐπίγνωτε νῦν διὰ τῆς νομοθεσίας ταύτης, ὦ Νοουατιανοί, Οὐαλεντῖνοι, Μαρκιωνισταί, Παυλιανοί, οἵ τε κατὰ Φρύγας ἐπικεκλημένοι, καὶ πάντες ἁπλῶς εἰπεῖν οἱ τὰς αἱρέσεις διὰ τῶν οἰκείων πληροῦντες συστημάτων, ὅσοις ψεύδεσιν ἡ παρ' ὑμῖν ματαιότης ἐμπέπλεκται, καὶ ὅπως ἰοβόλοις τισὶ φαρμάκοις ἡ ὑμετέρα συνέχεται διδασκαλία, ὡς τοὺς μὲν ὑγιαίνοντας εἰς ἀσθένειαν τοὺς δὲ ζῶντας εἰς διηνεκῆ θάνατον ἀπάγεσθαι δι' ὑμῶν. (...) (65, 1f) Τοιγάρτοι ἐπειδὴ τὸν ὄλεθρον τοῦτον τῆς ὑμετέρας ἐξωλείας ἐπὶ πλεῖον φέρειν οὐκ ἔστιν οἷόν τε, διὰ τοῦ νόμου τούτου προαγορεύομεν, μή τις ὑμῶν συνάγειν ἐκ τοῦ λοιποῦ τολμήσῃ. διὸ καὶ πάντας ὑμῶν τοὺς οἴκους, ἐν οἷς τὰ συνέδρια ταῦτα πληροῦτε, ἀφαιρεθῆναι προστετάχαμεν, μέχρι τοσούτου τῆς φροντίδος ταύτης προχωρούσης, ὡς μὴ ἐν τῷ δημοσίῳ μόνον, ἀλλὰ μηδ' ἐν οἰκίᾳ ἰδιωτικῇ ἢ τόποις τισὶν ἰδιάζουσι τὰ τῆς δεισιδαίμονος ὑμῶν ἀνοίας συστήματα συντρέχειν. πλὴν ὅπερ ἔστι κάλλιον, ὅσοι τῆς ἀληθινῆς καὶ καθαρᾶς ἐπιμέλεσθε θρησκείας, εἰς τὴν καθολικὴν ἐκκλησίαν ἔλθετε καὶ τῇ ταύτης ἁγιότητι κοινωνεῖτε... (65, 3) ὑπὲρ δὲ τοῦ τῆς θεραπείας ταύτης καὶ ἀναγκαίαν γενέσθαι τὴν ἰσχὺν προσετάξαμεν, καθὼς προείρηται, ἄπαντα τὰ τῆς δεισιδαιμονίας ὑμῶν συνέδρια, πάντων φημὶ τῶν αἱρετικῶν τοὺς εὐκτηρίους, εἴ γε εὐκτηρίους ὀνομάξειν οἴκους προσήκει, ἀφαιρεθέντας ἀναντιρρήτως τῇ καθολικῇ ἐκκλησίᾳ χωρίς τινος ὑπερθέσεως παραδοθῆναι, τοὺς δὲ λοιποὺς τόπους τοῖς δημοσίοις προσκριθῆναι, καὶ μηδεμίαν ὑμῖν εἰς τὸ ἑξῆς τοῦ συνάγειν εὐμάρειαν περιλειφθῆναι, ὅπως ἐκ τῆς ἐνεστώσης ἡμέρας ἐν μηδενὶ τόπῳ μήτε δημοσίῳ μήτ᾽ ἰδιωτικῷ τὰ ἀθέμιτα ὑμῶν συστήματα ἀθροισθῆναι τολμήσῃ. προτεθήτω.

Es ist zu beachten, daß dieser Erlaß über Versammlungsverbot und Beschlagnahmung der Kirchen hinaus keine Strafbestimmungen (Geldbuße, Gefängnis, Verbannung) enthält. Wie wenig das konstantinische Verbot im übrigen befolgt worden ist, veranschaulicht die bekannte Warnung des Cyrill von Jerusalem vor der Gefahr, unversehens in eine markionitische Kirche zu geraten, wenn man in einer fremden Stadt nur nach der Ekklesia und nicht nach der *katholischen* Ekklesia frage (cat. 18, 26). — *Literatur*: H. Kraft, Kaiser Konstantins religiöse Entwicklung (BHTh 20), Tübingen 1955, 246-248; H. Dörries, Das Selbstzeugnis Kaiser Konstantins (AAG Phil.-hist. Kl. 34), Göttingen 1954, 82-84; ders., Konstantinische Wende und Glaubensfreiheit, in: ders., Wort und Stunde I, Göttingen 1966, 1-117, v.a. 103ff; K.-L. Noethlichs, Die gesetzgeberischen Maßnahmen (s. Anm. 9), 12f.

[XI] *Theodosius II: Häretikergesetz vom 30-5-428* (CodTheod XVI, 5, 65) § 2 (edd. Th. Mommsen/P. M. Meyer, Theodosiani Libri XVI cum Constitutionibus Sirmondianis et Leges Novellae ad Theodosianum pertinentes. I, 2, Berlin [3]1962, 878).

Post haec, quoniam non omnes eadem austeritate plectendi sunt, Arrianis quidem, Macedonianis et Apollinarianis, quorum hoc est facinus, quod nocenti meditatione decepti credunt de veritatis fonte mendacia, intra nullam civitatem ecclesiam habere liceat; Novatianis autem et Sabbatianis omnis innovationis adimatur licentia, si quam forte temptaverint; Eunomiani vero, Valentiniani, Montanistae seu Priscillianistae, Fryges, Marcianistae, Borboriani, Messaliani, Euchitae sive Enthusiastae, Donatistae, Audiani, Hydroparastatae, Tascodrogitae, Fotiniani, Pauliani, Marcelliani et qui ad imam usque scelerum nequitiam pervenerunt Manichaei nusquam in Romano solo conveniendi orandique habeant facultatem; Manichaeis etiam de civitatibus expellendis, quoniam nihil his omnibus relinquendum loci est, in quo ipsis etiam elementis fiat iniuria.

Literatur: K.-L. Noethlichs, Die gesetzgeberischen Maßnahmen (s. Anm. 9), 165. 212; Th. O. Martin, Theodosius' Laws on Heretics, Am. Eccl. Rev. 123 (1950) 117-136, v.a. 117; C. Luibhéid, Theodosius II and Heresy, JEH 16 (1965) 13-38, v.a. 13f.

[XII] *Theodor von Mopsuestia Comm. in 1Tim (ad 1Tim 4, 1-3)* (ed. H. B. Swete, Theodori Episcopi Mopsuesteni in Epistolas B. Pauli Commentarii. II, Cambridge 1882, 139-141). Anfang 5. Jh.

euidens quidem quoniam haec dicit beatus Paulus non quia tunc iam apud aliquos coeperant ista profiteri, sed quod postea ista erant ab hominibus principium sumptura ... nam et Manichaeos et Marcionistas et eos qui de Valentiniana sunt haeresi et omnes qui eiusmodi sunt, similiter quis perspiciet et nuptias dampnare et escarum usum quasi inhonestum criminare; et quod adnitantur ostendere carnem a Domino non fuisse susceptam ... omnes isti Christianos se esse simulant et doctrina sua maiorem se tenere promittunt castitatem, multum uero pietatis contraria eos qui sibi obtemperant de Christo docere adnituntur; omnia uero illa quae luxuriae sunt plena, quae et omnem in se continent prauitatem, ipsi inter se agere cum omni properant sollicitudine, quae inprimis ad plenum silere uidentur; atubi uero per illam quam ineunt simulationem aliquem instanter suaderi sibi per omnia fecerunt, tunc illa sermonibus quibusdam adducunt ad medium, suadentes ut illa peragant quasi pietatis opera perficientes quae omnis sunt spurcitiae plena. et hoc inueniet quis si illa omnia quae praedicta sunt cautissime considerare uoluerit, licet non facile possint deprehendi, eo quod latere plurimos super talibus operibus adnituntur.

[XIII] *Theodoret von Cyrus ep. 81* (MG 83 1260/1264). 448.

Νόμῳ ὑπάτῳ. Ἐν βραχεῖ μὲν ἡμέρας μορίῳ τῆς ὑμετέρας μεγαλοφυΐας ἀπήλαυσα, βιαίας ἀνάγκης με στερησάσης τοῦ ποθουμένου. Ἤλπισα δὲ καὶ τὴν μικρὰν συνουσίαν ζώπυρον εὐνοίας καὶ θερμῆς ἔσεσθαι διαθέσεως· ἐψεύσθην δὲ τῆς ἐλπίδος. Δὶς μὲν γὰρ ἤδη γεγραφώς, ἀντιγράφων οὐκ ἔτυχον· βασιλικῇ δὲ ψήφῳ τῆς Κυρεστῶν χώρας τοὺς ὅρους ὑπερβαίνειν κεκώλυμαι. Αἰτία δὲ οὐδεμία τῇ δοκούσῃ πρόσκειται τιμωρίᾳ, ἀλλ᾽ ὅτι συνόδους ἐπισκοπικὰς συναθροίζω. ... Ἐγὼ δὲ οὔτε ἐρωτηθεὶς εἴτε συνάγω συνόδους, εἴτε μή, καὶ ἐπὶ τίσι συνάγω, καὶ τί τοῦτο λυμαίνεται ἢ τοῖς ἐκκλησιαστικοῖς, ἢ τοῖς κοινοῖς, τοῖς μέγιστα παρανομήσασι παραπλησίως τῶν ἄλλων εἴργομαι πόλεων· μᾶλλον δὲ τοῖς μὲν ἄλλοις ἅπασι πᾶσα πόλις ἀνέῳκται, οὐ μόνον τοῖς τὰ Ἀρείου καὶ Εὐνομίου φρονοῦσιν, ἀλλὰ καὶ Μανιχαίοις, καὶ Μαρκιωνισταῖς, καὶ τοῖς τὰ Βαλεντίνου, καὶ Μοντανοῦ νοσοῦσι, καὶ μέντοι καὶ Ἕλλησι καὶ Ἰουδαίοις· ἐγὼ δέ, τῶν εὐαγγελικῶν ὑπεραγωνιζόμενος δογμάτων, πάσης εἴργομαι πόλεως. (...)

Literatur: K. Günther, Theodoret von Cyrus und die Kämpfe in der orientalischen Kirche vom Tode Cyrills bis zur Einberufung des sog. Räuberkonzils, Aschaffenburg 1913, 5-8 (zur Datierung von ep. 81); 32-38 (zu Theodorets Internierung in Cyrus).

[XIV] *Timotheus von Konstantinopel De receptione haereticorum* (MG 86/1 9-68) p. 17. Um 600.

Ὁ μὲν Βασιλείδης ὁ Αἰγύπτιος ἀσώματον ἐν γῇ φανῆναι τὸν Χριστὸν ἐμυθεύσατο, πάθος οὐδὲν ὑπομείναντα· Σίμωνα δὲ τὸν Κυρηναῖον ὡς αὐτὸν νομισθέντα τῷ σταυρῷ προσπαγῆναι· τὸν Χριστὸν δὲ θεώμενον πόρρωθεν, γελᾶν τῶν Ἰουδαίων τὴν ἄνοιαν. Χρῆναι φάσκων οὐκ εἰς τὸν σταυρωθέντα πιστεύειν, ἀλλ' εἰς τὸν ἐσταυρῶσθαι δόξαντα. Ἡρνεῖτο δὲ τῆς σαρκὸς τὴν ἀνάστασιν, ἀθετῶν τὸν νόμον καὶ τοὺς προφήτας· μετέχειν δὲ ἀδεῶς εἰδωλοθύτων ἐπέτρεψε, καὶ πάντα πράττειν ἀδιακρίτως τὰ αἴσχιστα, γοητείας καὶ ἐπῳδὰς καὶ μαγγανείας τελεῖν. Ὁ Βαλεντῖνος δὲ βυθὸν καὶ σιγὴν προυπάρχειν πάντων ὑπέθετο· ἀσώματον δὲ καὶ αὐτὸς τὸν Χριστὸν τερατεύεται, σῶμα ψυχικὸν παρὰ τοῦ Δημιουργοῦ κομισάμενον, ὅπερ ἁπτὸν καὶ ὁρατὸν μὴ ὂν πρότερον, γέγονεν ὕστερον. Ἐκ τούτων Ἑρμαῖοι προσαγορεύονται, ἀπὸ τινος οὕτω κληθέντος λαχόντες τὸ ὄνομα. Πᾶσαν πρᾶξιν ἀπειρημένην ἐργάζονται, ἑορτὰς ἐκτόπους καλοῦντες, καὶ ἐσθίοντες εἰδωλόθυτα. Ἔτι δὲ λέγει τὸ σῶμα τοῦ Κυρίου ἄνωθεν κατενηνέχθαι, καὶ ὡς διὰ σωλῆνος ὕδωρ διὰ Μαρίας τῆς παρθένου διεληλυθέναι. Καὶ τοῦτο δὲ τερατεύεται, ἄλλο σῶμα ἐγείρεσθαι, ὅπερ προσαγορεύουσι πνευματικόν, καὶ οὐχὶ τοῦτο· καὶ τῶν γνωστικῶν δὲ λέγει ἑαυτὸν εἶναι. Καὶ ὁ Βαρδησάνης τὰ αὐτὰ λέγει Βαλεντίνῳ. Οὗτος δὲ ὁ Βαλεντῖνος, ἐπίσκοπος γέγονεν Αἰγύπτου.

Zu Timotheus s. H.-G. Beck, Kirche und theologische Literatur im Byzantinischen Reich, München 1959, 401f. — Der Traktat handelt von den verschiedenen Häresien und dem Rekonziliationsverfahren, das die Kirche ihnen gegenüber anwedet. Drei Klassen werden dabei unterschieden (p. 13A): 1. jene Häretiker, die (wieder-) getauft werden müssen, 2. jene, die gesalbt werden, sowie 3. jene, von denen verlangt wird, "die eigene sowie jegliche andere Häresie" zu anathematisieren. Die Valentinianer werden der ersten Kategorie zugerechnet, zusammen mit den Tascodrugi, Markioniten, Enkratiten, Nikolaiten (= Borborianer), Montanisten, Manichäern, Eunomianern u.a. Timotheus reproduziert bei der Wiedergabe der häretischen *Anschauungen* zweifellos einfach die Angabe älterer Ketzerbestreiter (im Allgemeinen wohl v.a. Theodoret und [?] Epiphanius). Doch spricht das nicht zwangsläufig gegen die Zeitgenossenschaft der betreffenden Häretiker. Auch Ambrosius, von dem wir die Nachricht über die Valentinianer in Kallinikon beziehen, folgt bei der Charakterisierung ihrer *Lehre* (ep. 40, 16; s.o.) der häresiologischen Tradition, und Gleiches tut Theodoret, der sich über die Bewegungsfreiheit der Valentinianer in seinem Gesichtskreis beschwert (ep. 81; s.o.), in seinem Haereticarum fabularum compendium (I, 7). Für den Fortbestand der Valentinianer spricht neben dem Kasus (Rekonziliationsverfahren) auch die Mitteilung, daß die Valentinianer auch unter dem Namen Ἑρμαῖοι bekannt seien; derartige Hinweise sollten ja die Identifikation erleichtern und finden sich auch bei anderen Häresien. So bei den Markioniten, die auch als Artotyriten bekannt seien (p. 16B); dieser Hinweis ist singulär und wird von A. v. Harnack, Marcion (s. Anm. 2), 381*f als Zeugnis einer sonst nicht belegten Fusion beider Sekten gewertet. (An anderer Stelle freilich sind derartige Hinweise bereits in der Tradition verankert, wie etwa die Benennung der Eunomianer als Troglitae oder Troglodytae [p. 24C], die bereits bei Theodoret (haer. fab. IV, 3 [MG 83 422B]) erwähnt wird; zur Geschichte der Eunomianer cf. M. Albertz, Zur Geschichte der jungarianischen Kirchengemeinschaft, Theol. Stud. u. Krit. 82 [1909] 205-278, spez. 261f. Doch ist die Benennung der Valentinianer als Ἑρμαῖοι und überhaupt Ἑρμαῖοι als Sektenbezeichnung m.W. sonst nicht bezeugt). Zu Timotheus cf. auch B. Altaner/A. Stuiber, Patrologie, Freiburg/Basel/Wien ⁸1978, 514: "Aufzählung und Charakterisierung der Schismen und Häresien des 6. Jahrhunderts"; O. Bardenhewer, Geschichte der altkichlichen Literatur. V, Freiburg 1932, 26: "Überblick über die Schismen und Häresien des 6. Jh.s"; sowie H. J. Vogt, Coetus Sanctorum, Bonn 1968, 287f (über die Novantianer bei T.); J. Danielou, RSR 48 (1960) 124f.

[XV] *Die Quinisexta (oder 2. Trullanische Synode) von 692: can. 95* (Text nach: F. Lauchert, Die Kanones der wichtigsten altkirchlichen Concilien, Freiburg/Leipzig 1896, 136f; ferner: J. D. Mansi, Sacrorum conciliorum nova et amplissima collectio. XI, Graz ᴺ1960, 984).

XCV. Τοὺς προστιθεμένους τῇ ὀρθοδοξίᾳ καὶ τῇ μερίδι τῶν σωζομένων ἀπὸ αἱρετικῶν δεχόμεθα κατὰ τὴν ὑποτεταγμένην ἀκολουθίαν τε καὶ συνήθειαν, Ἀρειανοὺς μὲν καὶ Μακεδονιανούς, καὶ Ναυατιανοὺς τοὺς λέγοντας ἑαυτοὺς Καθαροὺς καὶ Ἀριστερούς, καὶ Τεσσαρεσκαιδεκατίτας ἤγουν Τετραδίτας, καὶ Ἀπολιναριστὰς δεχόμεθα διδόντας λιβέλλους καὶ ἀναθεματίζοντας πᾶσαν αἵρεσιν μὴ φρονοῦσαν ὡς φρονεῖ ἡ ἁγία τοῦ θεοῦ καὶ ἀποστολικὴ ἐκκλησία, σφραγιζομένους ἤτοι χριομένους πρῶτον τῷ ἁγίῳ μύρῳ τό τε μέτωπον καὶ τοὺς ὀφθαλμοὺς καὶ τὰς ῥῖνας καὶ τὸ στόμα καὶ τὰ ὦτα. καὶ σφραγίζοντες αὐτοὺς λέγομεν· Σφραγὶς δωρεᾶς πνεύματος ἁγίου· περὶ δὲ τῶν Παυλιανιστῶν τῇ καθολικῇ ἐκκλησίᾳ ὅρος ἐκτέθειται, ἀναβαπτίζεσθαι αὐτοὺς ἐξ ἅπαντος· Εὐνομιανοὺς μέντοι τοὺς εἰς μίαν κατάδυσιν βαπτιζομένους, καὶ Μοντανιστὰς τοὺς ἐνταῦθα λεγομένους Φρύγας, καὶ Σαβελλιανοὺς τοὺς υἱοπατορίαν δοξάζοντας καὶ ἕτερά τινα χαλεπὰ ποιοῦντας, καὶ πάσας τὰς ἄλλας αἱρέσεις, ἐπειδὴ πολλοί εἰσιν ἐνταῦθα, μάλιστα οἱ ἀπὸ τῆς Γαλατῶν χώρας ἐρχόμενοι, πάντας τοὺς ἀπ' αὐτῶν θέλοντας προστίθεσθαι τῇ ὀρθοδοξίᾳ ὡς Ἕλληνας δεχόμεθα· καὶ τὴν μὲν πρώτην ἡμέραν ποιοῦμεν αὐτοὺς Χριστιανούς, τὴν δὲ δευτέραν κατηχουμένους· εἶτα τὴν τρίτην ἐξορκίζομεν αὐτοὺς μετὰ τοῦ ἐμφυσᾶν τρίτον εἰς τὸ πρόσωπον καὶ εἰς ὦτα· καὶ οὕτω κατηχοῦμεν αὐτοὺς καὶ ποιοῦμεν χρονίζειν ἐν τῇ ἐκκλησίᾳ καὶ ἀκροᾶσθαι τῶν γραφῶν, καὶ τότε αὐτοὺς βαπτίζομεν· καὶ τοὺς Μανιχαίους δὲ καὶ τοὺς Οὐαλεντίους καὶ Μαρκιωνιστὰς καὶ τοὺς ἐκ τῶν ὁμοίων αἱρέσεων [προσερχομένους ὡς Ἕλληνας δεχόμενοι ἀναβαπτίζομεν. Νεστοριανοὺς δὲ καὶ Εὐτυχιανιστὰς καὶ Σεβηριανοὺς καὶ τοὺς ἐκ τῶν ὁμοίων αἱρέσεων] χρὴ ποιεῖν λιβέλλους καὶ ἀναθεματίζειν τὴν αἵρεσιν καὶ Νεστόριον καὶ Εὐτυχέα καὶ Διόσκορον καὶ Σεβῆρον καὶ τοὺς λοιποὺς ἐξάρχους τῶν τοιούτων αἱρέσεων καὶ τοὺς φρονοῦντας τὰ αὐτῶν καὶ πάσας τὰς προαναφερομένας αἱρέσεις, καὶ οὕτω μεταλαμβάνειν τῆς ἁγίας κοινωνίας.

Die von Kaiser Justinian II berufene Synode, die im "Trullon" — Saal des kaiserlichen Palastes in Konstantinopel tagte, diente dem Erlaß disziplinärer Kanones in Ergänzung des 5. und 6. ökumenischen Konzils von 553 und 680 (daher der Name Quinisexta). Zum Inhalt und Text von can. 95 cf. C. J. v. Hefele, Conciliengeschichte III, Freiburg 1877,

342f. Die Häresienliste dieses Kanons spiegelt sicherlich in erster Linie kleinasiatische Verhältnisse wider ("... καὶ πάσας τὰς ἄλλας αἱρέσεις, ἐπειδὴ πολλοί εἰσιν ἐνταῦθα, μάλιστα οἱ ἀπὸ τῆς Γαλατῶν χώρας ἐρχόμενοι...") und wird von K. Holl zur Rekonstruktion der Sektengeographie Kleinasiens herangezogen (Das Fortleben der Volkssprachen in Kleinasien in nachchristlicher Zeit [in: Ges. Aufs. zur Kirchengeschichte. II, Tübingen 1928, 238-248] 247: "Man gewinnt fast den Eindruck, als ob das Innere Kleinasiens ein gelobtes Land der Dissenters gewesen wäre. Hierher zieht sich und hier hält sich, was sonst untergeht. Denn mit merkwürdiger Hartnäckigkeit haben sich die Sekten gegenüber der Kirche behauptet. Von den Montanisten haben wir noch Nachrichten aus dem 9. Jahrhundert ..., und die meisten der übrigen ebengenannten Sekten führt noch das Trullanum von 692 can. 95 auf"; zur Fortexistenz häretischer Gruppen in Kleinasien allgemein cf. auch: W. M. Calder, The Epigraphy of the Anatolian Heresies, in: Anatolian Studies presented to Sir W. R. Ramsay, Manchester 1923, 55-91; W. M. Ramsay, Phrygian Orthodox and Heretics 400-800 AD, Byzantion VI [1931] 1-35; H. Gelzer, Ausgewählte kleine Schriften, Leipzig 1907, 101f). Im vorliegenden Kanon 95 der Quinisexta ist der sog. siebte Kanon des zweiten ökumenischen Konzils von 381, der in Wirklichkeit dem späten 5. (oder dem 6.) Jh. zuzurechnen ist (s. C. J. v. Hefele, Conciliengeschichte II, Freiburg [2]1873, 26-28; H.-G. Beck, Kirche [s.o. Nr. XIV] 45; A.-M. Ritter, Das Konzil von Konstantinopel und sein Symbol [FKDG 15], Göttingen 1965, 123 Anm. 1; H. J. Vogt, Coetus Sanctorum, Bonn 1968, 248-256), aufgenommen. Die Erwähnung der Valentinianer findet sich in den nicht-identischen Textpartien.

INDEX

I. DIE BIBLIOTHEK VON NAG HAMMADI

II. BP 8502 (= BG)

III. CODEX BRUCIANUS 47

IV. CODEX ASKEWIANUS 47

V. GRIECHISCHE GNOSTISCHE TEXTE

VI. HERMETIKA 8. 8,13

VII. ALTES TESTAMENT

VIII. PSEUDEPIGRAPHEN DES ALTEN TESTAMENTS

IX. NEUES TESTAMENT

XIII. KONZILSAKTEN UND STAATL. GESETZGEBUNG

XIV. PAPYRI

XV. ANTIKE HEIDNISCHE LITERATUR

XVI. MODERNE AUTOREN

NAG HAMMADI STUDIES

Edited by

M. Krause, J. M. Robinson, F. Wisse

in conjunction with

A. Böhlig, J. Doresse, S. Giversen, H. Jonas, R. Kasser, P. Labib,
G. W. MacRae, J.-É. Ménard, T. Säve-Söderbergh, R. McL.
Wilson, J. Zandee

1. Scholer, D. M. Nag Hammadi Bibliography 1948-1969. 1971. (xvi, 201 p.)
[02603 7] *cloth* Gld. 92.—

2. L'évangile de vérité. [Trad. franç., introd. et commentaire]. Par J.-É.
Ménard. 1972. (x, 228 p.) [03408 0] *cloth* Gld. 84.—

3. Essays on the Nag Hammadi texts in honour of Alexander Böhlig. Ed. by M.
Krause. 1972. (vi, 175 p.) [03535 4] *cloth* Gld. 72.—

4. The Gospel of the Egyptians. The Holy Book of the Great Invisible Spirit,
from codices III, 2 and IV, 2 of the Nag Hammadi library. Ed. with transl. and
commentary by A. Böhlig and F. Wisse, in cooperation with P. Labib. 1975.
(xiii, 234 [115 Coptic t.] p.) (The Coptic Gnostic Library) [04226 1]
cloth Gld. 76.—

5. L'évangile selon Thomas. [Trad. franç., introd., et commentaire]. Par J.-É.
Ménard. 1975. (x, 252 p.) [04210 5] *cloth* Gld. 116.—

6. Essays on the Nag Hammadi texts in honour of Pahor Labib. Ed. by M.
Krause. 1975. (viii, 315 p.) [04363 2] *cloth* Gld. 144.—

7. Les textes de Nag Hammadi. Colloque du Centre d'Histoire des Religions
(Strasbourg, 23-25 octobre 1974). Éd. par J.-É. Ménard. 1975. (x, 203 p.)
[04359 4] *cloth* Gld. 92.—

8. Gnosis and Gnosticism. Papers read at the Seventh International Conference
on Patristic Studies (Oxford, September 8th-13th 1975). Ed. by M. Krause.
1977. (x, 233 p.) [05242 9] *cloth* Gld. 96.—

9. Pistis Sophia. Text ed. by C. Schmidt. Transl. and notes by V. MacDermot.
1978. (xx, 806 [385 Coptic t.] p.) (The Coptic Gnostic Library) [05635 1]
cloth Gld. 224.—

10. Fallon, F. T. The enthronement of Sabaoth. Jewish elements in Gnostic
creation myths. 1978. (x, 158 p.) (D) [05683 1] *cloth* Gld. 56.—

11. Nag Hammadi Codices V, 2-5 and VI with Papyrus Berolinensis 8502, I and
4. Volume ed. D. M. Parrott. Contributors: J. Brashler, P. A. Dirkse, C.
W. Hedrick, G. W. MacRae, W. R. Murdock, D. M. Parrott, J. M. Robinson, W. R. Schoedel, R. McL. Wilson, F. E. Williams, F. Wisse. 1979. (xxii,
353 [188 Coptic t.] p.) (The Coptic Gnostic Library) [05798 6] *cloth* Gld. 180.—

12. Koschorke, K. Die Polemik der Gnostiker gegen das kirchliche Christentum.
Unter besonderer Berücksichtigung der Nag-Hammadi-Traktate "Apokalypse

des Petrus" (NHC VII, 3) und "Testimonium Veritatis" (NHC IX, 3). 1978. (xiv, 274 p.) (D) [05709 9]   *cloth* Gld. 124.—

13. The Books of Jeu and the untitled text in the Bruce Codex. Text ed. by C. SCHMIDT. Transl. and notes by V. MACDERMOT. 1978. (xxiv, 345 [239 Coptic t.] p.) (The Coptic Gnostic Library) [05754 4]   *cloth* Gld. 120.—

14. Nag Hammadi and Gnosis. Papers read at the First International Congress of Coptology (Cairo, December 1976). Ed. by R. McL. WILSON. 1978. (viii, 178 p.) [05760 9]   *cloth* Gld. 96.—

15. Nag Hammadi Codices IX and X. Volume ed. B. A. PEARSON. Contributors: S. GIVERSEN and B. A. PEARSON. 1981. (xxix, 397 p.) (The Coptic Gnostic Library) [06377 3]   *cloth* Gld. 240.—

16. Nag Hammadi Codices. Greek and Coptic papyri from the cartonnage of the covers. Ed. by J. W. B. BARNS, G. M. BROWNE and J. C. SHELTON. 1981. (xix, 162 p.) (The Coptic Gnostic Library) [06277 7]   *cloth* Gld. 60.—

1981. Prices may be changed without notice.

E. J. Brill — P.O.B. 9000 — 2300 PA Leiden — The Netherlands

MEDE VERKRIJGBAAR DOOR BEMIDDELING VAN DE BOEKHANDEL